TWO MONTHS IN THE
CONFEDERATE STATES

TWO MONTHS IN THE CONFEDERATE STATES

An Englishman's
Travels Through the South

W. C. CORSAN

EDITED WITH AN INTRODUCTION BY
BENJAMIN H. TRASK

LOUISIANA STATE UNIVERSITY PRESS
BATON ROUGE AND LONDON

Copyright © 1996 by Louisiana State University Press
Originally published by Richard Bentley as *Two Months
in the Confederate States: Including a Visit to New Orleans
under the Domination of General Butler,* London, 1863
All rights reserved
Manufactured in the United States of America
First printing
05 04 03 02 01 00 99 98 97 96   5 4 3 2 1

Designer: Amanda McDonald Key
Typeface: Granjon
Typesetter: Impressions Book and Journal Services, Inc.
Printer and binder: Thomson-Shore, Inc.

Library of Congress Cataloging-in-Publication Data

English merchant.
    Two months in the Confederate States : an Englishman's travels
through the South / W.C. Corsan : [edited with an introduction by
Benjamin H. Trask].
        p.   cm.
    Previously published as: Two months in the Confederate States :
including a visit to New Orleans, under the domination of General
Butler.
    Includes bibliographical references and index.
    ISBN 0-8071-2037-5 (cloth : alk. paper)
    1. Confederate States of America—Description and travel. 2. New
Orleans (La.)—History—Civil War, 1861–1865. 3. British—Travel—
Confederate States of America.   I. Trask, Benjamin H.   II. Title.
F214.E54   1996
973.7′42—dc20   96-20861
                                                        CIP

Contents

Illustrations

Acknowledgments

To edit Corsan's book required mounting a letter-writing campaign. Much of my correspondence was to England, to gather information on the book's author, printer, and publisher, and on Victorian culture. Twelve librarians from the Lancaster County Public Library system responded quickly to my requests, several giving me suggestions on where to locate biographical data in various sources they had searched.

From Manchester, Anthea M. Jarvis, Keeper of Costume at the Gallery of English Costume, provided me with an explanation and copy of Thomas Hood's poem "The Song of the Shirt." From Liverpool, E. H. Seagroatt of the Athenaeum and Janet Smith of the City Library checked the trade directories and minutes of the Liverpool Cotton Association Ltd. I also wrote to the reference staffs of the libraries at Leeds University, Leeds Central Library, Oxford University, Cambridge University, and Birmingham University. All responded and provided encouragement and suggestions. Finally, Patrick Flood of Dublin was kind enough to contact the British Library for me when I first began this project.

In the United States, I received assistance by mail from the National Archives and numerous other institutions. William E. Lind of the military reference branch searched to document Corsan's contact with the Union provost marshal general in New Orleans. He also directed me to the British Public Record Office in London and possible leads at the Library of Congress. Angie S. VanDeerdt of the civil reference branch paved the way for me to locate "Mr. Corsen/Corsan" aboard the SS *Etna* and answered numerous questions about related materials at the National Archives. Betty Thomson of Surrey, England, located passport records related to Corsan at the Public Record Office in Richmond.

Most of my bread-and-butter research took place in the Earl Gregg Swem Library at the College of William and Mary, Williamsburg, Virginia. I am fortunate to have such a fine facility in my hometown. I would like to thank reference librarian Katherine Fuller McKenzie for all her help and Margaret C. Cook, curator of manuscripts and rare books, for allowing me to examine and reproduce parts of the Swem copy of *Two Months in the Confederate States.* The title page reproduced in this volume is taken from the Swem copy. Michael A. Ermilio, of the Philadelphia College of Pharmacy and Science, and George Griffenhagen, of the American Pharmaceutical Association, answered all my questions concerning nineteenth-century medicines. I also want to thank the staffs of the Library of Virginia, Virginia Historical Society, Massachusetts Historical Society, and New-York Historical Society for their assistance.

While I was in the Crescent City, associates of the Historic New Orleans Collection and the University of New Orleans' Earl K. Long Library directed me to sources and answered my many queries about the Bayou State during the last century. Lorna Higgins Hale of Midvale, Utah, checked the International Genealogical Index and Ancestral File for Corsan in all the counties in England. Doug Hindmarch of the Sheffield Public Library matched Hale's leads to Corsan and provided the obituary that pointed to the industrialist as the author of this book.

On a personal note, colleagues R. Thomas Crew, Jr., Dina B. Hill, and John R. Peacock III examined a draft and offered keen suggestions for revision. My sister-in-law Debra Jean Trask drew the map of Corsan's travels. Another sister-in-law, Karen M. La Paro, allowed me to stay at her home in New Orleans while I completed my Louisiana research and visited LSU Press. At the press, John Easterly, Catherine Landry, and Margaret Dalrymple offered nothing but words of encouragement for this project, and the remarks and corrections of my copyeditor, Sarah Whalen, have improved my effort immensely. Finally, my older son, Alex, managed to keep his hands off Daddy's books, my new daughter, Gwen, had the good timing to be born just a few days late, and my younger son, Evan, helped by being a good sleeper. My wife, Sue, assisted in innumerable ways, but I am sure she would want me to list a few, such as researcher, motivator, editor, typist, and adviser.

Editor's Introduction

In the fall of 1862, the British government was considering intervening in the bloodbath being waged between Union and Confederate forces in America. Those cabinet members who supported involvement hoped to gain France and Russia's backing before implementing a formal move, but the timing of such a move would be tricky and a united European front would be difficult to manage. A number of factors compelled the British to consider strongly calling for an armistice or recognizing the new southern government.[1]

These factors were both economic and humanitarian in nature. Many Europeans already saw the rebels as a viable independent people and no longer questioned the status of their nationhood. To them it seemed pointless for members of the two warring factions to slaughter one another by the thousands. Since many Americans shared a common heritage with John Bull, the tragedy was even more painful to those bystanders. From an economic point of view, as the blockade established by the United States Navy grew stronger each month, trade between the British Isles and southern ports was increasingly affected. Most important, cotton and cloth surpluses stored by mill owners in Lancashire County, England, were low, and workers felt the pinch in the county's twelve hundred-plus cotton mills. The laborers had already experienced shorter work hours and layoffs and leaned on governmental and private relief assistance.[2]

From the perspective of certain key Britishers, the Federals had lost any realistic chance of subduing their former countrymen that they might have once possessed. The possibility of conquering nine million white southerners in an area over half the size of western Europe seemed very

1. Howard Jones, *Union in Peril: The Crisis over British Intervention in the Civil War* (Chapel Hill, N.C., 1992), 1–5.
2. *Ibid.,* 54, 69, 90.

slim from the outset. Furthermore, English politicians blasted Abraham Lincoln's policy on slavery. His administration had not taken firm steps to liberate the slaves at the beginning of the war, and only after setbacks on the battlefield did Lincoln address the issue squarely. Unfortunately, his approach to the problem struck many on both sides of the ocean as ineffectual and hypocritical. The Great Emancipator's decree, which went into effect January 1, 1863, freed slaves only in the counties under Confederate control, so the document accomplished nothing unless slaves ran away from their owners to free territory or rose up and killed their masters. Consequently, since the northerners could not defeat the southerners on the battlefield, the Emancipation Proclamation would encourage chattels to topple the Confederacy from within its own southern boundaries.[3]

Amid this turmoil, an English businessman named William Carson Corsan came to America to judge firsthand the status of his firm's southern customers. Corsan, a Sheffield native of Scottish descent, was a hardware merchant and manufacturer. He lived in a single-family dwelling in the city of his birth with his wife, Ann; baby daughter, Mary Ann; and two young, unmarried servants hired as a cook and a houseservant.[4]

The firm of Corsan, Denton, and Burdekin, with two hundred employees, was just one of four hundred "American cutlery and edge tool establishments" that furnished the United States with whaling lances, clock springs, surgical instruments, mint dies, engraving plates, and cutting spades. By 1860, these Yorkshiremen were sending annually 21,998 tons of finished steel products to the States, which was one-third of their total yearly output. Companies like Corsan's were known locally as "American merchants." When the blockade slashed the commercial sinews that bound Sheffield to the agriculturally based South, Corsan took the drastic step of heading to America to check on the marketplace, and probably to see what new opportunities were available.[5]

Upon returning to Britain, Corsan penned an account of his observations, with running commentary, entitled, *Two Months in the Confederate States, Including a Visit to New Orleans Under the Domination of*

---

3. *Ibid.,* 140–44; Lynn M. Case and Warren F. Spencer, *The United States and France: Civil War Diplomacy* (Philadelphia, 1970), 347–73; Richard N. Current, ed., *Encyclopedia of the Confederacy* (New York, 1993), I, 71.

4. Great Britain Census of 1861, County of York, Town of Sheffield; D. Hindmarch to B. H. Trask, September 17, 1993, editor's files; Geoffrey Tweedale, *Sheffield Steel and America: A Century of Commercial and Technological Interdependence, 1830–1930* (Cambridge, Eng., 1987), 8.

5. Hindmarch to Trask, September 17, 1993; Tweedale, *Sheffield Steel,* 8.

General Butler. The original edition identified the author simply as "An English Merchant" on the title page. Throughout the text, the traveler avoided giving specific details about his timetable, objectives, and some of his professional contacts.

It was common during the Victorian era for authors to cloak their identity by using initials and pseudonyms. For example, in the decade before Corsan's book, other writers had identified themselves as "An English Churchman," "An English Critic," "An English Girl," "An English Lady," "An English Landowner," "The English Opium Eater," and simply "An Englishman." The reasons for donning these literary masks were many. Corsan's decision to remain anonymous may have stemmed from humility, fear he would upset his associates, or the desire to add mystery and sensationalism to his efforts; the last would show the hand of his publisher, Richard Bentley. Whatever the reason, Corsan has remained obscure for over 125 years. Fortunately, his sobriquet matched his actual profession, for "vast is the field of pseudonymous literature in which authors have adopted names that have no resemblance to or connection with those by which they are known in private life."[6]

It should be noted that British sources do not attribute authorship of this book to William C. Corsan. Those sources in Britain that do provide a name note that "Corsom" was the author, with no first or middle initials.[7] What the reader learns about the author from the text is that he had a keen interest in Confederate finance, agriculture, and consumer goods, the attitude of citizens, and conditions in blockaded ports. In my research I have come to believe that William Carson Corsan of Sheffield was the author, particularly because of the information provided in his obituary on December 5, 1876: "When the American civil war was at its height, and his own business engagements at a standstill, he paid a visit of two months duration to his customers in the Southern States, determined to see and judge for himself as to the state of affairs and the future prospects of trade. He was in New Orleans at the time of General Butler's rule of that city, and on his return to England published a small volume, in which he took a very sanguine view of the prospects of the South."[8]

Another cloudy area requiring research was when and where Corsan

6. William Cushing, *Initials and Pseudonyms: A Dictionary of Literary Disguises* (New York, 1886), 90–91; James Kennedy *et al., Dictionary of Anonymous and Pseudonymous English Literature* (Edinburgh, 1926–34), VII, xiii.

7. Michael L. Turner, *Index and Guide to the Lists of the Publications of Richard Bentley & Son, 1829–1898* (Herts, Eng., 1975), 57; G. Ridgley to Patrick Flood, September 3, 1992, editor's files.

8. Sheffield (Eng.) *Independent,* December 5, 1876.

departed for and arrived in the United States. On August 28, 1862, the British Foreign Office issued Corsan a passport (number 61696) for travel on the Continent. The banking house of Glyns served as a reference. Twice in his book Corsan mentions presenting his passport to Confederate and Union officials. Once underway, he documented his trek from October 12 in New York City to mid-December in Richmond, Virginia—just before the battle of Fredericksburg. Before the engagement, Corsan slipped through the lines to return north for passage back to England.[9]

A check of passenger lists coming into New York shows that a "Mr. Corsan or Corsen" arrived on September 23, aboard the SS *Etna* from Liverpool via Queensland. The voyage took twelve days. He was described as an English gentleman, age thirty-two years, who traveled cabin passage.[10] This information does not quite match what is known of Corsan, who would have been thirty-seven at the time. During his journey into the South, however, Confederate provost marshals attempted to draft him into the army, indicating that he had the appearance of a man between the ages of eighteen and forty-five. Furthermore, the passenger records from September 11 to October 11 do not reveal any other male with a similar name.[11] Corsan, however, did not have to sail directly to New York from Liverpool; he could have steamed from England to Boston or Philadelphia and then taken a train to New York. Nonetheless, the Liverpool–New York route was the one most traveled in those autumn months.

Because Corsan informed his readers that in October he boarded the SS *Marion* on the East River, bound for New Orleans, one would expect to find him listed as a passenger when the vessel entered the Crescent City. Unfortunately, the pertinent records at the National Archives are listed as missing for that year, but his name does appear in four New Orleans newspapers as "W. C. Corsan," first-class passenger.[12]

9. Pp. 119 and 121 herein; Passport Index, 1862, Public Record Office, London, Foreign Office 611/11 (Co to Co); Passport Register, 1862, PRO, FO 610/32, 106; E. F. Thomson to B. H. Trask, September 29, 1993, editor's files.

10. Passenger Lists of Vessels Arriving at New York, 1820–1897, Roll 223, September 11–October 16, 1862, Record Group 36, Microcopy 237, National Archives, Washington, D.C.; Sheffield (Eng.) *Independent,* December 5, 1876; New York *Herald,* September 23, 1862. The *Herald* lists a "Mr. Corsen" as a passenger on the *Etna.*

11. Patricia Faust, ed., *Historical Times Illustrated Encyclopedia of the Civil War* (New York, 1986), 161 (title hereinafter abbreviated as *HTIE-CW*); Passenger Lists of Vessels Arriving at New York, 1820–1897, Roll 223, RG 36/MC 237.

12. Passenger Lists of Vessels Arriving at New Orleans, 1802–1902, Roll 259, December 1, 1860–

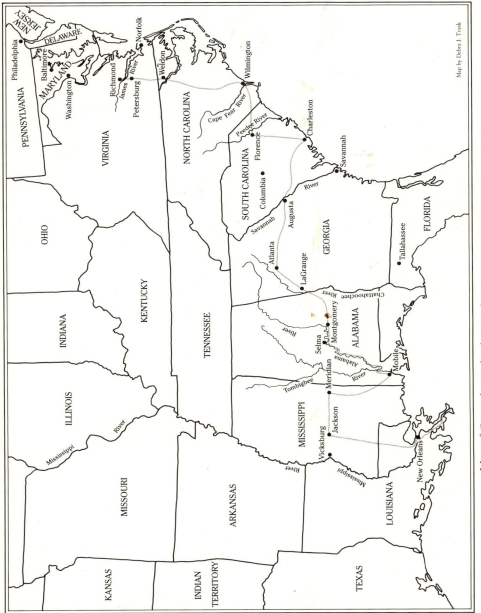

Map of Corsan's overland route from New Orleans to Richmond

It seems likely that Corsan returned to England in December, 1862, or early the next year. Sometime during 1863, the firm of Richard Bentley on New Burlington Street in London published Corsan's account. Bentley's house was well established but not always well respected. In 1829, Bentley had formed a partnership with Henry Colburn that lasted three years; Colburn then began his own press. About the time Bentley introduced Corsan's work, the business was on the rebound following two lean decades.[13]

Colburn and Bentley became rivals, and "their methods frequently caused them to be attacked; puffery and sharp dealing were not beneath their dignity, and some of their colleagues questioned whether they had any dignity at all." These harsh comments were more often applied to Colburn, "yet Colburn and Bentley were ahead of their time in their advertising methods."[14] These remarks are relevant in relation to Corsan's monograph because they may explain why General Benjamin F. Butler's name appears in the original subtitle. Corsan saw him only once, and the text concerns affairs in Richmond more than in New Orleans, where Butler was commanding general of the Union occupation forces. Butler's name, however, generated an emotional reaction like few other Civil War players. Over a period of months, Butler was involved in a number of imbroglios, some of them at the international level, and by 1863, his actions were well known in England.[15]

Butler's infamous "Women Order" (General Order No. 28), issued in the spring of 1862, called for his soldiers to treat the ladies of New Orleans like common prostitutes if they spurned the gentlemanly gestures of the Federals. This happened frequently, with the women of Louisiana even cursing and spitting on the soldiers at times. The British press misinterpreted the order "as an incitement to commit rape and other assorted atrocities on the flower of Southern womanhood."[16]

Butler also ruffled international feathers when he demanded that foreigners doing business in New Orleans take an oath of loyalty to the

March 31, 1866 (June, 1861, to February, 1865, missing), Record Group 36, Microcopy 237, National Archives. The *Daily Delta, Daily Picayune, Daily True Delta,* and New Orleans *Bee* all noted on October 21, 1862, the *Marion's* departure from New York harbor.

13. Patricia J. Anderson and Jonathan Rose, eds., *British Literary Publishing Houses, 1820–1880,* Dictionary of Literary Biography Series (Detroit, 1978–93), CVI, 49–50.

14. *Ibid.,* 39.

15. John D. Winters, *The Civil War in Louisiana* (Baton Rouge, 1963), 126–28.

16. Belle Becker Sideman and Lillian Friedman, eds., *Europe Looks at the Civil War* (New York, 1960), 148.

United States, which was part of his plan to undermine smuggling between the Union-held city and the Confederacy. Many foreigners had no
qualms about fostering commercial intercourse with the rebels even from
a port under Federal control. Butler's frustration with the situation was
understandable. Nevertheless, his efforts embarrassed the government in
Washington, and Lincoln checked his tack.[17]

The "Women Order," clashes with consuls and their countrymen, the
imprisonment of a former U.S. senator's wife, the arrest of British seamen
for singing rebel songs while in port, and the hanging of a New Orleans
citizen for defacing a United States flag were the sorts of incidents that
made Butler known in Europe and infamous in the South.[18] Therefore,
Bentley's use of the general's name in the title of Corsan's book revealed
his tendency toward sensationalism, as well as his book-trade acumen.

The original and, until now, only printed edition indicates that the
publisher moved quickly with the project. It had 299 arabic-numbered
pages with no chapter divisions, preface, introduction, frontispiece, index,
illustrations, or table of contents. The editors and I have imposed twelve
chapter divisions, changed the subtitle, created paragraph breaks, and
inserted a few words in brackets for readability. The volume sold for
eight shillings, six pence. In the three copies I examined, the original
binding consisted of green cloth coverboards with gilt lettering on the
spine. The firm of R. Clay, Son, and Taylor of Bread Street Hill in
London printed the book. Richard Clay's career as a recognized printer
dated from 1817 and his association with Samuel Burton at Bishopsgate.
All in all, the book's appearance was typical for the period.[19]

With so many long-standing, familiar bonds between the United
Kingdom and the States, British interest in the war was high. Entrepreneurs like Bentley offered numerous accounts about travel to the South

---

17. Winters, *Civil War in Louisiana*, 128–29.

18. *Ibid.*, 128; Stewart Sifakis, *Who Was Who in the Confederacy* (New York, 1988), 206, 224, Vol.
II of *Who Was Who in the Civil War*.

19. Sampson Low, comp., *The English Catalogue of Books with the Dates of Publication in Addition
to the Size, Price, Edition and Publishers Name* (1864–91; rpr. New York, 1963), II, 389; Philip Gaskell,
A New Introduction to Bibliography (Oxford, Eng., 1979), 245–46. The editor examined copies of the
book at the Virginia Historical Society, the College of William and Mary in Virginia, the Historic
New Orleans Collection, and the Library of Virginia, and a copy held by the proprietor of Henry
Stevens, Son and Stiles of Williamsburg, Virginia. In 1968, Lost Cause Press of Kentucky issued an
opaque microcard edition of the book. The Virginia Historical Society's copy contains the bookplate
of Charles Francis Adams, a New Englander who was American ambassador to Great Britain during
the Civil War; however, I could not link Adams to Corsan. William B. Todd, *Directory of Printers
& Others in Allied Trades, London and Vicinity, 1800–1840* (London, 1972), 40.

during the conflict, as well as memoirs by English-born southerners re-counting their experiences and their views on slavery in the antebellum period. A few appeared just after the war but may have been in press before Appomattox. One of interest that Bentley also produced was the Reverend William Wyndham Malet's *An Errand to the South in the Summer of 1862* (London, 1863), which covered the period from May to November, 1862, and recalled the reverend's efforts to visit his sister in South Carolina.[20]

Two frequently quoted travel accounts of activities in the Confederacy were written by British subjects Lieutenant Colonel Arthur James Lyon Fremantle and London *Times*'s special correspondent William Howard Russell. Though sympathetic to the South, Fremantle's effort is consid-ered the best of such accounts, while Russell's contribution to the litera-ture angered combatants on both sides of the Potomac. "He irked the North especially by his account of the rout of the Federals at First Ma-nassas. He stirred up hostility in the South by his phobia against slavery, which he denounced time and again as barbarism."[21] Both journals have been through several editions.[22] Critical bibliographies have commented favorably on Corsan's book as well. One remarked that "as a close-up view of economic and social conditions in the Confederacy it is a reliable account." Another claimed that "these observations . . . sympathetically reveal much of social and economic conditions in the wartime South."[23]

Corsan represented unofficially the expectations and prejudices of many of the British business class. He could not imagine the Federal government quelling a revolt by such a large number of English-speaking men and women who inhabited such a huge expanse of land. Corsan also revealed his prejudice against African Americans and Jewish Americans. In his mind, blacks who enlisted with the Union could not possibly go toe-to-toe with white southerners on the plain of battle, and Jews viewed the war only as a business opportunity.[24]

20. E. Merton Coulter, *Travels in the Confederate States: A Bibliography* (Norman, Okla., 1948), 173–74.

21. *Ibid.*, 222.

22. For the latest editions of these works, see Martin Crawford, ed., *William Howard Russell's Civil War: Private Diary and Letters, 1861–1862* (Athens, Ga., 1992), and Arthur James Lyon Fre-mantle, *Three Months in the Southern States: April–June 1863* (Lincoln, Nebr., 1991). I used an earlier reprint edition of the Fremantle (Westport, Conn., 1970).

23. Coulter, *Travels in the Confederate States,* 58; Allan Nevins *et al.,* eds., *Civil War Books: A Critical Bibliography* (2 vols.; Baton Rouge, 1967, 1969), I, 75.

24. See pp. 21, 61, 113, 116 herein.

Yet despite his opinion on the inferiority of blacks, he did not support the slave trade, with all of its suffering and selling of members of another race. Corsan's remarks about Jews are also telling. He portrayed them as greedy profiteers who exploited the needs of southern Christians squeezed by the Union naval blockade and pressured by oncoming armies from the North. Southern urban whites held this belief as well, a dislike that was reinforced as the situation worsened for the Confederacy. Corsan seemed to forget or ignore that he too was a businessman investigating opportunities for continued profits when the fighting ceased and perhaps during the conflict also. This would help explain why he made a personal trip instead of corresponding with his company's debtors, who would not be able to make payments until after the war regardless. It was odd that Corsan traveled such a long way only to confirm their intention to do so unless he hoped to resume trade during the conflict.[25]

Like other European travel journals of the era, Corsan's attempted to explain differences between northern and southern cultures. From New York's East River to the Mississippi Delta, Corsan saw much of the United States. Other English visitors gave southern society mixed reviews, but Corsan painted both white civilians and rebel troops as robust and earnest in their struggle to liberate themselves from the North at any cost.[26]

Corsan's "very sanguine view of the prospects of the South" probably went sour a year later. His poor prognostic skills indicated that he was a mediocre businessman. Corsan's obituary reported he "was of Scotch extraction, but his father carried on business in Sheffield for many years. In early life William Carson Corsan was brought up to the Sheffield trade, and gained considerable experience in transactions with America." Even with such experience, his partnership proved unsuccessful. "The American civil war destroyed all his calculations and frustrated his plans." Corsan's trip to the South may have been an act of desperation to save his firm; upon his return, however, the venture apparently failed anyway, as a result of the blockade and the Confederacy's loss. By 1868, he was in business for himself, but this too was not fruitful.[27]

In the 1870s, according to his obituary, "when he was able to pull himself together again, he went out to New York as the representative

25. *Ibid.;* Harold D. Woodman, *King Cotton and His Retainers: Financing and Marketing the Cotton Crop of the South, 1800–1925* (Lexington, Ky., 1968), 213–15.

26. Christopher Mulvey, *Transatlantic Manners: Social Patterns in Nineteenth-Century Anglo-American Travel Literature* (Cambridge, Eng., 1990), 33–48; pp. 28, 66, 93 herein.

27. Sheffield (Eng.) *Independent,* December 5, 1876; Hindmarch to Trask, September 17, 1993.

of the eminent house of Harrison Bros. and Howson." This firm was one
of the oldest cutlers and silversmiths in Sheffield, dating back to 1843,
when James William Harrison, John Sansom, and George Howson
formed a partnership. New York City directories listed Corsan as an
importer at 26 Cliff Street in Manhattan, between Fulton and John
Streets, with his residence in Brooklyn. Corsan returned home to Sheffield eighteen months before his death on December 2, 1876, at the age
of fifty-one. He left behind his wife and "several young children." His
obituary candidly remarks that "he was in many respects a man of note
in commercial circles, but perhaps a little too sanguine for the successful
carrying out of large undertakings." His strength was that "of a shrewd
observer of the business signs of the times," a trait evident in his travel
account.[28]

I hope that reprinting Corsan's book will help other students of the
Civil War and the Victorian era to recognize its value as a resource. When
Corsan accurately described his surroundings, he revealed much about
the Confederacy; when he was less accurate, he revealed much about
himself and the British merchant class.

For bibliophiles looking for a first edition of Corsan's account, the
going rate at this writing is between $300 and $585.[29] For those with more
modest tastes, what this reprint lacks in collectible value I hope is offset
somewhat by the additional commentary on Corsan's business trip of a
lifetime.

28. Sheffield (Eng.) *Independent,* December 5, 1876; Hindmarch to Trask, August 23, 1993, the
letter contains a photocopy of a post–World War II ad for the firm Harrison Bros. & Howson,
which gives some of its history.

29. Tom Broadfoot *et al., Civil War Books: A Priced Checklist with Advice* (Wilmington, N.C.,
1990), 107; Henry Stevens, Son and Stiles, *Catalogue New Series 101* (Williamsburg, Va., January,
1993), 15.

TWO MONTHS IN THE
CONFEDERATE STATES

TWO MONTHS

IN

THE CONFEDERATE STATES,

INCLUDING

A VISIT TO NEW ORLEANS

UNDER

THE DOMINATION OF GENERAL BUTLER.

BY

AN ENGLISH MERCHANT.

LONDON:

RICHARD BENTLEY, NEW BURLINGTON STREET,

𝔓𝔲𝔟𝔩𝔦𝔰𝔥𝔢𝔯 𝔦𝔫 𝔒𝔯𝔡𝔦𝔫𝔞𝔯𝔶 𝔱𝔬 𝔥𝔢𝔯 𝔐𝔞𝔧𝔢𝔰𝔱𝔶.

1863.

facsimile of original title page

ONE

Steaming from New York to New Orleans

O n a cold, wet, gusty day, early in October last, I waded through the liquid mud of the streets of New York to Pier No. 4, North River, alongside which lay "the fine steamship *Marion,* bound for New Orleans direct, without calling at Key West, Havanna, or any other port," as the advertisement truthfully stated. I had contrived to be so very nearly too late, as to have only time enough before starting to notice that the steamer was very much smaller than I had been led to believe, not by any means either a recently-built or imposing specimen of naval architecture, exceedingly crowded, but, on the whole, very clean, and sufficiently manned.[1]

Of course, the damp dirty wharf or pier was crammed, as usual, with cheerful, tearful, or stolid groups, either whispering "last words," mixed with sobs, in each other's ears, shouting "remembrances" for Bill or Jake to a friend on the hurricane-deck,[2] or staring gloomily at some acquaintance with whom hands had been shaken half an hour ago, but who could

---

1. Corsan probably applied for passage at the owner's office of Spofford, Tileston and Company on 29 Broadway. Built in 1851, the brig-rigged steamship made regular runs to New Orleans, Key West, and Havana early in the war. The *Marion* was about two hundred feet long with a breadth of beam of about thirty-one feet. On Corsan's trip, the ship left New York on October 11 and landed early on the evening of the twentieth.

Corsan's name appears in several sources as "W. C. Corsan," passenger on the *Marion:* in the *Daily Delta,* the *Daily True Delta,* the *Daily Picayune,* and the New Orleans *Bee,* all October 21, 1862; New York *Herald,* October 11, 1862; William M. Lytle *et al., Merchant Steam Vessels of the United States, 1790–1868* (Staten Island, N.Y., 1975), 137; *Marion* entry, in Eldredge Collection of Vessel Histories, Mariners' Museum, Newport News, Va.

2. The *hurricane deck* is "an upper deck of light scantlings above the superstructures"; a "promenade deck on passenger vessels" (René de Kerchove, *International Maritime Dictionary* [Princeton, N.J., 1961], 685).

be seen reciprocating the silent evidence of friendship by a returning stare over the bulwarks. As a matter of course, also, the ubiquitous newsboy was there with his everlasting cry of " 'Ere's the *'Erald, Tribune, Times, Express,* third edition![3] 'Ave a paper, sir? Three for a dime, sir! Thankee, sir! 'Ere's the *'Erald,*" &c.—the solemn nobody, who has neither friends going by the steamer, nor was a passenger himself, but who, nevertheless, had to be pushed or pulled off the gangway, every few minutes, to make way for the real traveller or traveller's friend—the apple-women, orange-girls, and crowd of New York loafers, whose solemnity of visage, intensity of curiosity, and seediness of dress, no language can describe.

Into the midst of this composite mass, every minute or two, would drive a "carriage," reckless of life or limb, so that the "fare" was not "left." Performing really the office of a cab only, though, with its pair of fine horses, bright harness-mountings, plate-glass, abundance of straps, fringe and varnish, and roomy interior, aping the size and style of the private carriage, two or three of these vehicles were sufficient to almost sweep the crowd of idlers into the water. But a crowd is not so easily driven into a corner; and that on Pier No. 4, North River, New York, continued to sob, whistle, shout, laugh, and stare, until a quiet gentleman, dressed in a suit of black broadcloth and a chimney-pot hat, who had been standing beside me, looking at the bustle below, and whom I took for a passenger, suddenly mounted the bridge, accompanied by another civilian (whom, from his inevitable dress-coat and black satin vest, I recognised in a moment as the true New York pilot), and alone, or with the assistance of the civilian aforesaid, proceeded to brawl some incomprehensible orders, which resulted, firstly, in convincing those who were not aware of the fact before, that our captain was aboard, and, secondly, in releasing the *Marion* from the pier exactly at the moment announced in the advertisement.[4]

---

3. Horace Greeley (1811–1872) founded the New York *Tribune.* He "did not hesitate to expound his own quite progressive views in his papers—particularly his opposition to slavery" (John S. Bowman, ed., *The Civil War Almanac* [New York, 1983], 340). James Gordon Bennett (1795–1872), the New York *Herald*'s founder, was "in favor of letting the seceding states go, and even proposed a reorganization of the Union under the new Southern constitution, with the New England states left out. With the actual firing on Fort Sumter, however, Bennett grasped the demands of public opinion and began to make the *Herald* a newspaper of acceptable loyalty, though sometimes copperhead [prosouthern] in tone" (*Dictionary of American Biography,* II, 195–99).

4. Charles Edward Russell's work, *From Sandy Hook to 62°: Being Some Account of the Adventures, Exploits, and Services of the Old New York Pilot-Boat* (New York, 1929), examines the role of these skilled pilots and includes a photograph of a dapper-looking guide sporting a top hat, vest, long coat, and heavy watch chain.

I have, of course, not the slightest intention of boring my readers with a description of a voyage from New York to New Orleans in October, 1862, by a mail-steamer. Not that there is not a mine of untold wealth in this as in many another bit of travel for the word-painter—in the busy, crowded harbour of New York, and her matchless bay—the glorious sunsets off the coasts of South Carolina and Florida—the strange approach to New Orleans up the muddy Mississippi—and in the Crescent City[5] herself, once so gay, prosperous, crowded, and high-spirited; now so deserted, pinched, silent, and cowed. All this, however, I must leave other writers to supply. My object and duty is specially to note the kind of men and women whom a traveller along these once almost hackneyed routes will meet in these changed days, what the motives are which take these people from home, and what their wishes and language on the momentous problems which are being worked out around them, and in the solution of which, no doubt, they are all unconsciously taking a part.

My own object in visiting the South is soon explained. The firm of which I was a member has for years dealt with many Southern merchants, from or of whom we had heard almost nothing since the commencement of the civil war. I was anxious, if possible, to ascertain whether our old friends were living or dead, and solvent or ruined. My intention was, if possible, to penetrate into and travel over the Confederate States, in pursuit of this perfectly innocent inquiry. I was told that it was just possible that I could get through the Federal and Confederate lines around New Orleans; and with this, I must own, very vague plan in my mind, I found myself steaming, as I have before said, on a cold, wet, gusty day, last October, down the bay of New York, on board the steamship *Marion,* bound to New Orleans.

I have said that the *Marion* was crowded: she was crammed full. I do not recollect how many passengers she really took, nor how many she was capable of accommodating comfortably. I do recollect, however, that we had on board just three times as many as we ought to have had, and that, consequently, the luggage-room forward (a kind of steerage quarter) had been shelved and curtained round with temporary berths, which were every one taken, and of which I occupied one.[6]

There was nothing in the absence of privacy, deficiency of pegs or

5. New Orleans is known as the Crescent City because of its location on a bend of the Mississippi.

6. *Steerage* is defined as "the part or space of a passenger vessel in the 'tween' decks, alloted to the passengers who travel at the cheapest rate." In British usage, steerage means all passengers except cabin passengers (De Kerchove, *International Maritime Dictionary,* 781–82).

chairs on which to put one's garments during the hours devoted to slumber, the economical supply of towels, soap, and water, or the presence of a barber, and mountains of luggage in the middle of the limited space—to terrify a traveller. The beds were clean, the food good and abundant, the stewards civil and attentive, and the ship in the hands of careful officers and men. But to sleep over a nest of boilers, in the month of October, south of Cape Hatteras, is no joke. If, in addition to being parboiled, one happens to be within a few feet of a sick German nurse, a crying child, a band of brothers who come rolling home from twelve to three A.M., and another set of monomaniacs who, with a view to securing the early worm, get up from four to six A.M.; my own impression is, that the pleasures of the day must be very peculiar to banish the recollection of the miseries of the night. I cannot say, however, that my New York friend and I, who ran against each other before we had been afloat half an hour, did not find sufficient to watch, and talk to or about, to make the trip, in spite of everything, a very pleasant one.

Our complement of passengers was made up of Northern invalids, seeking health during the impending winter in the sunny South[7]—Federal officers, returning from leave of absence—Southern merchants, going to watch over their property—ladies and children, seeking to rejoin their Northern or Southern protectors in New Orleans—confidential clerks, going to see how the land looked—Eastern manufacturers, big with the notion of putting the Butler[8] screw on some "rebel" debtor—Yankee speculators, who believed that the Union inhabitants of the Confederacy were beginning to send down their sugar and cotton in immense

7. Corsan's picture of health seekers going to the "sunny South" ran counter to other sojourners' overall view of Dixieland. "Most people of the antebellum period recognized that Southerners were not as healthy as Northerners. The rural character of the South, and the pervasive poverty, had produced a disease environment similar to those in developing countries today." Furthermore, the "climate in which the soldiers fought proved [also] to be a factor in the high rates of illness and mortality" (Judith Lee Hallock, " 'Lethal and Debilitating': The Southern Disease Environment as a Factor in Confederate Defeat," *Journal of Confederate History,* VII [1991], 51, 59).

8. Politically appointed, the Union general Benjamin Franklin Butler (1818–1893) became one of the most hated men in the Confederacy and the prosouthern sectors of Europe. His detractors accused him of stealing silver from civilians, allowing corruption and nepotism, encouraging slaves to run away from their masters, and abusing the honor of southern ladies. He was the commanding general when Corsan arrived in New Orleans (Faust, ed., *HTIE-CW,* 98–99; *DAB,* III, 357–59). The term "Butler screw" refers to an order Butler issued on July 9, 1862, that required payment of all debts and interests due companies or citizens of the United States within the Department of the Gulf (*The War of the Rebellion: A Compilation of the Official Records of the Union and Confederate Armies* [Washington, D.C., 1880–1901], Ser. I, Vol. XV, p. 518, hereinafter cited as *OR*; unless otherwise indicated, all citations are to Series I).

quantities to New Orleans, in spite of Jeff. Davis—and broken-down New York and Boston commercial hacks, with misty plans of setting up in New Orleans as auctioneers, commission-agents, or politicians, and having a pull somehow, by virtue of their "loyalty," on the prostrate carcase (as they were told in the *Herald*) of the "played-out" Confederacy.

A more heterogeneous mass could not well be imagined, nor one under the crust of which raged more irreconcileable opinions, more opposite hopes, nor more implacable hatreds. Notwithstanding, however, that politics were by no means tabooed, we had not one angry discussion during the whole trip. With that absence of anything like violent feeling, and that moderation of language which, some may think singularly enough, I have found to characterise the conversation of all Federal officers, or, indeed, of any American entitled to the name of American, on the present troubles, dangerous ground was mutually avoided.

New Orleans, of course, was spoken of as a city finally and for ever annexed to the Union; her inhabitants were evidently believed to be rebels, to a man and woman, at heart; and it seemed to be a settled conclusion in every Northern man's mind that coercion, confiscation, and abolition, administered by such a master as General Butler, were not only what the inhabitants of New Orleans and the whole South deserved, but that no system of government would be effective which was not saturated with this policy. Nobody seemed to have any misgivings about the *policy* of "crushing out the rebellion" in this way—much less about the *power* of the North to do it. The ill success of her armies in the field—the hopeless financial ruin which was at her doors—the peculations, injustice, and misery which filled the land, counted for nothing with these optimists.

"In ninety days, sir," they would invariably end by saying, "we shall have Charleston, Savannah, Mobile, and Richmond; the Mississippi will be opened from Cairo to New Orleans; the Confederate armies will be broken up; and we shall have all the South making the best terms they can. We shall then retain at every point of strategic importance in the South bodies of Northern troops sufficiently imposing—appoint Northern military governors to each State—and treat them as territories until one by one they sue in proper form for re-admission to the Union and give ample proofs of their loyalty and sincerity. Of course the property of all contumacious rebels will be confiscated and divided among loyal Northern and Eastern men, who will thus gradually leaven the whole South with Yankee enterprise, industry, and religion. No doubt slavery will be soon abolished, and of course the South must bear her share of taxation, of which a high tariff must be a part; while we shall refuse to recognise one cent of the notes or bonds the rebel Government has issued. Thus, in a few years, we shall again be an united, prosperous, and powerful people, not to be trifled with."[9]

Such was the fate promised the unhappy Southerner. How thankful should those Southerners be, that between them and designs begotten of such sublime conceit and marvellous ignorance Providence has placed the gulf of "possibility"!

As we steamed south of Cape Hatteras and along the "rebel" coast, officers and men began to speculate on their chance of falling in with the dreaded *Alabama*. The *Marion* had some half-dozen light pieces on board, with ammunition and everything necessary, but to any kind of war-vessel she would have afforded a very easy prey. When the idea had been put into one's mind by the fears of the crew, it did certainly seem strange that two or three steamers per week could be plying between New York and New Orleans unmolested. With the exception, however, of two or three distant sail, we never saw a vessel of any description from Cape Hatteras to New Orleans.[10]

At length, on the morning of the eleventh day after leaving New York, we found ourselves, as the mist rose from the flat wooded country ahead of us, steaming round the last point in the river which concealed New Orleans from our view. We had entered the muddy Mississippi the previous afternoon by the South-West Pass, threading our way with great difficulty among the projecting masts of the vessels which the Confederates had sunk on the bar to prevent the Federal fleet coming up the river.[11] The point where water ends and solid land begins is so indefinite

9. On July 28, 1868, the Fourteenth Amendment to the U.S. Constitution formally "repudiated the Confederate debt." Instead, it was Union citizens who demanded and eventually obtained more than $15 million for losses inflicted on American vessels by Confederate raiders built and outfitted in Great Britain. British diplomats negotiated for almost $2 million for losses suffered by the Queen's subjects (Faust, ed., *HTIE-CW*, 170, 263).

10. To protect the *Marion* from the commerce raider CSS *Alabama*, the U.S. Navy assigned its personnel to master and man guns mounted on the ship. Corsan was correct in observing that such a crew would be no match for rebel raiders. A year earlier, the *Marion's* contingent was just "four ordinary seamen, 4 seamen, 1 quarter gunner, 1 gunner's mate, 4 landsmen," and a master (*Official Records of the Union and Confederate Navies in the War of the Rebellion* [Washington, D.C., 1894–1927], Ser. I, Vol. I, p. 85, hereinafter cited as *OR, Navies;* unless otherwise indicated, all citations are to Series I).

11. Coming from the east, a ship entering the "South-West Pass" required a little extra time to reach the entrance; however, this channel was the deepest and the tides varied little at that time of year. Edmund M. Blunt and G. W. Blunt, *The American Coast Pilot* (New York, 1857), 396–97; A. A. Humphreys and H. L. Abbot, *Report upon the Physics and Hydraulics of the Mississippi*

on the Mississippi, that night had set in before we had reached any of the rich plantations which line a great portion of the river-banks between New Orleans and the Gulf of Mexico. As far as I could see while daylight lasted, the land on either side was a mere flat, low, swamp, covered with tall reeds, and filled, no doubt, with alligators, mosquitoes, and similar abominations.[12]

In the way of shipping we met nothing except a few schooners clustered round a tug, and one small steamer loaded with United States' troops. It was impossible to believe that this was the river down which was shipped one half the whole cotton crop of the continent, besides sugar, molasses, corn, pork, &c. &c. in enormous quantities. Instead of our meeting hundreds of ships going to sea—steamers bound to New York, Havanna, Texas, and heaven knows where besides—and coasters innumerable, the river was as silent and deserted as when first discovered.[13]

River . . . (Philadelphia, 1861), xvii, Appendix G, [1]; Gerald M. Capers, *Occupied City: New Orleans Under the Federals, 1862–1865* (Lexington, Ky., 1965), 32.

The sunken vessels with their "projecting masts" were part of a series of barriers set up to snag Union warships. The ships were part of a floating system of chains and hulks, in this case, *hulk* being defined as "an old ship converted for some use which did not require it to move" (Peter Kemp, ed., *The Oxford Companion to Ships and the Sea* [London, 1976], 406). The ranking officer of Forts Jackson and St. Philip reported that the schooners were afloat before the battle. Also David G. Farragut, the federal flag officer, in his report noted the "chain which crossed the river and was supported by eight hulks, which were strongly moored" (*OR, Navies,* XVIII, 155–56; *OR, IV,* 546–49).

12. Corsan's use of the word *alligator* is notable and correct as compared with earlier European travelers and explorers who used *crocodile* (Vaughn L. Glasgow, *A Social History of the American Alligator: The Earth Trembles with His Thunder* [New York, 1991], 7, 23–37).

13. Truly, New Orleans was a great port. One business guide called it "the grand emporium of all the vast tracts traversed by the Mississippi, the Missouri, and their tributary streams, enjoying a greater command of internal navigation than any other city, either of the Old or New World" (J. Smith Homans and J. Smith Homans, Jr., eds., *A Cyclopedia of Commerce and Commercial Navigation* [New York, 1859], 1417). By the 1850s, however, receipts of goods from the nation's interior began to decline, with the exception of tobacco and cotton, because of the growth of trade in Cincinnati and St. Louis and the use of railroads and canals elsewhere. Finally, many of the related financial transactions involving cotton shipped from New Orleans occurred in New York City. Thomas E. Redard, "The Port of New Orleans: An Economic History, 1821–1860" (Ph.D. dissertation, Louisiana State University, 1985), I, 173–94; James H. Soltow, "Cotton as Religion, Politics, Law, Economics, and Art," *Agricultural History,* LXVIII (Spring, 1994), 11–12.

Before the outbreak of war, thousands of citizens were employed in the cotton business as draymen, stevedores, pilots, and factors, and in labor gangs. Thirty-six countries had consuls in the city, no doubt because of the importance of trade. In 1859–60, the city exported $96,166,118 in cotton; far more of the fiber left New Orleans than from any other American port. See U.S. Treasury Department, *Report of the Secretary of the Treasury Transmitting a Report from the Register of the Treasury of the Commerce and Navigation of the United States for the Year Ending June 30, 1860*

During the night we stopped at Forts Jackson and Philip, in which the Confederate authorities had placed so much reliance when the city was threatened by the Federal fleet. From the fires burning, both forts seemed full of men, and all on the alert. When morning broke, we were, as I before said, rapidly nearing New Orleans, and soon were steaming slowly along the river-front of the city to our station at Front Levée.[14]

As most people know, New Orleans is built on the low land, between the river Mississippi and Lakes Pontchartrain and Maurepas. The general shape of the city is that of a fan, the river flowing round the outer edge and all the streets running from a centre-point towards that edge. The population of the city was something over 170,000 people before the war.[15]

By far the greatest portion of the swamps, on which the city is built, is on a lower level than the full waters of the river, which, in fact, are only prevented from drowning the inhabitants out by solid artificial banks, or levées, which perform the double duty of keeping the Mississippi within bounds, and providing a splendid wharf, nearly nine miles long, fronting the river.

In times of peace, this immense area would have been piled up from end to end, in the month of October, with cotton, sugar, and provisions of all kinds; while the river would have been crowded with steamers, barges, canal-boats, cotton-boats, and all kinds of craft, anxiously seeking

---

(Washington, D.C., 1860); Charles Gardner, comp., *Gardner's New Orleans Directory for the Year 1859* (New Orleans, 1859).

14. Forts St. Philip and Jackson, twelve miles above the Head of Passes, where the Mississippi branches to the Delta, were the anchors of the Confederate defense of New Orleans. Jackson, on the right bank, was begun in 1822 and completed ten years later; St. Philip, its twin masonry structure, rested on the opposite bank. The forts, a line of hulks, and a patchwork fleet made up the rebel contingent; on April 10, 1862, however, high waters washed away every part of the barrier and flooded the forts. After a heavy shelling, Union commander David G. Farragut's fleet rushed through the Confederates. On April 25, Farragut landed in New Orleans prepared to accept the surrender of the city. *OR*, VI, 512; Faust, ed., *HTIE-CW*, 281–82; Zed H. Burns, *Confederate Forts* (Natchez, Miss., 1977), 54–59; Terry L. Jones, ed., *The Civil War Memoirs of Captain William J. Seymour* (Baton Rouge, 1991), 15–40.

The Front Levee borders directly on the Mississippi River. The *Marion* landed at William J. Reid's dock in New Orleans' first district (*Daily Delta*, October 21, 1862).

15. New Orleans' population in 1860 consisted of 144,601 whites, 10,689 free blacks, and 13,385 slaves, for a total of 168,675 residents (Department of the Interior, *Population of the United States in 1860: Compiled from the Original Returns of the Eighth Census* [Washington, D.C., 1864], 195).

Lake Pontchartrain (Poncharterain) was named for Louis, Comte de Pontchartrain (1643–1727), and Lake Maurepas honored Comte J. F. P. de Maurepas; both men were French political officials (George R. Stewart, *American Place-Names: A Concise and Selective Dictionary for the Continental United States of America* [New York, 1970], 286, 382).

an opening along the crowded levée to unload. As soon as ever day broke, this immense extent of wharf would swarm with negroes, dock-labourers, sailors, carmen, clerks, and merchants; and probably no spot in the world would present a more active and stirring spectacle than the levée of New Orleans, when the crops were being received.[16]

How different was the sight which met our eyes on that fine October morning, as we steamed slowly along this levée to our station! Half a dozen paltry coasters, seeking a freight which was not to be found; some six or eight Federal gunboats, which really were nothing more than ordinary passenger-steamers, iron-plated, with a few guns on board; and a Federal steam-ram, called the *Essex,* were all the shipping which occupied the river: while neither a bale of cotton, a hogshead of sugar, a bushel of corn, a packet of merchandise, or a man at work, could be seen from end to end of that levée, nearly nine miles long.[17]

As we glided along past the ends of the streets of the French city,[18] which ran at right angles with the river, groups of idlers stared, without any sign of interest, enthusiasm, or dislike, at the stars and stripes which our steamer showed. Occasionally the glistening of bayonets showed when the Federal pickets were keeping or relieving guard. But the stores seemed all closed; neither dray nor carriage could be seen on the move; and, in fact, the city seemed deserted. Gradually we passed the Mint,[19]

16. In 1860, over thirty-five hundred steamboats arrived in New Orleans (Louis C. Hunter, *Steamboats on the Western Rivers: An Economic and Technological History* [Cambridge, Mass., 1949], 644–45).

17. Local papers for the month included listings for a few schooners and international packets (*Daily Delta* and New Orleans *Bee,* October 1–31, 1862). Union naval forces in the area included screw gunboats, the USS *Kineo,* USS *Sciota,* USS *Katahdin,* and USS *Itasca,* and support vessels like the *St. Maurice* and *Iberville.* The USS *Essex* was converted from a civilian vessel to an ironclad. *OR, Navies,* XIX, 247–50; Paul H. Silverstone, *Warships of the Civil War Navies* (Annapolis, 1989), 155.

18. "In 1731 Louisiana reverted to the French crown.... In 1763 France ceded New Orleans and Louisiana west of the Mississippi to Spain.... Following secret negotiations in 1800 to regain Louisiana from Spain, Napoleon decided to sell it to the United States in 1803" (David C. Roller and Robert W. Twyman, eds., *The Encyclopedia of Southern History* [Baton Rouge, 1979], 900).

19. The Mint on Esplanade Avenue, which was designed by William Strickland, was begun in 1835 and completed in 1838. The E-shaped structure has an Ionic portico and remains an impressive edifice. After seizing the building and its contents, the state of Louisiana turned the operation over to the new Confederate government. On March 18, 1861, a sum of $389,267.41, known as the "Bullion Fund," was accepted by the secretary of the Confederate treasury. Edward H. Hall, *Appleton's Handbook of American Travel: The Southern Tour* (New York, 1866), 102; Mills Lane, *Architecture of the Old South: Louisiana* (New York, 1990), 101; James M. Matthews, ed., *The Statutes at Large of the Provisional Government of the Confederate States of America* (Richmond, 1864), 57, 93, 94. "Soon after the authority of the Union was re-established at New Orleans, a special agent was appointed to

where Mumford[20] was hung, by order of General Butler, because he assisted to haul down the United States' flag, which had been hoisted over that building by a boat's-crew before the city was surrendered by the mayor; then past the quaint Cathedral,[21] built by the Spaniards, standing in an old-time-looking square, ornamented by an equestrian statue of Jackson, in bronze;[22] then past the Custom House, a massive granite building, very extensive, and about two-thirds completed, but now crowded by Federal soldiers, who used it as a barracks;[23] and then slowly to our landing at Front Levée.

As we were being made fast to the wharf, I noticed a Federal officer in undress push quietly through the few score staring Irishmen and ne-

---

examine the condition of the branch mint in that city, and its machinery. The machinery proved to have been greatly injured, and portions of it were found distributed and secreted in various parts of the city. The portions were collected and replaced in the mint, and the necessary repairs are in progress. The operations of the branch mint, however, have not been, and for the present at least, will not be resumed" (U.S. Treasury Department, *Report of the Secretary of the Treasury, on the State of the Finances, for the Year Ending June 30, 1862* [Washington, D.C., 1863], 26).

20. In April, 1862, William B. Mumford (1820?–1862), a professional gambler, lowered the Federal flag that had been raised over the Mint by a party of marines. At the time, Farragut was negotiating for the formal surrender of the city. For his actions, Butler ordered Mumford tried for treason, and in short order he was found guilty and was hanged in front of the Mint. The outraged Confederates claimed the city had not yet been officially surrendered to Federal authorities. For this and other actions, Jefferson Davis branded Butler an outlaw. See Hall, *Appleton's 1866*, 102; Winters, *Civil War in Louisiana*, 98; Roller and Twyman, eds., *Encycl. of Southern History*, 868.

21. The structure is the St. Louis Cathedral, which was officially dedicated on December 7, 1851. See Leonard V. Huber and Samuel Wilson, Jr., *The Basilica on Jackson Square: The History of the St. Louis Cathedral and Its Predecessors, 1727–1987* (New Orleans, 1987), 33.

22. Jackson Square is at the heart of the French Quarter; it was laid out by the French in 1721 as the Place d'Armes. The Spanish called it Plaza de Armas, and the Americans knew it as the Public Square. Natives dubbed it Jackson Square, honoring the hero of the Battle of New Orleans during the War of 1812, who later became president. The Jackson Monument Association had begun efforts by 1851 to create a bronze sculpture of Andrew Jackson on horseback, mounted on a stone base, and in 1856, sculptor Clark Mills's rendition of "Old Hickory" was unveiled (Edward J. Cocke, *Monumental New Orleans* [New Orleans, 1968], 1, 56, 79–81).

23. The U.S. Customs House covers a city block (about two acres) and was one of the largest granite buildings in the country when it was finished. Construction began in 1848 and had not been completed by the time Corsan arrived. Just before the war, the future Confederate general Pierre Gustave Toutant Beauregard (1818–1893) held the position of supervising architect. Not until 1881 was the third story completed (Lane, *Architecture,* 137, 140; Faust, ed., *HTIE-CW,* 51–52).

The customs office for the District of New Orleans had 227 employees, an indication of the port's value to the U.S. Treasury. The Customs House, fronting Canal Street, also contained a court and post office. The structure suffered from rough use and the elements, but the Unionists constructed a temporary roof that provided some protection (Hall, *Appleton's, 1866,* 102; U.S. Treasury Dept., *Finances, 1860,* 92–93).

groes, who stolidly watched our vessel, and slip on board, followed by a sort of serving-man. This, I found, was no less a personage than General Butler himself, who had come from his office (where he was usually to be found as soon as day dawned, and often sooner) to meet his wife, who, it seemed, had been our fellow-passenger, though very few of us knew it.[24] He seemed a spare man, of middle height, quick and nervous in his movements, and, at a glance, very much more like a lawyer than a soldier. His face is distinguished by nothing more unusual than what the boys called a "cock" eye; and with its thin compressed lips, livid complexion, almost, if not entire, absence of beard, moustache, or whisker, and thin grey hair thrown back over his ears, impressed me simply as the face of a restless, earnest, decided, and possibly abrupt man; but with no special bias towards, nor familiarity with, evil, rather than as that of the cruel, cunning, unprincipled scoundrel which, by common consent, so many millions of people believe him to be.

I could not help looking almost with pity on that one unarmed man, for whose blood a whole nation was thirsting; who is never spoken of by half his own countrymen but as "the beast;" who is probably hated more intensely than any other living man, and by more people; and against whose dying quietly in his own bed there are so many untold chances.[25]

Finally, we landed without trouble, examination of baggage, or any demand for names, business, or intentions, and soon found ourselves in the only hotel then open—the "City Hotel."[26] It was very plain that there was neither business nor pleasure going on in New Orleans. The day was intensely hot, the mosquitoes abundant, and the streets deserted. Of course the ubiquitous newsboy was there, and active; but the newspapers he vended were, without exception, the most wretched representatives of the press I ever saw, their publishers being compelled, I found, to abstain

24. Sarah Hildreth Butler (d. 1877), a former actress, was listed in a local paper as "Mrs. Major General Butler and servant." Actually, she was returning to New Orleans, as her first visit of the war was in May, 1862, when she joined the general at the St. Charles Hotel (Benjamin F. Butler, *Butler's Book: A Review of His Legal, Political, and Military Career* [Boston, 1892], 79, 374; Orleans *Bee,* October 21, 1862; *DAB,* III, 357).

25. Butler was so hated, southerners called him "Beast"; he was also known as "Spoons" because he reportedly took silverware from pro-Confederate citizens (Faust, ed., *HTIE-CW,* 99).

26. The City Hotel, built about 1831, was located on Camp Street on the corner of Common Street. After the war, one travel guide pointed out that it was much frequented by merchants and steamboat men. Hall, *Appleton's, 1866,* 101, 296; *Hellier's New Orleans Business Directory for 1860 and '61 with Commercial Register of Business Men of New York City* (New York, 1860), 301; Mary Louise Christovich *et al.,* eds., *New Orleans Architecture: The American Sector* (Gretna, La., 1972), 47, 70, Vol. II of Christovich *et al.,* eds., *New Orleans Architecture.*

entirely from comment unfriendly to the Federal Government, and even submit to a military censor the news they intended to publish.[27] Beyond a trifling, retail trade, all commerce seemed extinct; certainly all of a wholesale kind. Subsequent experience proved, that since the occupation of the city by the Federals, commerce had been extinct.[28]

Although a Military Governor of Louisiana[29] had been appointed, and the fiction was kept up officially, that the whole state was subjugated, the truth was, that the Confederate pickets were within ten miles of the city in one direction, and held in heavy force all the north shore of Lakes Pontchartrain and Maurepas, between which and the river, as I said before, New Orleans is situated. The consequence, of course, was, that no produce was permitted by the Confederates to enter, nor merchandise to leave, the city, and New Orleans was really blockaded by her friends.[30]

So long as transit with the interior was possible, a brisk trade had gone on, and the stocks of groceries and dry goods especially had been almost entirely sold out at enormous prices in Confederate money. These funds, as fast as they accumulated, had been despatched by the hands of trusty agents into the interior, and invested in sugar or cotton, at eight to ten cents per pound, on the plantations. As a rule, only such lots of cotton were purchased as either were then, or could easily be, removed from twenty-five to fifty miles from river, road, or railway.[31] It was considered

---

27. In 1862, the local papers included the New Orleans *Bee,* New Orleans *Crescent, Commercial Bulletin,* and *Daily True Delta.* Butler clashed with the editors immediately, and eventually the general forced all the papers to cease their operations for various periods of time. Billy H. Wyche, "The Union Defends the Confederacy: The Fighting Printers of New Orleans," *Louisiana History,* XXXV (Summer, 1994), 280–81; Capers, *Occupied City,* 240; Roller and Twyman, eds., *Encycl. of Southern History,* 901.

28. The use of the word *extinct* is a misstatement on Corsan's part. Legal and illegal trade, although limited, continued under Butler (Walter E. Pittman, Jr., "Trading with the Devil: The Cotton Trade in Civil War Mississippi," *Journal of Confederate History,* II [1989], 133–39).

29. George Foster Shepley (1819–1878) served as the military governor of the federally occupied parishes of Louisiana. He was a Maine attorney and had been a regimental commander before his appointment in the summer of 1862 to brigadier general and military governor. Despite his qualifications, Shepley was little more than an aide to Butler. Glenn R. Conrad, ed., *A Dictionary of Louisiana Biography* (New Orleans, 1988), II, 739; *Who Was Who in America: Historical Volume, 1607–1896* (Chicago, 1963), 430.

30. "By the end of 1861 the Union blockade had cut exports to a trickle. Though the blockade from the gulf was lifted after the city's capture in the spring of 1862, the situation worsened during the next year because the Confederates then imposed a similar blockade from the north" (Capers, *Occupied City,* 146). *OR,* Ser. IV, Vol. II, 126; Matthews, ed., *Statutes of the Confederate States,* 152.

31. Corsan's discussion of cotton stored in small troves near transportation routes points out just one of the methods used by factors and planters to maintain their businesses. "Prosperous wartime

prudent, also, not to have in any case more than fifty bales stored in one place. The result of all this was, that all the principal houses in the city had realized very large fortunes, and invested the bulk in cotton, at about threepence sterling per pound.[32] There can be no doubt that eventually every debt in New Orleans may be paid in full; and I could not hear of a solitary instance, where the slightest disposition was manifested to repudiate, or even compromise either a Northern or a foreign debt. While I was there, however, trade was annihilated. Firms, whose sales would add up to millions of dollars per annum, were not selling enough to pay a porter's wages; and depression, sullen and hopeless, weighed down the spirits of a commercial community usually the most sanguine and cheerful in the world.[33]

About the real sentiments of the population there could be no doubt. Such a thing as an "Union" party outside the *employés* of the Federal Government does not exist.[34] Deprived of their arms, their property liable to confiscation, every negro turned into a Federal spy, cut off from their Confederate friends, with near 20,000 Federal troops and several thousand armed "contrabands" in their midst, and their river held by Federal ships of war, which in a few hours could flood the city by cutting the banks and letting the Mississippi in upon them,—against such odds re-

---

trading, profits judiciously invested, cotton hidden and saved—these are the recurring themes in the histories of those who saved themselves from ruin. To these must be added others—trade with the enemy, fraud, and theft. In all these activities cotton assumed a leading role. If the war had proved that King Cotton's power was far from absolute, it did not topple him from his throne, and many found it advantageous to continue to serve him" (Woodman, *King Cotton*, 216).

32. Sale of cotton in very small quantities did attract public attention. Thirty-six slightly damaged bales sold for $155 a bale during Corsan's visit. The average bale of cotton weighed about four hundred pounds and sold for about eleven cents a pound before the war. Cotton sold for $155 a bale would be about four cents a pound. If these bales were of normal size, this would indicate that prices actually may have fallen at this time, even in Union-held areas, or more likely there was an artificial lack of demand in New Orleans. *Daily Delta,* October 22, 1862; *Daily True Delta,* October 21, 1862; Roller and Twyman, eds., *Encycl. of Southern History,* 300; James M. McPherson, *Battle Cry of Freedom: The Civil War Era* (New York, 1988), 100.

33. The 1860 census revealed 1,232 manufacturing establishments in Orleans Parish, the most numerous being clothing and shoe manufacturers and cooperage and truck works, as well as other critical war industries such as metal shops and shipbuilding yards. The total annual value of production was $11,373,265. Despite these figures, the cotton trade was the major industry (Department of the Interior, *Manufactures of the United States in 1860: Compiled from the Original Returns of the Eighth Census* [Washington, D.C., 1865], 199–200).

34. New Orleans did in fact have its share of Unionists. The *Daily Delta* ran ads for Union men to meet in Jefferson City and for the Union Association of the Second District (*Daily Delta,* October 21, 1862).

sistance was not to be thought of. No language, however, could convey an adequate idea of the loathing with which the hated Yankee was regarded, and that, too, without regard to age, sex, or condition. Of course the ladies were less guarded than the gentlemen,[35] but beyond either keeping indoors, or avoiding the streets when the Federal officers and men were likely to be met with, declining without distinction any social acquaintance or intercourse with them, refusing to countenance anything like balls, operas, or theatricals, and perhaps singing the "Bonnie Blue Flag"[36] with more frenzied energy, I neither saw nor heard of any act of which any gentleman would take cognisance. The middle and upper classes of New Orleans, in brief, seemed to me to be alternately ashamed of the discreditable defence which she had made against the enemy, and amazed at the cool manner in which step by step General Butler had disarmed them, and placed them at his mercy; but after this state of mind would come such expressions of smothered hate, and longings for deliverance in any way, as showed plainly that, though helpless and cowed, they were worse "rebels" than ever.

"If the men had half the spunk which the women have," said a pretty Creole lady, "New Orleans would soon be ours again. Oh! how I hate the Yankees! I could trample on their dead bodies and spit on them! Why *don't* you help us?" "What could we do?" an old and wealthy merchant said. "The Confederate Government never could be brought to believe that New Orleans could be taken, and therefore saw no necessity for extreme haste in completing the rams we had building. Then, again, the contracts for the machinery for the rams were given out to favourites of parties in power, and no great pressure put on them. The result was that, when the Federal fleet came up, we had only Forts Jackson and Philip to depend upon, and the boom across the river. The boom

---

35. From the time the Federals landed, the white women of New Orleans were openly hostile. Navy officer George Hamilton Perkins recounted how the women vocalized their dissent and shook Confederate flags when the Yankees landed. Julia Le Grand remembered that during the early occupation "the whole city, both camp and street, was a scene of wild confusion. *The Women only* did not seem afraid. They were all in favor of resistance, *no matter how hopeless* that resistance might be" (Henry Steele Commager, ed., *The Blue and the Gray: The Story of the Civil War as Told by Participants* [1950; rpr. New York, 1982], 810, 811).

36. The "Bonnie Blue Flag" seemed to be a favorite in New Orleans. "Written early in 1861 at Jackson, Mississippi, and presented as the highlight of [Harry B.] Macarthy's 'Personation Concerts,' 'The Bonnie Blue Flag' was sung in the New Orleans Academy of Music in September, 1861. The house was filled with soldiers en route to Virginia and the song was, in the phrase of the day, received with unbounded applause" (Richard Harwell, *Confederate Music* [Chapel Hill, N.C., 1950], 56).

was passed in consequence of treachery; and one fine morning, after repeated assurances by telegraph from the forts all the previous day that the defences could not be passed, we woke up and saw a Federal fleet off the levée, and troops landing opposite the Custom-house.[37] Of course all our young men left when the city was taken. Then the city was surrendered to save property; then we were disarmed; then we were compelled to take the oath of allegiance; and then negroes were encouraged to run away, enlist, and bear arms; and now, if for no other reason than to save our families from outrage and death, we *must* grin and abide our time. But the day of reckoning *will* come, and then—look out!"

Even the Irishmen and Germans, who are usually employed as dock labourers, carmen, porters, &c., but whom General Butler has wisely set to work to clean out the canals, sewers, and streets of the city, and to repair the Levée—even they seem to hate the Yankee. "What will a dollar and a half a day do towards keeping a man and his family?" one man indignantly exclaimed, who had just emerged from the slime of one of the canals. "Sure, we was a dale bitter off with the ould sett than this. Thim d— niggers will starve a poor white man out of house and home, if they sits them free, and be d—d to them."[38]

The fact is undeniable that the Northern Conqueror is hated cordially by every class of residents, and that nobody looks upon the occupation of their city as a thing which can last. It is borne as an evil which will soon be abated. When I was there, the only hotel open for travellers, as I said before, was the "City Hotel," the St. Charles[39] being closed, and others used either as hospitals or as headquarters of some Federal departments. The Custom-house was being used as barracks and offices; pickets patrolled the adjoining streets, cannon commanded the approaches; and a constant communication by signal was kept up with the gunboats and troops across the river and elsewhere. Merchants, commission-agents,

---

37. The obstruction across the river was swept away by heavy rains flowing down the river or removed by Farragut's men; it was not removed as the result of treachery or deception (Capers, *Occupied City,* [32]). Other defenses in southern Louisiana in various states of readiness included Chalmette Battery and Forts Bienvenu, Pike, Livingston, and Macombe (*OR,* VI, 819).

38. Despite the image of New Orleans as an old French and Spanish city, by 1862 there were far more Germans, Irish, and African Americans. And to no surprise, "election riots involving Irish immigrants in the mid-1850s fueled nativism" (Francesco Cordasco, ed., *Dictionary of American Immigration History* [Metuchen, N.J., 1990], 365–70); Capers, *Occupied City,* 5–6.

39. The official name of the St. Charles was the St. Charles Exchange, and it was located between Common and Gravier on St. Charles Avenue. Christovich *et al.,* eds., *New Orleans Architecture: The American Sector,* 70; *Hellier's New Orleans Business Directory for 1860,* 30. The directory lists fourteen other major hotels.

brokers, and tradesmen lounged about their empty stores and offices until about two P.M., taking occasional drinks with quiet toasts, and then went home to curse the common foe in peace. Ladies ventured out as little as possible; and the half-empty streets were left to Federal officers and soldiers, negroes, curious nurse-girls, dogs, and mosquitoes. By eight P.M. the city seemed fast asleep; not twenty people apparently being abroad after that hour. By ten P.M. even the few bar-rooms and billiard saloons which had been open would be deserted and closed; no theatre, opera, or social gathering could be sustained; people seemed pleased another day was gone; and New Orleans, in October 1862, exceeded in dulness any little country-town I ever saw the day after market-day.

It would be tiresome to repeat the charges of oppression, peculation, and bad morals with which the Federal officials were charged. General Butler and his brother Colonel Butler came in for the largest share of abuse, the former on account of his "orders," and alleged brutality of speech and manner; the latter because of his monopoly of the supplies to the city in the way of bread-stuffs, groceries, medicines, and all staples and imported necessaries.[40] They were accused of having made jointly from 3,000,000 to 6,000,000 dollars out of this monopoly. The sugar and cotton, seized "as rebel property" by the Federal forces, was said to be sold to Colonel Butler at absurdly small prices, and shipped to New York; ransom-money taken for setting persons at liberty who had previously been locked up for nothing; hush-money taken for the suppression of threatened confiscation; share-money of debts collected for Yankee creditors at frightful sacrifices to the Southern debtor; proportion of profit on cargoes of salt, medicines, and clothing, run into the Confederacy by their

40. Butler's brother, Andrew Jackson Butler (1815–1864), was not a colonel in the U.S. Army but did serve as an unofficial aide. One source shows that his commission as a captain was rejected on February 6, 1862, by the U.S. Senate (Thomas H. S. Hamersly, comp. and ed., *Complete Regular Army Register of the United States: For One Hundred Years (1779 to 1879)* [Washington, D.C., 1881], 16). Also see *Butler's Book,* 41. Nevertheless, he remained very active in the region and worked as a shipping agent and procurement officer; he made money as a middleman for cotton, cattle, and other supplies. Edward Bacon, an officer from Michigan, recalled shortly after the war, "We learn[ed] that General Butler's brother, Andrew J. Butler, and Colonel Shaffer, Chief Quartermaster, are supposed to be the best intercessors to obtain some favor for us with the Major-General" (Edward Bacon, *Among the Cotton Thieves* [1867; rpr. Bossier City, La., 1989], 26). Also see Dick Nolan, *Benjamin Franklin Butler: The Damnedest Yankee* (Novato, Calif., 1991), 72, 172. Andrew Butler died February 11, 1864, in the St. Denis Hotel, New York City, at "age 49, less two days" (New York *Herald,* February 13, 1864). The newspaper also lists him as a colonel, an indication of militia rank or honorary title.

consent; and in fact money taken for every conceivable violation of duty and character of which man is capable.[41]

If one tithe of what was openly asserted was true, death was too mild a punishment for the perpetrators. And still, strange to say, both the General and the Colonel could be seen any day riding up and down the street, sometimes with, but often without escort; and in fact acting as though they were the most pure and popular rulers the city ever knew.

I must add, that the inexpressible disgust with which the two Butlers were regarded did not extend to any other Federal officers, or only to very few of them. Brigadier-General Shipley [sic], the Military Governor of Louisiana, and Major Strong,[42] were especially spoken of as gentlemen who were fulfilling difficult duties in a gentlemanly manner; and I must confess that the same tribute seemed justly due to all the Federal officers with whom I came in contact. The soldiers also were certainly very well behaved, and free from disorder. I never saw a case of drunkenness or bullying among them while in the city, though all the bar-rooms were open, and the pleasures of the city accessible to all.[43]

---

41. Butler "expected the war to advance his political fortunes and the financial fortunes of his family and friends" (DAB, III, 34). However, the trade could not have flourished without the corruption of southern officials and residents. "Private citizens disregarded government policy with impunity; additionally, Confederate officials accepted bribes to let cotton marked for destruction fall into Union hands" (Roller and Twyman, eds., Encycl. of Southern History, 271).

Salt became a precious commodity in the South. Before the war, the United States imported twelve million bushels of salt annually with a "striking proportion" going to southern states. Almost a quarter, or about 350 tons a day, "entering from England was brought to the port of New Orleans." The English used the sacks as ballast and traded for cotton. Salt consumption was roughly thirty pounds per person; it was used for seasoning, preserving meat, and as a dietary requirement (Ella Lonn, Salt as a Factor in the Confederacy [1933; rpr. University, Ala., 1965], 14–15).

A sampling of prices fixed by the acting mayor, Colonel Henry C. Deming, included $9.50 for a barrel of flour, twenty cents for 52 ounces of bread, ten cents for 26 ounces, and five cents for 13 ounces. Within ten days, the price had risen to twenty cents for 46 ounces of bread, ten cents for 23 ounces, and five cents for 12 ounces (Daily True Delta, October 16, 26, 1862). Local papers did advertise medicines such as opium, quinine, chloroform, and morphine for sale but did not provide their costs to the consumer (Daily True Delta, October 22, 1862).

42. Major George C. Strong was assistant adjutant general under Butler (OR, IV, 707).

43. "The first of the tenderloin districts of New Orleans to attain special notoriety was the 'Swamp,' an area bounded by South Liberty and South Robertson Streets, and by Girod and Julia streets. It was an incredible jumble of cheap dance halls, brothels, saloon and gaming rooms, cock-fighting pits, and rooming houses. A one-story shantytown jammed into a half-dozen teeming blocks, the Swamp was the scene of some eight-hundred known murders between 1820 and 1850." Later, "during the late 1850s and early 1860s the Swamp declined for purely geographical reasons, as its inhabitants drifted downtown into Gallatin Street behind the French Market, a location even more convenient, now that pretense of legal control had been demolished, and where the pedestrian traffic

The acts of the Federal officers which seem to have most exasperated the New Orleans people are, the execution of Mumford; the orders against the "women of New Orleans," against "assembling in groups on the side-walks," against "singing treasonable songs," and so on;[44] the enforced oath of allegiance on all males and *females* over eighteen years of age, without distinction;[45] the taking away of arms, followed by the arming of negro regiments raised from the runaways of the city and state, who of course were the refuse of all the gaols and plantations in the neighbourhood; the deposition of all their local governments, and imprisonment of their mayor and other officials for treason;[46] the forcible seizure and occupation, without pay, of some of the most magnificent residences in the city by Federal officers as a "military necessity;" the placing of negroes on a level with white men in courts of justice, as regards the horse-cars they should ride in, &c.; the closing of churches; confiscation; forcible collection of debts; and general insolence and hectoring whenever opportunity occurred.

It is not my province to discuss the question as to whether such a city so seized and held could be rightfully so treated: of this, however, I am certain, that no other plan could have been devised which would so effectually alienate all latent Union feeling, and exasperate beyond redemption all sentiments of enmity as the policy which General Butler inaugurated and pursued, and which the Washington Government sanc-

---

was heavier" (Al Rose, *Storyville, New Orleans: Being an Authentic, Illustrated Account of the Notorious Red-Light District* [1974; rpr. Tuscaloosa, Ala., 1989], 7, 9).

44. The infamous "Women Order" went into effect on May 15, 1862, infuriating southerners. Pleas from the mayor went unheeded as Butler ordered that a lady showing disrespect to Union troops and ignoring courtesies of these gentlemen "shall be regarded and held liable to be treated as a woman of the town, plying her avocation" (*OR*, LIII, 527); Faust, ed., *HTIE-CW*, 840; Winters, *Civil War in Louisiana*, 132.

In 1862 Union officials arrested a Royal Navy officer from the HMS *Galatea* for singing "The Bonnie Blue Flag." In the summer, a similar incident occurred when the officers and crew of the HMS *Rinaldo* sang the tune (Regis A. Courtemanche, *No Need of Glory: The British Navy in American Waters, 1860–1864* [Annapolis, 1977], 148; Winters, *Civil War in Louisiana*, 128).

45. As a result of foreigners' continued trade with the rebels, Butler demanded they too take the oath. This directive angered consulates and diplomats stationed in the city and in Washington (Winters, *Civil War in Louisiana*, 128–30).

46. John T. Monroe (1822–1871), a former stevedore, was elected mayor in 1860, having already served as an assistant alderman. He continually demonstrated his prosouthern leanings by openly opposing imprisonment of his fellow citizens and by contact with Confederate leaders. Eventually, Butler imprisoned him in Fort St. Philip and later Fort Pickens, near Pensacola. After the war, he once more became mayor, but Union officials again removed him from office (*OR*, IV, 707; *Dictionary of Louisiana Biography*, I, 575; *Gardner's New Orleans Directory*, 212).

tioned. "If you visit Mobile, Savannah, Charleston, or Richmond," several gentlemen said before I entered the Confederacy, "tell them to blow up or burn down their cities, and perish, man, woman and child in the ruins, rather than run the risk of suffering what we suffer!" I am satisfied that General Butler's conduct has, by intensifying the feeling of the Confederates, been as good as 50,000 additional troops arrayed against the Union cause.

While I was in New Orleans two events occurred which would certainly have provoked an outbreak, if the population had been armed. The first was the marching of a negro regiment about 800 strong,[47] down the whole length of Canal-street at noon on a fine Saturday, with flags flying, bayonets fixed, drums beating, the band playing "Yankee Doodle," and Colonel Stafford, a white man, at their head.[48] One negro, as the regiment passed the store of his former master, who was then in the Confederate army, shook his rifle at the name over the door, and shouted, "Dat's de man *I* wants to meet on de field ob battle!" at which of course his company grinned a frightened grin. The bulk of the men seemed either fagged, sheepish, or afraid of the scowling line of white faces along which they passed. Any three white men in the crowd could have dispersed the whole regiment with a good cart-whip each, and a few yells.

The other event to which I allude was the despatch as prisoners to Fort Lafayette of three episcopal clergymen because they refused to pray for the President of the United States in the proper portions of the service.[49] For this offence these three gentlemen were forced from their fam-

---

47. At first Butler, in a wise and technically correct move, recruited for the Union black regiments that already existed, not individual African Americans. The regiment Corsan mentions here was part of the "Native Guards," originally formed in April, 1861, as part of the state militia to protect the city from invasion. Butler persuaded these units to switch to the Union cause under new leadership. In endeavoring to place African Americans in a more active role, he pushed the limits of his authority.

On August 22, 1862, General Order No. 63 went into effect, calling upon "the free colored militiamen of Louisiana to enroll in the volunteer forces of the Union" (Dudley Taylor Cornish, *The Sable Arm: Negro Troops in the Union Army, 1861–1865* [1956; rpr. New York, 1966], 65); *OR,* Ser. III, Vol. II, 436–38.

48. Colonel Spencer H. Stafford transferred from a New York regiment to join Butler's staff. He served as assistant provost marshal and later as acting provost marshal. On October 31, 1862, he took command of the 1,637 soldiers of the First and Second Louisiana Native Guards (African descent). *Butler's Book,* 896; *OR,* Ser. III, Vol. III, 1115.

49. The ministers—William Thomas Leacock (*ca.* 1810–1884), Charles Goodrich (b. *ca.* 1805), and John Fulton (d. 1907)—also refused to take the oath of allegiance. Butler branded Goodrich "an active and violent secessionist" and claimed Fulton had served as a private in the Confederate

ilies, which in two cases sorely needed their presence; at a few hours'
notice, sent to a prison over 2,000 miles away, and their churches closed.
So completely cowed, however, were the inhabitants, that not over 150
or 200 people, chiefly ladies and idlers, assembled to bid them farewell.
They went off, however, in good spirits, one of their number declaring
loudly and cheerfully that they would "soon be back, with the stars and
bars flying at the peak!" Such was the state of New Orleans in October
1862, and such the dead lock to which both parties had arrived.

Having at length brought my own business to a conclusion in New
Orleans, it became necessary to find out some mode of getting into the
Confederate States. Every one agreed that, unless the consent of the Federal authorities could be obtained, the only three ways open from New
Orleans were, by going to Havannah, and taking passage on board one
of the vessels which regularly ran the blockade from that port to Mobile;
crossing the Mississippi to Algiers, and skulking north through the forests
and swamps on the west bank of that river, until an opportunity occurred
of again crossing at a point above the Federal pickets; or, taking a skiff,
and putting out boldly across Lake Poncharterain, the north shore of
which was in the hands of the Confederates. Fortunately for me, I was
not compelled to adopt any of these hazardous plans; though in one of
these three modes, undoubtedly, a stream of intelligence, and everything
else, sets steadily and daily, out of New Orleans into the Confederate
lines.

---

army; Leacock had published a sermon before the war that was "highly incendiary in its nature"
(OR, Ser. II, Vol. IV, 650); DLB, I, 350, 493–94. The trio were taken to New York and delivered to
a U.S. marshal, who paroled the clergymen and sent them back to New Orleans. Once within view
of the city, they were required to take the oath. When they refused, they were transported back to
New York (Hodding Carter and Betty Werlein Carter, So Great a Good: A History of the Episcopal
Church in Louisiana and of Christ Church Cathedral, 1805–1955 [Sewanee, Tenn., 1955], 133–35).

TWO

Sailing into the Confederacy

I *was told, in confidence, that instructions had been given to issue passes,* quietly, to a limited number of troublesome and "disloyal" citizens, to cross the Lake into rebeldom, and stay there; and that, if I chose to join them, we should be taken across somehow. I accordingly walked up to Brigadier General Shipley's office, at the City Hall,[1] was very politely received, explained my wish and object to the General's A.A.A. Adjutant;[2] and, after a close cross-questioning and some very sensible advice, received a pass, authorizing me to cross the Lake, on parole of honour, not to give "information, aid, or comfort, to the enemies of the United States."[3] The next question was, how to get across; but I was assured that in a few days a schooner would probably be advertised. The very next day an advertisement appeared in one of the papers, stating that the "schooner *Locust Tree* would sail on——instant, for Ponchiatonla, across the Lake."[4] As Ponchiatonla [*sic*] was about ten miles *inside* the

1. The City Hall rested opposite Lafayette Square at the intersection of St. Charles and Lafayette (formerly Hevia) Streets. As expected, it was a marble structure looking much like a Greek temple. Christovich *et al.,* eds., *New Orleans Architecture: The American Sector, 42; Appleton's Illustrated Hand-book of American Travel* (New York, 1857), 297.

2. The rank should be "Acting Assistant Adjutant"; Corsan has added an extra "A." Neither Bernhard Pretz's *A Dictionary of Military and Technological Abbreviations and Acronyms* (London, 1983) nor Joseph H. Crute, Jr.'s *Confederate Staff Officers, 1861–1865* (Powhatan, Va., 1982) indicates that the rank of "A.A.A. Adjutant" was in use during this period.

3. A check of records at the National Archives did not reveal documentation of Corsan's pass (William E. Lind, Military Reference Branch, National Archives, to Benjamin H. Trask, March 11, 1993, editor's files).

4. The ads for the schooner *Locust Tree* appeared in the *Daily Picayune,* informing interested parties that the boat would sail on October 30 at 10:00 A.M. from the New Basin Canal to Ponchatoula (*Daily Picayune,* October 26, 28–30, 1862). In 1851, shipwrights at Sharon, Pennsylvania, constructed

Confederate lines, it seemed to me very singular that her departure should be permitted; and, on application for a passage, I was told that she might, or might not go—that I had better come down to the basin, where she laid as quietly as possible—and that no promise could be given as to when we should land, nor how long the trip would take. The difficulties seemed to be, that we might either be taken by the Federal gunboats, which were scouring the Lake, and between whose commanders and the military authorities in New Orleans the widest difference of opinion existed about the propriety of issuing these passes at all; or that we might be fired into by the Confederate pickets on the other side of the Lake, and compelled to return.[5]

Being, however, resolved upon crossing, I presented myself at the appointed hour at the basin, and found about a dozen negroes and idlers, staring at a small dirty schooner, no better, in fact, than a common oyster-boat, which turned out to be the *Locust Tree.* She was loaded deep with salt, pork and general merchandise, apparently, and her decks were piled several yards deep with all kinds of luggage, among which sat huddled some forty or fifty ladies, gentlemen, and children, who seemed to be trying to look sorry until they dare look as they felt. No one could tell us how long the trip would probably take us; but, as there was no cabin, not a square yard of spare deck room, nor awning, nor protection of any description whatever from sun, wind, rain, or dew, I could only hope, as our good-humoured captain said, that "we *might,* with a fair wind, run across in a few hours."

Among our number was Mrs. Philips, her husband and family, who had just been set at liberty by General Butler, from Ship Island, where he had sent her, some months before, for laughing as the corpse of a Federal officer was borne past the balcony of her house in New Orleans. My own impression is, that if Mrs. Philips (hating a Yankee, living or dead, as she did) was tempted to laugh at his funeral, she would do it without thinking of consequences. But it would be the uniform, and the

---

the *Locust Tree.* It was roughly 56′ × 19′ × 3′ with one deck and two masts. At the time Corsan was a passenger, the owner may have been William Wagner, and John Regnaud or John Carr its master. Very soon after Corsan left the vessel, Confederate authorities seized the schooner "for coming from the enemy with enemy's papers" (*OR,* Ser. IV, Vol. II, 172). Federal Archives in Louisiana, *Ship Registers and Enrollments of New Orleans, Louisiana* (Baton Rouge, 1942), V, 158, VI, 175.

5. A direct sailing route across Lake Pontchartrain to the Passes would be about twenty-three statute miles (U.S. Department of War, comp., *The Official Military Atlas of the Civil War* [1891; rpr. New York, 1978], CLVI, hereinafter cited as *OM Atlas*).

cause in which it was worn, and not the poor dead soldier, which provoked the demonstration, I am inclined to think; for, though evidently a
fiery partizan, possessed of a superior intellect, a sharp tongue, and a
decidedly demonstrative manner, Mrs. Philips was plainly a lady, and a
kind-hearted lady too.[6]

The remainder of our passengers were nothing less than respectable
refugees, to whom a residence in New Orleans had become intolerable,
and who were seeking congenial sentiments and friends across the border.

After innumerable farewells and parting messages, a couple of mules
were "hitched on," and in about three or four hours towed us to Lake-
port, where the canal emptied into Lake Poncharterain, about six miles
from New Orleans. Here we were stopped by the Federal pickets, and
the whole of the baggage mercilessly opened and examined, chiefly for
medicines. This involved another delay of several hours, so that the whole
day was really consumed in getting some six miles on our way. By midnight a fair but light wind had carried us about ten miles from land,
when it fell off completely, and we lay becalmed, under a brilliant moon
and unclouded sky, a prey to cramped limbs, empty stomachs, and mosquitoes.

It was very plain now that we were *not* going to cross the lake in a
few hours; and those who had come away without eatables (and they
were the majority,) began to wonder where their next meal was to come
from. By borrowing from each other, however, this difficulty was sur-
mounted in a way, and everybody tried to sleep where they sat, for cabin,
covering, or privacy of any kind was not to be had. It was well for the
ladies and children that it did not rain.

Soon after midnight a light chilly wind sprang up from the north, and
in another hour it had risen to a smart breeze, under the influence of
which a very nasty chopping sea began to be felt on the shallow lake. Of
course, our tub behaved as all such craft do under similar circumstances,

6. Eugenia Levy Phillips (b. 1819), wife of a former U.S. senator and mother of nine, had been
deported from Washington, D.C., for encouraging her children to spit on Union soldiers. In New
Orleans, she again angered Federal authorities when it was alleged she laughed at the funeral
procession of an officer. Butler could not make her apologize, so he banished her to Ship Island,
Mississippi, for two years on soldier's rations. Later, he commuted her sentence and sent her into
Confederate-held Louisiana. "The incident received international attention" (Sifakis, *Who Was Who
in the Confederacy,* 504). Her sister, Phoebe Yates Pember, showed the same strong will serving as a
matron at Chimborazo Hospital in Richmond. *OR,* Ser. I, XV, 511, Ser. II, Vol. II, 237; Phoebe
Yates Pember, *A Southern Woman's Story: Life in Confederate Richmond,* ed. Bell Irvin Wiley (1959;
rpr. St. Simons Island, Ga., 1980), 2–3. Ship Island was a yellow fever station in the Mississippi
Sound about eighty miles from the river's mouth.

ʀoiling and pitching as if she were working wonders in the way of pro-
gression, whereas every successive tack really brought us within a very
few yards of the place we had left. What with half-empty stomachs, a
touch of nausea and even sea-sickness, want of sleep, and a now piercingly
cold wind, from which there was no shelter, the ladies and children, and
even many of the gentlemen, passed a wretched night.

I was never more thankful in my life to see any day dawn than that
which found our overloaded craft, with her hungry, seedy, shivering,
silent passengers, staggering and pitching in a gale on Lake Poncharterain. Presently the sun rose; provisions, such as they were, were shared;
and a pull at a flask, and the thought that Butler was far behind, seemed
to impart new life and spirits to all. The northern and western shores of
the lake, one unvarying stretch of flat swamp, covered with cedars, pine,
and thick undergrowth, soon came in sight.

Our captain told us that he was making for Pass Manjac, through
which we were to thread our way into Lake Maurepas.[7] After hours of
almost fruitless tacking, we accomplished this, and very shortly glided
past the deserted block-house, which, with a few cannon, once commanded the entrance. By this time the wind had fallen, and the day was
as hot as yesterday. As ladies, gentlemen, and children had now been
huddled together on an open deck for over twenty-four hours, it was
deemed desirable to land for half an hour. This we did, in the cane-
brake, and then continued our way through the pass, which had the
appearance of a river about a mile or two wide, lined on either side with
cedars and pines, from whose branches hung festoons of moss, and which
seemed to grow out of the water, so dead a level was the swamp, for
many many miles, on which the forest stood.

We were told that, in times of peace, the New Orleans, Jackson, and
Great Northern Railroad[8] crossed this pass, a little further down, on a
trestle-bridge, but that the Confederate general burned it behind him
when leaving New Orleans; and very soon we descried, in the distance,
the lines of blackened piles, on which the rails had rested, stretching
across our path ahead of us. An opening had been left for vessels to pass;
and here we felt certain of being stopped either by the Federal or Con-

7. Pass Manchac (Manjac) is a navigable waterway about six miles long that connects Lakes
Pontchartrain and Maurepas.

8. Before the war, the New Orleans, Jackson and Great Northern Railroad ran from the
Crescent City to Canton, Mississippi. The stops in Louisiana included Kenner, Frenier Station,
Manchac, Ponchatoula, Tickfaw, Amite City, and Tangipahoa (G. F. Thomas, comp., Appleton's
Illustrated Railway and Steam Navigation Guide [New York, 1859], 248).

federate pickets. However, having now got a brisk leading wind, we made boldly for the opening. When within a few hundred yards of it, the glistening of the sun on a line of bayonets, among the trees on the bank to our right, distant some half-mile, showed us that the Confederate pickets had seen us; and very soon a score or two of men, who could scarcely be distinguished from the trees behind them, were seen waving their hats, and hallooing for us to heave to.[9] This was too much for the pent-up feeling of my fellow-passengers. In an instant, every handkerchief, hat, and even coats, were being frantically waved to the welcome "rebels," and such a succession of hurrahs for "Jeff. Davis and the Southern Confederacy" were given as I never heard surpassed at home, even for our beloved Queen.[10]

Of course the man at the helm must go wild, like everybody else, and neglect his duty, the consequence of which was, that in a very few minutes our precious craft ran butt against one of the piers of the old bridge, smashed in her forward bulwarks, and sent half a dozen of us sprawling among splinters and falling tackle. The upshot of this was that we were jammed fast. A boat was put out to shore, to get the assistance of our new friends. In about half an hour she returned, with the first three of the renowned Confederate soldiers I ever saw. Anything less like the received notion, at home, of how a soldier should look, or even less like the well-found, natty, Federals we had left behind, never met my eye, than the three youths who were pulled on board from their half-swamped canoe, amid the cheers and tears of our passengers.

There was no getting a sight of them when they were on board, much more a chance of speaking to them, for a good hour. Everybody wanted to give them something, and ask some question. I began to fear the women would eat them. As much food and drink were thrust on them as would have surfeited or "corned"[11] a dozen men. The lads fingered their rifles and accoutrements; the ladies "God blessed!" and "Poor thinged!" them until even the victims themselves smiled; and the men plied them with endless varieties of such questions as, "What's the news

9. The units along the north shore of Lake Pontchartrain could have been the Caruthers' Sharpshooters Company Infantry (Livingston Parish), Louisiana Scouts and Sharpshooters Company Infantry (Orleans Parish), and the Ninth Battalion Partisan Rangers (Arthur W. Bergeron, Jr., *Guide to Louisiana Confederate Military Units, 1861–1865* [Baton Rouge, 1989], 59, 176, 177).

10. Corsan is referring to Queen Victoria, who reigned for over fifty years and was one of the most beloved monarchs of all times.

11. This Scottish and northern English idiom means "to provision with corn or grain"; it provides a clue to Corsan's background (*Oxford English Dictionary*, III, 939).

from Bragg's army?" "Anything new from Richmond?" "How about
that little affair at Bayou Lafourche?" &c.&c.[12] But the young men knew
very little news; they had been down at the point where we saw them
some time; had not seen a paper for a month; and didn't seem to care
much how their compatriots went on, so that no Yankees got across Pass
Manjac alive. They asked few or no questions in return, modestly selected
a few sandwiches and apples from the abundance offered, took such a
long pull and a strong pull at the black bottle, as showed they had not
seen anything better to drink for a long time than water, and quietly
withdrew to themselves, after telling all they knew in a manner so re-
spectful, intelligent, and unassuming, as won my admiration. They said
they were going with us to Ponchiatoula, where we should find a pretty
heavy force, to which they belonged, and which was attached to the army
of the Southern Mississippi, encamped at Camp Moore, some thirty miles
from Ponchiatoula.[13] When it was possible to speak to them, I found
them to be three very quiet, sensible young fellows, from eighteen to
twenty-three years of age, all sons of respectable planters, all volunteers,
all "full of fight," and determined to perish rather than submit. Their
dress, arms, and accoutrements were the same as those of all the military
I ever saw in the Confederacy, so that our description here will suffice
for all.

They wore suits (that is, a jacket and trousers) of "homespun" cotton,
either grey or a dingy brown; a woollen shirt; rough strong shoes; and a
sort of "billy-cock" hat, all of course much the worse for wear.[14] They

12. Bayou Lafourche was one of the richest sugar plantation regions in Louisiana. From late
October to early November, Union operations in the area netted "thousands of hogsheads of sugar
of the value of at least a million dollars" (*OR*, XV, 592). By April, 1863, Federals had these parishes
under their control. See Thomas A. Becnel, *The Barrow Family and the Barataria and Lafourche
Canal: The Transportation Revolution in Louisiana, 1829–1925* (Baton Rouge, 1989), 74–75; *OR*, XV,
158–67, 592–94.

13. Ponchatoula (Ponchiatoula) most likely takes its name from the Choctaw phrase meaning
"falling hair," a reference to the abundance of Spanish moss in the vicinity (Kelsie B. Harder, ed.,
Illustrated Dictionary of Place Names: United States and Canada [1976; rpr. New York, 1985], 433).
Corsan had arrived at the newly formed Confederate Department of Mississippi and East Louisiana.
There was no "army of the Southern Mississippi," but there was a Confederate Army of Mississippi.
On October 1, 1862, the state became part of the Department of Mississippi and East Louisiana.
This department and the Department of East Louisiana formed the new and larger Army of Mis-
sissippi (Mark Mayo Boatner III, *The Civil War Dictionary* [New York, 1987], 555; *OR*, XV, 820,
840).

14. At the beginning of the war, Confederates wore a wide variety of uniforms or homemade
clothing. As the years advanced, "butternut" became very common—"uniforms colored a yellowish-

each had a splendid rifle and bayonet, in beautiful order; and cartridge-box, &c. of strong plain leather; but no sword, revolver, or bowie-knife.[15] This, with a blanket rolled up and strapped to their shoulders, completed their equipment. Of course they were strangers, evidently, to razor, comb, brush, or even soap, I fear; but they spoke good English, in a quiet, determined manner, and *not* through their noses.[16] They were small, lithe men; not much of them, but all game. I could very soon see why President Lincoln had not "subjugated the South," if the South was made up of such men as these; and, in the long run, I found that was actually the fact.

By their assistance we got our schooner free very soon, and proceeded into Lake Maurepas, across it, and, late in the afternoon, entered the Tickfaw river, one of the many sluggish streams which flow through the densely-wooded swamp into Lake Maurepas. The lofty cedars, which lined the low banks, shut out what little wind we had felt on the Lake, and there was nothing for it but pulling, if we ever intended to get up the narrow, tortuous stream. The heat was intense, and the stillness awful, but the situation was novel and exciting. Every log beside the bank had its alligator, snapping-turtle, or heron, perched or stretched on it; the woods were filled with brilliant-plumaged birds, solemn-looking owls, and enormous bats; and above all, we were in "Dixie."[17]

---

brown by dye made of copperas and walnut hulls" (Faust, ed., *HTIE-CW*, 101); James I. Robertson, Jr., *Soldiers Blue and Gray* (Columbia, S.C., 1988), 16. For the rebels, "every shape and form of hat was in evidence from the snappy French-inspired kepi to huge broad-brimmed coverings that resembled inverted coal scuttles" (Robertson, *Soldiers Blue and Gray* 17). A "billy-cock" was a round, low-crowned felt hat worn by men and occasionally young women. It may also refer to wearing the hat cocked like a bully (*OED*, II, 196).

15. The bowie knife had "a blade from ten to fifteen inches long above an inch broad, curved and double-edged near the point, carried as a weapon in the wilder parts of the United States" (*OED*, II, 457). Immortalized by Colonel James Bowie (1799–1836), the knife was also known as an "Arkansas toothpick" (Robert Hendrickson, *Whistlin' Dixie: A Dictionary of Southern Expressions* [New York, 1993], 12–13).

16. "In general, Southern dialect is best characterized by a slower enunciation than is common in most of the country combined with the gliding or dipthongization of stressed vowels." The variation of the dialect that Corsan described can be found today in tidewater Virginia to South Carolina as well as other spots in the Old Dominion. It is described as a "pleasing soft dialect with little nasalization" (Hendrickson, *Whistlin' Dixie*, xxv, xiii). "When the speech of the South became distinctive is unclear, although the first half of the 19th century, the period when the region achieved its fullest expression of regional consciousness, would make the most sense" (Charles Reagan Wilson and William Ferris, eds., *Encyclopedia of Southern Culture* [Chapel Hill, N.C., 1989], 763).

17. To most people the word *Dixie* (also *Dixey* at one time) means the South. It was forever fixed in the American psyche by the song "Dixie's Land," popularized by Ohioan Daniel D. Emmett

Night, however, soon overtook us; and long after we had composed ourselves to sleep again, as well as we could, in the heavy dews and chilly river air, we were roused by the shouts of the pickets, and saw a line of camp-fires on shore. We found ourselves among a cluster of schooners and barges, at a small village called Spring-field,[18] I believe, and were told that we could not go any higher up the river, but must either walk or be "hauled" from that point, through the woods, some six miles, to Ponchiatoula, on the New Orleans, Jackson, and Great Northern Railroad. I found that we had gradually left the low swampy land behind us, and were now in a well-wooded and rolling country. Most of our number determined to stay where they were during the night, but about half a dozen of us preferred landing and walking through the woods to Ponchiatoula, in hopes of finding food and a bed, and, possibly, teams and oxen to bring up the women, children, and baggage, on the morrow.

We found the village where we had landed deep in sleep, except some fifty or a hundred uncouth, but armed and vigilant figures, who glided round the blazing pine-knots, which they had lighted to drive off fever and ague.[19] The bank was covered with hogsheads of sugar and piles of

---

(1815–1904) just before the outbreak in hostilities. Whether the minstral wrote the tune or learned it from the Snowdens, an African American family from Knox County, Ohio, is the subject of recent debate. The earliest known printed use of the word is in an 1850 playbill titled "The United States Mail and Dixie in Difficulty." See Current, ed., *Encycl. of the Confederacy,* I, 488; Howard L. Sacks and Judith Rose Sacks, *Way Up North in Dixie: A Black Family's Claim to the Confederate Anthem* (Washington, D.C., 1993), 1–23.

The origins of the term *Dixie* are also subject to debate. One explanation is that the former slaves of a "Mr. Dix" of Manhattan Island, New York, coined it to describe an earthly paradise for African Americans. Another story points to the Mason-Dixon line between Maryland and Pennsylvania as the boundary between North and South and that the term came from the latter surveyor's name. Another version suggests *dixes* as the source word; this refers to bilingual (French and English) ten-dollar bank notes issued from New Orleans, with the French side using *dix* (ten) to denote the denomination. From this the Crescent City, and by extension the South, became known as Dixieland. Wilson and Ferris, eds., *Encycl. of Southern Culture,* 364, 1052; Hendrickson, *Whistlin' Dixie,* 86–87; Stewart, *American Place-Names,* 138.

18. The Springfield area, to no surprise, had a number of springs; it was an inlet on the Tickfaw River for schooners sending cotton to New Orleans (Clare d'Artois Leeper, *Louisiana Places: A Collection of the Columns from the Baton Rouge "Sunday Advocate," 1960–1974* [Baton Rouge, 1976], 225).

19. According to one mid-nineteenth-century account, "The exhalations from the marshes in the long hot summers poison the atmosphere, and make Louisiana, in much of its territory, dangerous to the acclimated, and quite unapproachable to strangers, at the season when the landscapes may be seen in all their greatest glory" (*Appleton's, 1857,* 294). Ague (intermittent fevers and chills) and, more specifically, yellow fever were thought to be spread by these dangerous gases generated

cotton bales, but I saw sufficient of the preparations made for defending it to convince me that it would not very easily be seized by General Butler.

After floundering for fully two hours through the forest and swamp, we came, more by good luck than design, on the outskirts of Ponchiatoula, which we found to be a straggling neat village, of white-painted wooden houses, with probably five hundred inhabitants, and the last depôt or station, as I have before said, on the New Orleans, Jackson, and Great Northern Railroad, before that line crosses Pass Manjac and enters New Orleans. Having very imperfect information as to where we should find either bed or food, we of course roused half a dozen families before we came to the hospitable widow's house where eventually we found shelter. A vigorous knock or two at the door usually brought a woman's head from some window, and, our request for accommodation having been arranged, the questions invariably followed: "Where do you come from?" "Are the Yankees coming?" and then, when assured that they were not to our knowledge, "Thank God for that!"

It seems that a small body of the Federal forces had pushed up the Tickfaw river a few weeks before, made a stealthy march through the woods, and come on Ponchiatoula and its then trifling defence unawares. The result had been a very harmless skirmish on both sides, from behind houses and trees; after which, the Federal forces burned some small quantity of stores, cotton, and sugar, and retreated to their boats in considerable haste. These poor women had, probably for the first time in their lives, seen the blood of their relatives, spilt in their own quiet village, and were half sick with fear that the tragedy might be repeated.

Very early the following morning, a sufficient force of oxen and waggons went down to the schooner, and brought up the remainder of our passengers, baggage, and freight. The news that a cargo had come across the Lake seemed to have been communicated by magic to the villages and plantations for miles round; for, long before the salt, pork, medicines, &c. &c. with which the schooner seemed to have been loaded could be hauled to the wooden "depôt," which served as railway station, post-office, exchange, and public store, many scores of farmers had ridden in, "hitched" their Creole ponies to the most convenient tree, and were waiting, cash in hand, to buy all up.[20]

---

from swamps and the decay of flesh and garbage. Butler and his troops feared the fever and hoped that by sanitizing New Orleans, epidemics could be avoided. E. H. Barton, *The Cause and Prevention of Yellow Fever at New Orleans and Other Cities in America* (New York, 1857), 10–48 *passim;* Winters, *Civil War in Louisiana,* 127–30.

20. The word *creole* is "commonly applied to things native to the New World, such as creole

Ponchiatoula is only some forty miles from New Orleans, yet so completely is intercourse cut off between the two places, that I saw salt, which had not cost over one dollar per sack in New Orleans, sold at one hundred and thirty dollars per sack; bacon, hams, and shoulders, which may have cost ten cents per pound, sold at seventy-five cents per pound; and sulphate of quinine, purchased in New Orleans at two or three dollars per ounce, sold at eighteen and twenty dollars per ounce.[21] Who pocketed these enormous profits I cannot say—the owner of the cargo, the owner of the schooner, or the Federal and Confederate officers, by whom the traffic was permitted. One thing is certain, the poor farmer, planter, and soldier had to pay. He paid, of course, in Confederate Treasury notes, or in State, City, Bank, or "personal" shin-plasters.[22] But as Confederate money was worth from fifty to sixty cents on the dollar in "greenbacks" when I left New Orleans, and as that would make a sack of Liverpool salt, say, for instance, worth about 9*l.* to 10*l.* sterling in gold,[23] it was evident that there was a great and pressing want to be supplied, and wealth for those who could trade on that want.

"Nothing like being on the *inside track,* stranger, in times like these!" said an unfortunate wight, who had ridden probably twenty miles in sun and dust to buy some brown, tempting hams, which he had just been

---

cuisine and creole horses" (William H. Harris and Judith S. Levey, eds., *The New Columbia Encyclopedia* [New York, 1975], 679–80).

21. Salt prices skyrocketed during the war. "For purposes of comparison it might be well to recall pre-war prices. On the eve of the conflict, Liverpool salt sold in New Orleans at fifty cents a sack on board the vessel, one-fourth of a cent a pound, including the cost of the sack" (Lonn, *Salt as a Factor in the Confederacy,* 43). Sulphate of quinine looked like "needles of a pearly and satiny appearance" and "came from boiled tree bark and other elements." It was used to control intermittent fever (R. Eglesfeld Griffith, *A Universal Formulary: Containing the Methods of Preparing and Administering Officinal and Other Medicines* [Philadelphia, 1850], 344–45; Robley Dunglison, *A Dictionary of Medical Science* [Philadelphia, 1855], 737).

22. "Usually, shinplasters referred to low-value paper money issued by state banks during the free banking era (1837–1863), to virtually all small change bills, and during the war in the Confederacy, to any paper money (except Confederate notes) that circulated at a high rate of depreciation to gold" (Current, ed., *Encycl. of the Confederacy,* IV, 1424). In the spring of 1862, Butler outlawed their use. In Montgomery about the same time, a Georgia soldier reported to the folks back home that "the shinplaster mania in Alabama is unparalleled. Brokers are growing rich on these liliputian [*sic*] bills of exchange, and some of them will not pass outside of 'horn-blow' of the place of issue" (Allen W. Jones, ed., "A Georgia Confederate Soldier Visits Montgomery, Alabama, 1862–1863," *Alabama Historical Quarterly,* XXV (Spring/Summer, 1963), 104); *OED,* XV, 267; Winters, *Civil War in Louisiana,* 127.

23. Corsan's publisher has used the symbol *l* to denote the British pound currency, rather than the pound symbol more commonly used today. The pound was worth 240 pence, or twenty shillings.

told were "all cleared." He thrust his well-stuffed wallet of notes into his pockets, squirted a few rivulets over the "stoop," testily mounted his pony, and in a very few moments could be seen flying over the sandy track, through the "piney" wood, his broad-brimmed hat, and loose, homespun coat flapping and streaming after him, bound for the next nearest cargo which he had been informed had "run the blockade," fully bent on not being too late again.

I soon found that the two great wants of the South were salt and medicines, especially quinine, morphine, calomel, and chloroform.[24] The Southerner cares nothing for poultry or fresh meat. "Pork and hominy" is his national dish. Give him plenty of Indian corn, salt pork, sweet potatoes, and whisky, and, as a rule the rural Southerner asks for nothing more, either for himself or his negroes.[25] Without salt, however, his pork could not be cured, and at the time I speak of, salt being an article for which the Southerner had depended on foreign countries and the North, the want of it was a very pressing difficulty. Since that time the price has set thousands of people to work to make and collect it; its use has been carefully regulated and economised by the Confederate Government, and the want is in some degree alleviated. The universal statement was, "We have corn enough to feed the North as well as ourselves, we have all the hogs we need, but no salt. Beef and mutton our people don't like, and won't take to if they can avoid it.[26] But we must take to it if we can't get salt." This I found to be literally the fact all over the Confederacy. In every direction where I went, tens of thousands of acres of Indian corn might be seen ungathered in the fields. If it was dear in any locality, as it often was, and oppressively so too for the poor, this was owing to the want of transportation. I always found the railroad and river-boats

---

24. Calomel came in several forms and was "used in almost every disease either as purgative, alternative, [or] anthelmintic." It was also known as mercurous chloride. Unfortunately, it "breaks down into highly poisonous components in the intestine, [and] was a particularly nasty and dangerous staple in the average medicine chest" (Hallock, "Lethal and Debilitating," 60; Griffith, *Universal Formulary*, 238–40). Chloroform was "a transparent, heavy fluid of a peculiar, fragrant, ethereal, apple-like odor," which was used as a stimulant, sedative, and antispasmodic (Griffith, *Universal Formulary*, 159). Also see Dunglison, *Medical Science*, 198.

25. Mainstays of the southern diet were pork (especially bacon), salt, molasses, whiskey, and corn. The swine's "importance in the domestic economy was overwhelming" (Sam Bowers Hilliard, *Hog Meat and Hoecake: Food Supply in the Old South, 1840–1860* [Carbondale, Ill., 1972], 92, 186–91).

26. "The use of meat other than pork by the white people of the South is easy to underestimate. Such meats were commonly consumed but the total quantity was small." Beef was usually eaten fresh because southerners found it hard to preserve to suit their tastes. Also, there was a "strange prejudice . . . against mutton" (*ibid.*, 44, 45).

blocked up by the transport of troops and military stores in enormous quantities. It was the old story over again—the food was in one place, and the mouths in another.[27]

As for hogs, their name certainly was legion. Every village, town, country-house, cottage, and depôt swarmed with them—arch-backed, sharp-nosed, long-legged rascals, who seemed capable of living on a rock, and about whose daily food nobody seemed to trouble themselves. I am satisfied that, if the war goes on a year or two longer, the Southerners will raise all the hogs they need, and do without the Western States in future. I often asked the question, while South, why, with woods crammed with game, and rivers with fish, the population should live so much on pork, but could get no better answer than that they "hated yer darned beef and fixins! Give 'em a cut of well-cured pork, and ye may take all the rest." While shot is three dollars per pound, and gunpowder wanted for winning their independence, of course deer, partridge, snipe, 'possum, rabbit, squirrel, and every other wild luxury, which swarm in the Southern woods and mountains, may breed with impunity; but when peace comes it is to be hoped that the traveller will see less pork, and more beef, mutton, fish, and game, on a Southern table than has usually been the case.

For medicines, of course, the South is mainly dependent on running the blockade, and immense quantities find their way thus into the country. But the Southerners consume a great deal of medicine at the best of times—much more now. The fevers and other diseases incident to a country like the South, with her immense swamps, dense forests, and undrained towns and villages, all baking under an almost tropical heat, would tax the skill of an army of accomplished physicians. But medical skill is not a commodity often met with. A few radical recipes, a limited list of medicines, some notion of how to bleed, &c., and a man is allowed to be a "doctor." Perhaps he keeps the post-office, a general "grocery," does a bit of law, and is a politician besides. Be that as it may, the agricultural Southerner, his family, and negroes must take him or none; and if they have good constitutions they survive, that is all.

---

27. The Confederacy had to overcome many transportation problems, one of these being the configuration of the railroads. From Norfolk to Savannah, the lines branched out to the fertile valleys and developed agricultural lands to take the harvest to the ports. In the Deep South, the location of cotton plantations dictated the route of railroads. Throughout the entire area, little effort was made to connect different rail lines, and only moderate means were available to transport goods and individuals long distances from south to north (George Edgar Turner, *Victory Rode the Rails: The Strategic Place of the Railroads in the Civil War* [Westport, Conn., 1972], 29–30).

As for whisky, or in fact any kind of "drink," that I found, even at Ponchiatoula, was not to be had. The President, as Commander-in-Chief, had interdicted the sale of liquor of any kind, on any pretence, in any part of the Confederacy, and I never saw half a dozen men the worse for liquor while in the South; and where *they* got the means of becoming drunk I cannot tell.[28] After endless inquiries, and many hours of watching, a "thirsty soul" told me that if I chose to go with him, he knew where he *thought* he could get a drink. For the sake of seeing what men will do to get liquor, I went with him to a cottage on the outskirt of the village, where we were thrust into a dirty bedroom in the dark, locked in, and then by the light of a "dip" in a bottle served with about a table-spoonful of rye-whisky, perhaps a week old, for which we paid a dollar, and departed, with tears in our eyes and very warm in our throats.

Before leaving Ponchiatoula, we all had to present ourselves before the Provost-Marshal, a large, jolly man, who bothered us with very few questions about our errand, and never asked to examine our baggage. He would give us passes no further than Camp Moore, near Tangipahoa, some thirty miles north, where the body of the Army of the Southern Mississippi then was encamped. We found out his reason afterwards, some of us to our sorrow. I happened to say, "People say you are starving in the South," when he beckoned a negro, said a few words, and sent him off. He returned very shortly with a potato (not a sweet potato), which weighed on trial nine pounds and a half, and which he said was only one out of hundreds such grown near Ponchiatoula.[29] "We can't starve, I think," he said, "in a country which will grow these. Any way, we will risk *that*."

As far as I could learn, all the passengers who crossed the lake with us were permitted to proceed, except a young man and young woman, whom I had supposed to be a newly-married pair, but whom several refugees in the village, and others we brought with us, swore to be spies

28. "Liquor was eagerly sought by many of the soldiers, and it was frequently available" (H. H. Cunningham, *Doctors in Gray: The Confederate Medical Service* [1958; rpr. Gloucester, Mass., 1970], 211). The restriction Corsan refers to may be General Order No. 3, which reads in part: "The introduction of spirituous liquors into any camp, barrack, or station of the Army, except for medicinal purposes, duly recommended by the senior medical officer and approved by the general or other officer in command is hereby expressly prohibited" (*OR*, Ser. IV, Vol. I, 835). Also, some states imposed a form of prohibition on liquor "but without much success" (Current, ed., *Encycl. of the Confederacy*, III, 1285). It is important to note that alcohol was allowed when prescribed by a physician.

29. Corsan's remark about potatoes is notable because farmers in the Deep South planted more sweet potatoes than the white, Irish variety (Hilliard, *Hog Meat and Hoecake*, 173–77).

sent out by Butler. The affidavits to that effect were sworn to, as soon as the guilty couple arrived in the waggons from the schooner, and, for the whole of that hot, dusty, weary day did these two wretched-looking creatures sit on a wooden bench in their tawdry finery, locked in a room in the depôt, and stared at like wild beasts through the windows by every man, woman, and child in the village. The last I saw of them was, when, the following day, they were being rudely thrust out of the cars and along the platform at a small station on the railway, some distance past Camp Moore. The man was said to have been one of Butler's "detectives," and to have done his master good service against scores of refugees then in Ponchiatoula. If that was proved against him, he would have short shrift enough. I know no more than that he was spoken of as a "gone coon" when he left the railway car.[30]

30. To understand the expression "gone coon," imagine "yourself in the place of a raccoon finally treed by the hunting dogs, and you'll see why this phrase is used for a person in dire peril" (William Morris and Mary Morris, *Morris Dictionary of Word and Phrase Origins* [New York, 1977], 252).

THREE

Riding the Rails to Jackson

A s soon as the *Provost-Marshal at Ponchiatoula could arrange the* passes before-named, a train of cars came up, and we started for Jackson, Miss. *viâ* Tangipahoa and Camp Moore.[1] As might be expected, after nearly two years' uninterrupted use, without painting, upholstering, or even glazing, these cars are not in very good repair. This was the case, I found, on all the main lines of the South. Perhaps one or two cars in a train would be kept decently clean and in fair order. These were invariably reserved for ladies, children, and their male appendages. Everybody else, without distinction—soldiers, officers, civilians, sick and wounded— were thrust into carriages with no more comfort than mere horse-boxes, and even into common freight-cars. Broken seats, unglazed windows, which would either not shut or not open, doors that could not be persuaded to remain closed, added to a floor strewn with apple-parings, chewed sugar-cane, bones of fowls, scraps of pork, and tobacco-juice everywhere, did not make a slow jolting pace any the more tolerable.[2]

1. Camp Moore, named in honor of the state's governor, Thomas Overton Moore, was seventy-eight miles from New Orleans in present-day Tangipahoa Parish. Its function was that of a training base and staging area for operations against the enemy. Like many facilities of its kind, it contained a parade ground and a hospital (Powell A. Casey, *Encyclopedia of Forts, Posts, Camps Names, and Other Military Installations in Louisiana, 1700–1981* [Baton Rouge, 1983], 122–24). *Tangipahoa* may be a Choctaw word for "corn gatherers." The specific tribe's name has disappeared. The river with the same name flows generally southeast to Lake Pontchartrain (Harder, *Place Names,* 539).

2. The British traveler's fascination with southern tobacco chewers was well documented by the time Corsan visited the Confederacy. During a tour of a tobacco factory in Richmond, Charles Dickens recalled, "All the tobacco thus dealt with was in course of manufacture for chewing; and one would have supposed there was enough in that one store house to have filled even the comprehensive jaws of America" (Charles Dickens, *American Notes* [1842; rpr. Gloucester, Mass., 1968], 159).

The only care the railroad officials seemed to have was to keep the cars and locomotives in *running* order. Any attention to appearances or comfort was out of the question. Such things were of secondary importance, and no one ever grumbled at their absence. So that large bodies of men, with their munitions and equipments, could be passed rapidly, and without excessive fatigue, from point to point, both civilians and shareholders were satisfied.

I might as well mention here, to prevent the necessity of recurring to this point again, that the various railroad companies seemed to have resolved to use up their present stock of cars, without expending much, if anything, except to keep them in good running order; and to replace them with plain, strong, substantial cars of their own make, which, in the better times coming, might at least do for negro cars. In times of peace, of course, every car, locomotive, and, in fact, the whole rolling-stock, of their lines came from the North. Being cut off from this supply, they had no choice but to be content with the old cars as long as they lasted, and then with the best they could make themselves. I saw in the South many hundreds of Southern-made cars, for both freight and passengers, and very useful things they seemed.[3]

The worst feature in the management was, that in no case was accommodation provided for more than half or two-thirds of the passengers offering. The result was, that the passages down the centre of the cars, the platform, and even the roofs, were often crowded, to the intense suffering of many a thousand sick and wounded men, to save whose fluttering lives far more than common skill and care were needed.

The speed of the main lines had been gradually reduced, first from twenty to fifteen, and subsequently to twelve and a half, and even ten miles per hour. At the last-named rate of speed, the belief was that the rails then down would last about two years longer. At the end of that time, it was calculated that the companies would be able entirely to relay those lines essential to their military operations, from the new rails in stock, those being made in the Confederacy, those taken from unimpor-

3. Southern antebellum industries did produce locomotives and railroad cars. J. R. Anderson and Company (Tredegar Iron Works) in Richmond had "delivered its last locomotive in December 1860 to a Tennessee railroad." During the conflict, however, production did not resume, as these workers and their machinery built cannon and gun carriages. In Tennessee, foundries also built locomotives, but parts of the Volunteer State fell into northern hands. See Charles B. Dew, *Ironmaker to the Confederacy: Joseph R. Anderson and the Tredegar Iron Works* (New Haven, Conn., 1966), 86, 127; Angus James Johnston II, *Virginia Railroads in the Civil War* (Chapel Hill, N.C., 1961), 10–14.

tant lines in the interior, and those also taken from the horse-railroads in the streets of the various cities.[4]

Such was the sort of railroad accommodation to which the South was driven, and into such cars were we crammed, that hot afternoon, at Ponchiatoula. The line ran through what are called "piney woods," or forests chiefly of pine, mixed with hickory and oak. As we proceeded, we were soon clear of the swampy portions of the State, and rapidly neared the rich, rolling uplands, which distinguish that portion of the States of Louisiana and Mississippi.

The little villages through which we passed (Tickfaw, Amite, &c.) were nothing more than thin straggling lines of wooden houses and small stores, all painted white, running parallel with the railroad, with a few divergent roads at right angles, equally straggling, and ending very soon in the pine forest. Sugar, cotton, and Indian corn were evidently the staple productions,[5] in perhaps the same succession of importance that they are now named. At every depôt hogsheads and bales could be seen piled up, with the inevitable crowd of negro idlers—cadaverous citizens in broad-brimmed hats, chewing tobacco and spitting as for dear life—and the Creole ponies, fretting at their tether under the trees.

At last we began to pass lines of campfires in the woods; some we could see were made up before the entrance of ordinary tents, others opposite cozy-looking bowers made of branches, and very many in the open. The unkempt figures flitting about, the glistening of arms, and the challenges of pickets, showed us that we were passing the outlines of Camp Moore, and the army of Southern Mississippi.

---

4. Mechanics assembled and repaired railroad cars in Richmond, Atlanta, Charleston, and Augusta, Georgia. The Tredegar mills turned out spikes, bridge bolts, axles, and wheels. See *OR*, Ser. IV, Vol. I, 881; Dew, *Ironmaker to the Confederacy*, 127; John F. Stover, *The Railroads of the South, 1865–1900* (Chapel Hill, N.C., 1955), 17. For the most part, southern leaders such as Jefferson Davis did not understand the true value of the railroads or have a reliable long-range transportation plan. As a result, stopgap moves plagued the industry. Furthermore, railroad operators were shackled with a plethora of troubles, such as skilled-labor shortages and disputes, inferior rails and rail shortages, gauge differences, limited access to isolated regions of the country, and inflated prices for fuel, wages, nails, wheels, and lubricating oil. See Stover, *Railroads of the South*, 16; Roller and Twyman, eds., *Encycl. of Southern History*, 1018; Turner, *Victory Rode the Rails*, 233–46; Richard M. McMurry, *Two Great Rebel Armies: An Essay in Confederate Military History* (Chapel Hill, N.C., 1989), 61–63.

5. Planters invested very heavily in cotton in northern Louisiana and Mississippi. Corn appeared only in moderation in this region, while 95 percent of the South's sugar crop was grown in the southern half of the Bayou State. See Sam Bowers Hilliard, *Atlas of Antebellum Southern Agriculture* (Baton Rouge, 1984), 66, 71, 77; Current, ed., *Encycl. of the Confederacy*, IV, 1559.

Presently we stopped at the village of Tangipahoa; and, as half an hour elapsed without any sign of proceeding, I got out to ascertain the reason, and was told that we went no farther that night. As no one seemed to be looking out for beds, I asked where we were to sleep; and was told, "In the cars, of course."

Not being inclined to go to bed, even in a railway-car, without supper, two of us determined to scour the village in person. But it was vain. Neither high words, soft words, nor promises of liberal pay, would even open a door, much less obtain food. Sometimes a shrill, snapping treble, sometimes a muttered curse, accompanied by a suspicious clicking that sounded like a revolver being got ready, drove us away; and eventually we had to retrace our steps through the inhospitable street, without seeing even a light—hungry, cold, and vexed—scramble into an empty freight-car, and make the best bed we could on the floor through the frosty night.

Hungry men do not sleep soundly nor long, and we were up very early, and on the look-out for an hotel and breakfast. But we might have been asking for the Koh-i-noor,[6] instead of food for which we were willing to pay, so amused did every white and black native seem at the idea of our getting anything to eat at Tangipahoa. All the food in or about the place, they said, was wanted for the army. They had none to sell—scarcely enough for themselves.

For hours we bullied, begged, and attempted to bribe; until I began to think we should have to go all day without food. Not having eaten for about fifteen hours, however, we grew desperate, and made final overtures (after having been repulsed at least ten times by him) to a native, who was sunning himself, in his shirt-sleeves, on his "stoop," and squirting tobacco-juice all round; explained that money was no object, but food we must have; and finally got for a dollar as much coffee (made out of burnt rye), warm corn bread, beefsteak (which no steel could cut, nor tooth masticate), and bay-salt, as we could eat. How much we did eat and drink, I knew not then; but "hunger is a sharp thorn," and no doubt we ate a dollar's worth.[7]

We had taken our places in the cars, and were ready to start, when I noticed that a guard was being placed at the door of each car, with fixed

6. The Kohinoor is a very large diamond from India that in 1849 became a British Crown jewel (*OED*, VIII, 525).

7. Southerners did produce their own salt once their usual sources were depleted. One method was to dam sections of saline water in lowlands and allow the water to evaporate, hence "bay-salt." They also tapped salt springs and mined the mineral (Humphreys and Abbot, *Mississippi River*, xvi; Lonn, *Salt as a Factor in the Confederacy*, 207–15).

bayonets, and that a well-dressed, dapper Confederate officer, evidently a Frenchman, was demanding some paper or other in succession from each passenger. Some were able to produce what he required; others were not. These last were at once ordered out of the car, and despatched, under guard, up the village.

When he came to me, I found that orders had been issued by the General in command of the army (who was also Governor of the State, I believe) to conscript every man, without distinction, between the ages of eighteen and forty-five, and put them in a camp of instruction, unless he could produce papers which would exempt him. I showed my British Foreign Office passport. It produced no effect.[8]

"How could I prove," he asked, "that I was the person named in the passport? If I could not do that, I was a conscript. That I must make out to the satisfaction of the Conscript Judge."

And accordingly I was marched off to a wooden hut, which had once been a sort of small grocery, where that most potent functionary for the time being, the Conscript Judge, sat in state. Half-a-dozen trembling fellow-travellers, who had left home, no doubt, under the impression that they could come back when they wished, were rapidly disposed of before my turn came.

"You are a conscript, sir!" were the few pregnant words which, after a few pertinent questions, condemned them one by one to military duty, and out they were marched, free men no longer.

My case was soon disposed of. My personal cards, letters addressed to me—which I fortunately happened to have in my pocket—and such proofs of identity soon dissipated the rather silly doubts and quibbles, which the free-and-easy bench suggested as we lolled on the unplaned deal counter and discussed the question. Eventually I received my "discharge as a conscript," and was not sorry in another half-hour to leave Tangipahoa, with its swarms of troops, negroes, pigs, and officials, far behind.[9]

8. Corsan had trouble because General Daniel Ruggles, commander in the area, enforced the South's Second Conscription Act that went into effect that autumn. Corsan's status as a British subject did not protect him from the draft, as it potentially applied to all white males who were residing in the Confederacy. See *OR*, Ser. IV, Vol. II, 160–62, Ser. I, Vol. XV, 768; Faust, ed., *HTIE-CW*, 647.

9. The Confederacy's secretary of war, George Wythe Randolph, informed the British consul at Mobile that "foreigners are not subject to conscription unless permanent residents of the Confederate States, and are invariably discharged when improperly enrolled" (*OR*, Ser. IV, Vol. II, 84). Corsan may have been discharged on these grounds because he was simply traveling through the South on business. *OR*, Ser. IV, Vol. I, 1126–27.

It occurred to me, as we rode along, that, in the matter of food, the troops of the army of the Southern Mississippi were at least as well off in time of war as in peace. During my morning-stroll in the woods which hemmed in the scattered village, I had seen the men all round cooking their breakfast in companies, and uncommonly savoury breakfasts they were; pork, fowls, coffee, and corn bread; fare certainly as good as most of them were accustomed to at home, and perhaps better than either they or any other Confederate army could always command. The men were a fine sturdy set of fellows; quite unlike the wiry, cadaverous type with which the word "Southerner" is usually associated. They were of course destitute of any regular uniform, dressed as a rule in homespun of all colours, and looked as if they had slept in the woods for six months. Their arms were in good order, and all I saw had Northern or British rifles.[10] The men seemed healthy and contented; were waited on, hand and foot, by troops of negroes, who seemed to look upon themselves as part of the army, and did any task eagerly; and, if well handled, in such a country, I am satisfied there was plenty of mischief in them.

We took with us from Camp Moore a large body of soldiers, and received considerable additions at all the side stations we came to, all the way to Jackson. I was told that reinforcements were being pushed up to General Bragg, at or near Holly Springs, on the Mississippi Central and Tennessee Railroad, near which a pitched battle was daily expected with the Federals under General Buell, who was said to have 80,000 men.[11] I cannot describe the alacrity and enthusiasm with which these men moved up or spoke of the chance of meeting the foe. They were, as they said, "dying for a fight," and any notion of having the worst of it never entered their heads.

It was Sunday, and at every little village we came to, Osyka, Magnolia, Summit, Bogue Chitto, Collamer, Crystal Spring, &c., the whole of the

---

10. Despite Corsan's observation, "A lifetime of exposure to these health factors appears to have left Southerners less able to fight disease, and more likely to succumb to wounds" (Hallock, "Lethal and Debilitating," 52). The "health factors" referred to are "adverse effects of the heat [and] climate-related diseases" carried by insects, bacteria, and viruses, for example, "with no winter killing-off as there was in the colder North" (*ibid.*).

The weapons he saw most likely were the British Enfield or the United States Rifle models 1841, 1855, or 1861, Boatner, *Civil War Dictionary,* 266, 557; Bowman, ed., *Civil War Almanac,* 287.

11. Holly Springs, in far northern Mississippi, was about the midway point of the Mississippi Central Railroad, which ran from Jackson to Canton (Thomas, *Appleton's Railway Guide,* 239). On October 8, 1862, Union general Don Carlos Buell and his blue-clad columns drove General Braxton Bragg's Army of the Tennessee out of Kentucky. Buell's army numbered about fifty thousand, and when he failed to follow up his victory, he was replaced (Faust, ed., *HTIE-CW,* 75, 88, 576–77, 643).

inhabitants, male and female, black and white, young and old, were assembled to cheer the men going up to the fight, say good-bye to those leaving their own village, and hear the news generally.[12]

The country through which the line passed to Jackson, struck me as being very fine. Gradually it became more and more uneven, the woods less dense, the land more fertile, until, very soon, it became one magnificent rolling upland, with fine woods of oak, maple, ash, and other trees, very generally cultivated, and evidently well watered. Cotton was plainly "king" in Mississippi. Round every little dépôt, and in every village, the precious staple was piled, baled ready for transport. Every available corner was choked with it.[13]

The villages were of the usual type: a straggling line of neat, wooden, one-storied houses and stores, painted white, running parallel with the line for perhaps a quarter of a mile, with divergent roads, at regular intervals, of similar residences rather more imposing; side-walks made out of planks; sand knee-deep in the roads; perhaps one or two "hotels," from which a negro emerged the moment the cars appeared, beating a gong to announce "dinner ready for passengers wishing to dine;" and of course the usual crowd of negresses, with pumpkin pies, cold chicken, baked 'possum, apples, cracked corn, sweet cake, green sugar-cane, m'lasses cake, and so on for sale. The day was fine and hot, and crinolines, parasols, and fans were in full play, both among the black and white female natives. The negro was dressed quite as well as his master, and the negress, I think, as a rule, outdressed her mistress. They had either just "been to meetin'," or were just going; and, as we glided away, we could see black dress-coats, satin vests, and fancy "pants" giving their arms to hooped muslins, bonnets *à la* Paris, fans and parasols, and strolling up the sandy road, just as though there were no great battles coming off anywhere, that they knew of, and certainly not within two or three hundred miles of their own village, and to which their own brothers, lovers, and friends were rushing as fast as steam could take them.

We reached Jackson late in the evening, and our train stopped in the midst of a dense mass of soldiers, mostly waiting to push on northward to Holly Springs by trains, which were being prepared and despatched

12. Corsan was still on the New Orleans, Jackson and Great Northern Railroad. The stops beyond Tangipahoa were Osyka, Magnolia, Summit, Bogue Chitto, Brookhaven, Bahala, Collamer, Hazelhurst, Crystal Springs, Terry, Byram, and Jackson, Mississippi, a total trip of about one hundred miles (Thomas, *Appleton's Railway Guide,* 248; OM Atlas, CLV).

13. In 1860, Mississippi produced 1,203,000 bales of cotton, more than any other state (Roller and Twyman, eds., *Encycl. of Southern History,* 301).

as fast as possible. Some of the men, however, were going west to Vicksburgh—and others east to Mobile. There was also a very considerable
number of paroled Confederate prisoners, who had been sent down from
Cincinnati and Louisville, *via* the Ohio and Mississippi, past Cairo, to
Vicksburgh. These men were on their way to their various homes, and
were one and all furious at the infamous manner in which they said they
had been housed and fed while prisoners, and treated while on their way
down the river to Vicksburgh. They complained bitterly that they had
been so crowded in temporary huts, and so neglected, that they were
almost eaten alive with vermin; that their rations had been a handful of
crackers or a small slice of dry bread and a mug of coffee twice per day
only, with about a couple of ounces of bad pork and another small piece
of bread at mid-day, not altogether more than enough for one meal for
a strong man; that no matter what money, clothing, or comforts their
friends or sympathizing inhabitants sent them, they never reached the
intended recipients; and that, when paroled and on their way down the
river, they had had to rise *en masse* and seize provisions to prevent actual
starvation.

What seemed most important to me were their statements, that the
vast bulk of the Western troops with whom they came into contact
seemed tired of fighting, wanted to "go to work, and trade" with the
South as before, hated and ridiculed the abolitionists, as they called the
Republican party, and confessed the South could not be beaten. "Remember the —th Illinois, boys!" they reported regiment after regiment of
their enemy as shouting, as they left or passed them. "*We* don't mean to
shoot you, so don't you shoot us! We shall give in, and get paroled, and
get home to the old woman and children as soon as we can. D—n this
work to h—l, say we!"

Such a shouting, hustling, dusty, perspiring mass of "butternuts," niggers, rifles, bayonets, blankets, cannon and ammunition waggons, tents,
cavalry horses, hacks, ambulances, omnibuses, and all the heterogeneous
accompaniments of an army on the move I never saw, as crammed that
ample sandy space about the railway depôt at Jackson that hot evening.
I very soon found that to obtain a bed or supper at any hotel or boarding-
house was out of the question.

Jackson is the capital of the State of Mississippi, has over 5,000 inhabitants, and, owing to its wide, sparsely-built streets, and numerous parks
and open spaces, covers a very considerable quantity of ground on the
banks of the Pearl River. It is built on a series of bold swelling hills, and
its situation is both commanding and picturesque. Most of the side-walks

are of brick or wood, and the streets, as is generally the case in all second-class Southern cities, knee-deep in loose sand.[14]

Many of the buildings, public as the City Hall, State House, and several churches, are imposing at a distance. But as a Southerner, after having once built a place and set it going handsomely in the world in the matter of fencing, garden, glass, and paint, never seems to think the plumber, gardener, joiner, or painter can by any possibility be needed again, the public edifices of Jackson, Mississippi, do not, on closer inspection, quite redeem the promise of neatness and perfection which they make at a distance. Broken fences, cracked stucco, overgrown walks and beds, patched and broken window-glass, and an utter absence of paint, make a poor show on a near acquaintance. Every excuse must, however, be made for times of war and a trying climate. In the "good time coming" I hope to see Jackson very very much improved.

As I said before, bed and supper could not be had until two paroled Kentuckians and myself had toiled for hours through the sandy streets, when eventually we were lucky enough to share a very dirty garret with four or five other military men, among whom were a major, a captain, and a first lieutenant. I was rather amused, when listening the following day to a very hot discussion among my roommates as to the comparative merits of Generals Beauregard, Lee, and Johnson, [sic] to notice the perfect equality on which officers and privates regarded themselves as standing. Subordination *on duty* is, I am told, and believe, complete and perfect in the Southern armies; but when squatted cross-legged on beds, certainly the rank-and-file can curse his officer's eyes and limbs as handsomely as ever I believe one officer could similarly accommodate another.[15]

In Jackson, for the first time, I saw the melancholy signs of what wounds, death, and disease were doing. I never saw a female who was not in mourning.[16] Every large or public building was turned into a

---

14. In 1860, Jackson had a population of 3,199 persons (one-third African American), but like other southern cities, its population would fluctuate with soldiers, refugees, wounded, and camp followers during the war. Along with the Great Northern, the Southern [Mississippi] Railroad cut through the capital. Dept. of Interior, *Population 1860*, 95; Thomas, *Appleton's Railway Guide,* 246, 248.

15. Corsan is referring to General Joseph E. Johnston, not Johnson. As citizen soldiers, many recruits considered themselves the equal of any officer. "Hence, maintaining firm control over the rank and file was a critical problem on both sides, especially in the first years of the war" (Robertson, *Soldiers Blue and Gray,* 123).

16. "Compared to Northerners, Southern families stood a much better chance of having a relative wounded or killed." As the battles continued, the suffering rose. "So quickly did one death follow

hospital, and lines of ambulances and litters were creeping slowly but continually from the railway depôt along the road. These men were being brought down chiefly from the Confederate armies in Kentucky and Tennessee; and such wrecks of human beings I never wish to see again. My own conviction is, that bungling surgery and incompetent physicians killed as many men as the sword, bullet, or disease. Like all overworked departments, the medico-military authorities in Jackson could only half do their work.[17]

Hundreds and hundreds of sick and wounded men, limping weakly on crutches, writhing with chronic diarrhœa, coughing their lungs out almost in consumption,[18] or pale as ghosts and helpless as infants from recent fever half cured, would be turned out of the cars arriving in the evening, and left to find bed and supper as they could. For hours they would be met wandering about, repulsed from every hotel or lodging-house, until some officer, whose duty it was to have been at the depôt and met them, directed them, as he should have done at first, to the extempore wooden hospitals which, with every comfort, the authorities had kindly provided for such men near the depôt. No one but a sick soldier can tell what a luxury a hot cup of coffee and a mattress are after a long, cold, weary ride, or how grateful he feels for it.

Probably Jackson never was so full of people before as when I was there. The streets swarmed with officers and men; the hotels had to put down mattresses even in their halls and on the landings of the stairs; to almost every available fence strong, useful-looking cavalry-horses were hitched, saddled and bridled; and the whole place had the appearance of being the head-quarters of some immensely important movement.

Most of the stores were closed, not because the owners had failed, but because they had sold out their stocks, and realized immense profits, and could not replace them. Those that were open had the most mixed lot of

---

another, that most people had neither the time nor the emotional energy to become obsessed with a single tragedy." One visitor observed fourteen women in black at a neighboring plantation. (George C. Rable, *Civil Wars: Women and the Crisis of Southern Nationalism* [Urbana, Ill., 1989], 69).

17. "Southern medical development on the eve of the Civil War was at least as far advanced as that in the Northern states. . . . Unfortunately, there were also certain depressing features manifesting themselves late in the ante-bellum period, such as the relaxing of licensing laws and the concomitant flourishing of quackery, which boded ill for many of the ensuing war's sick and wounded" (Cunningham, *Doctors in Gray,* 20).

18. Consumption, "to waste away," was the condition that "precede[d] death in the greater part of chronic diseases, and particularly in *phthisis pulmonalis.*" In many cases this would mean tuberculosis (Dunglison, *Medical Science,* 233).

goods I ever saw—the odds and ends, in fact, of their used-up neighbours' stocks—medicines, dry-goods, books, hardware, and tobacco being a common assortment. As for the prices which these enterprising shop-keepers were getting, they were simply amusing. I paid thirty-five cents (one shilling and fourpence) for a square of "Confederate-" made soap, about the size of a small billiard-ball, the colour of clay, and the consistency of stiff curds; fifty cents (two shillings) for two small boxes of "Confederate" matches, of which the seller candidly told me not one in five would light ("but," he added, "we shall improve gradually, sir!"); and five cents (twopence) for an envelope made out of a sort of slate-coloured grocer's paper[19] (also a Confederate production), with the words printed on it—

"Stand firmly by your cannon,
Let ball and grape-shot fly,[20]
Trust in God and Davis,
And keep your powder dry!"

I defy any man to repress his admiration of the enthusiasm, patience, and

19. Like so many things, writing and printing supplies became scarce and the demand increased. There were shortages of ink, type, and all kinds of paper. To counter the deficiency, southerners imported machines that reportedly created thirty-five thousand envelopes a day. Printers experimented in making ink and advertised for clean cotton and linen rags to make paper; the rags fetched a nickel a pound. Because typefaces wore smooth and were not cast by printers of this period, the clever compositor could take a *q* and invert it to make a *b*. See T. Michael Parrish and Robert M. Willingham, Jr., *Confederate Imprints: A Bibliography of Southern Publications from Secession to Surrender* (Austin, Tex., 1987), 11–14; Mobile *Register and Advertiser,* October 22, 1862.

With legions of soldiers in the field, there was great demand for personal stationery. To meet the demand, one supplier recycled items such as railroad tickets and wrappers from cartridges to make envelopes; however, the effort was so makeshift one can still read the ticket and identify the rounds' manufacturer on existing samples (Morris Everett, "Confederate 'Rag Tags,'" *Confederate Philatelist,* XXXVI [January–February, 1991], 27–30).

The "slate-coloured" envelope could be the result of dirty water in the paper's slurry, impure pulp, or the failure to bleach the paper. To examine an excellent collection of this genre, see Civil War Pictorial Envelopes, 1861–1865, Collection No. 3409, at the Southern Historical Collection, Chapel Hill, N.C. The 515 items are "decorated with patriotic and polemic sentiments, mottoes, cartoons, and emblems." See Susan Sokol Blosser and Clyde Norman Wilson, Jr., *The Southern Historical Collection: A Guide to Manuscripts* (Chapel Hill, N.C., 1970).

20. Grapeshot, a form of artillery projectile sometimes quilted in cloth, normally "consisted of nine solid iron balls, top and bottom plates, two rings, all of iron, and rope handle on top" (Warren Ripley, *Artillery and Ammunition of the Civil War* [New York, 1970], 265–68; this source has a photograph of Confederate-manufactured grapeshot). The term *grapeshot* has been used interchangeably with *canister,* but although similar, the latter had a slightly different configuration. It is possible Corsan saw a prewar manufactured stand of grapeshot or canister. See Thomas S. Dickey and Peter C. George, *Field Artillery Projectiles of the American Civil War* (Mechanicsville, Va., 1993).

good-tempered endurance of inevitable, though self-inflicted evils, which these people exhibited. Committed to a course, and in a cause which they believed just, it was plain they had counted the cost, and were prepared for death or victory.

FOUR

From Mobile to Montgomery

*I*n *a few days I obtained a pass to go to Mobile, and proceeded by the* Southern Mississippi line to a wretched place called Meridian, where we spent another miserable night (two and three in a bed, and several beds in a room); and thence, on the morrow, by the Mobile and Ohio line, crossing frequently a fine stream, called the Chickasawha River, to Mobile itself.[1] The country through which these lines run is a cotton country, almost exclusively, though of course fully four-fifths of the lands in the South usually devoted to cotton were, in 1862, set to grow corn, and wheat, &c.[2]

The land seemed very fertile, uneven, and rolling, well-watered, and covered with fine woods of pine, oak, hickory, ash, &c. with thick underwood, which, under the influence of frosty nights, now presented almost every shade of colour. The most considerable towns or villages on the way, as Decatur, Manai, Quitman, Winchester, &c., were not places of over perhaps 1,000 inhabitants, but neat and evidently thriving. There

1. The Mobile and Ohio Railroad ran from Mobile, Alabama, to northern Mississippi. From Meridian to Mobile the distance was about 133 miles. In Mississippi, Corsan would have passed through Enterprise, Quitman, DeSoto, Shubuta, Red Bluff, Waynesboro, Winchester, and Buckatunna before crossing the state line into Alabama. From there, he would have journeyed through Deer Park, Citronelle, Beaver Meadow, Chunchula, Kushla, and Whistler. What Corsan refers to as Manai may really be Mauvila or Manville, Alabama. See Thomas, *Appleton's Railway Guide,* 244; *OM Atlas,* CXXXV-A, CXLII. The Chickasawhay (Chickasawha) flows southward and meets the Lead River to form the Pascagoula River (Harder, *Place Names,* 100).

2. A Confederate agent in Demopolis, A. S. Gaines, made the same comment as Corsan to his seniors in Richmond, when he remarked that most of the planters in the area had abandoned cotton for corn. *OR,* Ser. IV, Vol. I, 1091; Woodman, *King Cotton,* 209; Robert B. Ekelund, and Mark Thornton, "The Union Blockade and Demoralization of the South: Relative Prices in the Confederacy," *Social Science Quarterly,* LXXIII (December, 1992), 900.

was the same rush of soldiers joining the train at every station; the same leave-taking, in which black and white joined; the same queer assortment of eatables and refreshment peddled along the cars by negresses wherever we stopped; the same piles of cotton-bales, anywhere and everywhere; the same eager rush for news; and the same fixed notion, that if, in consequence of a gong being sounded, the unwary traveller put his head inside the "hotel," and *looked* at the table, spread with little plates of cold fowl, beef-steak, pork, corn-cake, &c., he must inevitably pay a dollar to the man behind the door.

The number of troops which we had gradually accumulated since leaving Jackson was very large, our train consisting, when we arrived at Mobile, of over forty cars, crammed to suffocation inside and loaded outside as well. We were followed by trains of similar dimensions, besides long lines of freighted cars, filled with field-pieces, ammunition, tents, and all kinds of outfit. At that time, all troops or stores going east from Vicksburgh, or west from Charleston, had to turn south at Montgomery or Meridian, respectively, thus making a detour of fully 600 miles, and losing two days at least in time. This was owing to the fact, that the line between Selma and Meridian was not completed, some thirty to fifty miles between Union-town and Meridian being in course of construction. It was said that President Davis saw, very clearly and very early, the vital necessity of this new line, and urged its construction by the Confederate Congress on that body, during its sitting in the spring of 1862. Their consent, however, was obtained with very great difficulty, and only after threats, it was said, that the line *must* be made as a military necessity, whether they consented to advance the funds or not. Once at work, however, no time was lost. Over 2,000 men were reported to be at work in November upon it, and it has since been opened, and found of essential service to the Confederate generals.[3]

---

3. Corsan may be referring to Davis' efforts during his tenure as the Union secretary of war (1853–1857) to have the transcontinental railroad pass through the Deep South. To make this possible he persuaded Federal officials "to acquire from Mexico the region now known as the Gadsden Purchase" (*DAB*, V, 126). Nevertheless, railroad transportation was not appreciated by many Confederate authorities.

The sluggish construction of the Alabama and Mississippi Rivers Railroad line between Meridian and Selma, Alabama, illustrated the Confederates' lack of vision and their numerous problems. Railroad executives had requested a government grant of $150,000 in aid, but because Congress and the president were slow to act and prices rose, the executives had to request an additional advance. By April, 1862, the line had almost reached Demopolis from Selma (*OR*, Ser. IV, Vol. 1, 1048–49, 1060, 1171–73; Matthews, *Statutes of the Confederate States*, 276). To fight shortages of materials, the

Mobile, as every one knows, is a handsome city, of over 30,000 inhabitants, built at the head of Mobile Bay, where the Tombigbee and Alabama rivers enter it.[4] The ground on which it is built is quite flat, and many of the business-streets are flooded when certain gales blow. The Bay is probably thirty miles long, and ten wide, very shallow, the east shore bold and commanding, and the west shore mostly flat and swampy. The entrance to this Bay is protected by the Confederate forts, Gaines and Morgan, under whose powerful batteries any vessel attempting to enter by the made ship-channel (and there is only that one in existence) must pass very carefully.[5]

Mobile is considered by the inhabitants, and the military and naval Confederate authorities, quite impregnable. Of course I am not at liberty to disclose all I saw, but I may say, that, what with a bay so shallow that nothing drawing much over six or eight feet can sail in any part, except in the artificial ship-channel, which can be blocked and destroyed in half an hour; the forts at the entrance of the bay; shore batteries all the way up; then lines of obstructions, sunk, one within the other, across the channel below the city, these commanded in turn by water-batteries, mutually protecting each other all across the bay; with floating batteries and iron-clad rams waiting inside to pounce upon any assailant; the city covered, on the land side, by huge semicircles of earthworks, one within the other, all heavily armed; and to crown all, the power of concentrating

company hoped to strip less productive lines of their rails and rolling stock. To make matters worse, in the fall of 1862, local planters withdrew their slaves from the labor gangs that had laid tracks and ties. Officials were unsuccessful in winning their return, so they appealed to George Wythe Randolph, the Confederate secretary of war, to use his influence (*OR*, Ser. IV, Vol. I, 1060, 1089–91, Vol. II, 106). "When the Confederacy finished this road late in 1862, it provided an all rail route (with the exception of a steamboat connection on the Alabama River between Montgomery and Selma and a ferry crossing of the Tombigbee River) from Vicksburg to Richmond, entirely south and east of the mountains" (Stover, *Railroads of the South*, 17).

4. Before the war, Mobile's seven wards held 29,258 people, of which 7,587 were slaves. Mobile was a very important port for the Confederates, especially after the fall of New Orleans, with shoals and "dangerous sands" offering a natural protection (Blunt and Blunt, *American Coast Pilot*, 391). The southerners also built or improved existing man-made defenses. Most important were two old, incomplete fortifications—Forts Morgan and Gaines at the entrance to Mobile Bay. Construction on the pair began in the early 1800s (Dept. of Interior, *Population, 1860*, 9; Burns, *Confederate Forts*, 58, 86; Arthur W. Bergeron, Jr., *Confederate Mobile* [Jackson, Miss., 1991], 6–7).

5. Antebellum pilots, with the aid of buoys, lighthouses, and a knowledge of tides, could enter the bay from more than one direction. To make navigation as difficult as possible, Confederates destroyed lighthouses, removed buoys, laid mines, sank hulks in the channels, and ran chains across narrow passages. For a description of peacetime navigation around the bay, see Blunt and Blunt, *American Coast Pilot*, 391–93.

an army of 100,000 men at Mobile, by railroad, in a very few days;[6] make up such a collection of difficulties, as may well deter the Federal Government from trying to take Mobile.

Still the inhabitants are not foolishly confident. They seemed to despise any known navy or army which President Lincoln could send, but what the Monitors, Montauks, Ironsides, &c., could do was to be tried, and in the event of their being able to take the city, the resolution was unanimous to rase it to the ground, rather than permit it to harbour the hated foe.[7] All repairs, whitewashing, painting, or in fact any kind of work on property which could be avoided was avoided, on the ground that *if* the place *might* be taken, why spend money on what would certainly be burned?

I found Mobile just as overrun as Jackson. Not a bed could be had for love or money in hotel or lodging-house. The hall, steps, office, and corridors of the "Battle House," and every other hotel, were crammed with officers and men, clamouring for supper and a mattress to sleep on.[8] Hundreds stood in the street and stared at the warm lighted rooms and

6. Although the Confederates could have massed thousands of troops in lower Alabama in days, it would have been to the detriment of other vital regions. In the fall of 1862, the District of the Gulf had 9,129 troops present, with 1,484 of the defenders at Forts Morgan and Gaines (*OR*, XV, 850, 853).

7. Army and navy officials exploited various resources to defend the city. They impressed hundreds of slaves to dig entrenchments, laid in cannon, and employed a host of defensive measures. When Union troops assembled in Pensacola, Florida, in October, the Confederates anticipated that Mobile would be their target. General John Horace Forney, commander of the District of the Gulf, requested reinforcements, and although by the end of the month, the threat had passed, troops had been positioned in Alabama and Mississippi in case of attack. See *OR*, XV, 833–42; Faust, ed., *HTIE-CW*, 268–69; Jeffrey N. Lash, "A Yankee in Gray: Danville Leadbetter and the Defense of Mobile Bay, 1861–1863," *Civil War History*, XXXVII (September, 1991), 203, 207. Following the success of the ironclad USS *Monitor* in neutralizing its counterpart, CSS *Virginia*, the North put great stock in the new ships and launched a number of them. The *Monitor* was commissioned in December, 1861; eight months later the USS *New Ironsides* was commissioned (Faust, ed., *HTIE-CW*, 504; Silverstone, *Warships*, 4, 8, 15).

8. Earlier, Mobile had been painted as "pleasantly situated on a broad plain, elevated 15 feet above the highest tides, and has a beautiful prospect of the bay from which it receives refreshing breezes" (*Appleton's, 1857*, 290). Like New Orleans, it was a cotton port, with over three hundred vessels clearing customs each year just before the war (Bergeron, *Confederate Mobile*, 6). The Battle House was a favorite gathering place for off-duty soldiers and was known for its oysters, which were plentiful in the area; before the war, epicureans enjoyed the local delicacy both pickled and spiced. Located on the southeast corner of Royal and St. Francis Streets, the Battle House was supposedly named after its proprietor; the city directory listed it as a restaurant, not a hotel. See Bergeron, *Confederate Mobile*, 6, 93; *Appleton's, 1857*, 288; Sidney Adair Smith and C. Carter Smith, Jr., eds., *Mobile, 1861–1865: Notes and a Bibliography* (Chicago, 1964), 3; Henry Farrow and W. B. Dennett, *Directory for the City of Mobile, 1859* (Mobile, 1859), 53.

signs of eating and drinking, until, hours after, they were stowed away, somehow, up and down the city. I had the pleasure of sleeping at a boarding-house in the outskirts of the city, in a little room, about ten feet square, with four other men, a negro, and a dog; but we had a good warm supper, and that was an improvement on the past.

I found Mobile, the following day, a very busy place, the streets being crowded with soldiers, the stores filled with merchants purchasing what stocks were left, and the ladies and children out in full force. The stocks of goods were at a low ebb. Most of the dry-goods, hardware, boots and shoes, crockery, and colonial-produce merchants had sold out their stocks and closed their stores. The goods which were left were being dribbled out as a favour, for cash, at enormous profits, ranging from 750 to 1,500 per cent. advance. As far as possible, the stocks of goods which the smaller interior towns held, had been repurchased by the Mobile merchants, and were being resold at further advances.[9]

The truth was that everybody who had goods to sell was making money as fast as they could count it, and then investing it in State, Bank, or Railway Bonds, Confederate 8 per cent. Government Bonds, or in cotton, at about fifteen to twenty cents per pound. This cotton was carefully stored far from any water-course, road, or railway, and never more than twenty-five bales in one place.[10]

9. The Mobile *Register and Advance* of October 23, 1862, advertised sugar, stationery, bacon, blockade matches, salt, rice flour, sheet music, opium, Virginia tobacco, lamp black, soap, and teas.

10. In the beginning of the war, railroad companies did make a profit, and with the government's need for their service, they appeared to be an attractive investment. Roller and Twyman, eds., *Encycl. of Southern History*, 1018; Stover, *Railroads of the South*, 15. The Confederate Congress authorized the issue of "certificates of stock or bonds to the amount of $15,000,000 bearing 8%, payable semi-annually in specie. Bonds were issued for ten years but could be redeemed by the Government any time after five upon giving three month's public notice" (Richard Cecil Todd, *Confederate Finance* [Athens, Ga., 1954], 26); Matthews, *Statutes of the Confederate States*, 117.

Great Britain consumed 80 percent of the South's exported cotton; British dependency on American cotton was so great, in fact, that southerners assumed the Europeans would openly intervene on their behalf. Therefore, individuals and governments encouraged destruction of the white gold and growing other crops, hoping to force the British to enter the war for the South. Sometime late in 1862, when the British did not break the blockade, southerners started to realize that cotton was the medium they could use to purchase desperately needed materiel. See Frank Lawrence Owsley, *King Cotton Diplomacy: Foreign Relations of the Confederate States of America* (1931; rpr. Chicago, 1959), 43–49; Current, ed., *Encycl. of the Confederacy*, I, 180; David G. Surdam, "Cotton's Potential as an Economic Weapon: The Antebellum and Wartime Market for Cotton Textiles," *Agricultural History*, LXVIII (Spring, 1994), 141–45.

As a result of curtailed cultivation and decrease in the surpluses held by northern and European mills, cotton demand grew. The Confederates then "valued [cotton] as a means of supporting gov-

The greatest anxiety existed here that their foreign and even Northern creditors should know that they had not repudiated, and did not intend to repudiate, a single debt, but could and would pay every cent and interest. This, I firmly believe, is within their power, and is their intention.

The Confiscation Law, passed early in 1861 by the Confederate Congress, was explained to me to be simply a restraint on their paying any debt *while the war lasted,* but no seizure of property by the Government for its own use.[11] Government, in fact, became for the time the trustee of the Northern and foreign creditor.

I frequently inquired from all sorts of people likely to know, what their notion was of the amount of cotton then in the Confederacy. The reply usually was: "Well, there are the remains of the crop of 1860, all the crop of 1861, and that of 1862 when gathered—probably 750,000 to 1,000,000 bales; in all, I should say, we shall have, in the spring of 1863, from 4,000,000 to 4,500,000 bales. But if there is no chance of peace before next planting (April), we shall not sow a single seed."[12]

The losses by burning were not considered heavy, nor was it deemed probable that any further incursions could be made into the cotton districts by the Federal troops, which would cause any important diminution of the stock. The planters were becoming less reckless; the troops cared little about the gunboats, which at first spread terror through their ranks; and the whole country was keenly cognisant of the fact, that two years of the blockade had not enabled the North or Europe either to obtain,

---

ernment credit, whereas the War and Navy departments wanted to exchange it for urgently needed supplies. All bought cotton in large quantities, often in competition with one another, as well as states and private citizens, thus driving up prices" Roller and Twyman, eds., *Encycl. of Southern History,* 271). Finally, to coax livestock, tobacco, and cotton from planters and farmers, the Confederate Congress granted the secretary of the treasury the power to accept bonds for same with the rates to "be adjusted between the parties and the agents of the Government" (*OR,* Ser. IV, Vol. I, 1079).

11. On May 21, 1861, the Confederate Congress passed an act prohibiting its citizens from paying debts to corporations or individuals in the United States (with the exception of Delaware, Maryland, Kentucky, Missouri, and Washington, D.C.) while war was being waged (Matthews, *Statutes of the Confederate States,* 151). Corsan later referred to these acts as "stay laws."

12. "The cotton crop of 1862 certainly felt the weight of all this agitation in favor of curtailment. Only about a million and a half bales were produced as compared with four and a half million for 1861. And hundreds of thousands of bales were put to the torch during the spring and summer of 1862. Every newspaper—southern, northern, and English—carried the story of burning cotton and the reduction of the crop" (Owsley, *King Cotton Diplomacy,* 48, 49). The next year the crop was only 449,059 bales, barely enough for home consumption (Current, ed., *Encycl. of the Confederacy,* I, 419).

or see much chance of obtaining, such a supply of cotton from any other source than the South as to diminish the value of their stock. Half-a-crown per pound for American cotton in Liverpool said more plainly to them than mountains of books and figures could gainsay: "We can get no supply of cotton unless the South can send her crop; whenever she can send it, we will buy it in preference to any other, take all she can send, and pay her in gold for it if she will have nothing else."

Of course this tended daily to make them care more for their cotton, and I believe will cause it to be planted in 1863 extensively, even if the war goes on for twelve months more. That the war has confirmed the monopoly of the cotton supply to the Southern States, in a manner which nothing for years can undo, is certain; and what with the fact that the Confederate Government know they may safely put an export duty upon it, and that the planters know they really hold the supply in their power, it is plain that cotton will not touch the prices of 1860, nor anything near it, for many a long year.[13]

The people of Mobile seem to drive a thriving trade with Havannah by running the blockade—their swift, well-handled steamers going in and out just when they please. The newspapers announced daily sales of clothing, boots and shoes, hats and caps, hardware, hosiery, &c. &c. all of which had run the blockade, and everything was snapped up at ridiculous prices;—shoes 25 dollars per pair, long boots 40 dollars per pair, overcoats 75 dollars each, caps and hats 15 to 25 dollars each, and so on.[14]

Owing to the blocking-up of the railroads and rivers with troops and military stores, flour had risen to 45 and even 60 dollars per barrel; Indian corn to 3 dollars 25 cents per bushel; butter to 1 dollar 75 cents and 2 dollars per pound, and so on. Coffee was 3 dollars 25 cents per pound; tea, anything between 12 and 20 dollars per pound; and all colonial pro-

---

13. In 1860, cotton sold for about ten cents a pound. This figure is based on a value of $191,806,555 estimated for 1,767,686,338 pounds of Sea Island and other strains exported for the fiscal year. This represented 3,812,345 bales of about four hundred pounds each (McPherson, *Battle Cry of Freedom*, 100; Roller and Twyman, eds., *Encycl. of Southern History*, 300; Treasury Dept., *Report of Commerce and Navigation, 1860*, 316–17).

14. Havana, Cuba, like Nassau in the Bahamas and Matamoras, Mexico, became a haven that harbored blockade runners, crews, and cargoes before the dash to blockaded southern ports. Shortly before Corsan's arrival, two ships, the *Cuba* and the *Alice* (the *Matagorda* until August, 1862), reached Mobile from Havana. Generally speaking, however, Gulf Coast blockade runners did not compare to the East Coast versions. The Federal navy manned a heavy blockade near Mobile, and because of shallow bars and channels, smaller vessels that carried less cargo had to be used (Stephen R. Wise, *Lifeline of the Confederacy: Blockade Running During the Civil War* [Columbia, S.C., 1988], 167–68, 267).

duce in proportion. Hotel-board, however, was only 3 dollars 50 cents
per day; but, as far as eating went, it was far too much, for a more
miserable bill of fare than that once-famous hostelry the "Battle House"
offered, except that at the "Exchange" in Richmond, I never saw. The
will was there to do better, but the market really contained nothing to
choose from.

The absence of wine at the hotel tables, of bar-drinking, and, in fact,
drinking in any form or degree except of water, kept the city and troops
in excellent order, but was really rather hard on the traveller and the
men themselves. However, no one complained: whatever "Government"
did, said, or wanted was all right, and conceded without a murmur. Did
any one want to purchase a tempting lot of iron, boots or shoes, hosiery,
&c., ten to one the answer would be, "We don't know yet what the
departments may want out of these, and until we do know we cannot
sell anything to any one else."

After nearly a week's pleasant sojourn in Mobile, I embarked, early
one cold morning, with several thousands of troops and a vast number
of other passengers, on board a steamer, which took us some distance up
the Alabama River, where we landed, and entered the cars on a line
which joined the Alabama and Florida Railroad at Greenville, reaching
Montgomery, the State capital of Alabama, and the cradle of the Confederate Government, late the same night.[15]

For half this distance the line ran through an uneven, gently-swelling
prairie; well and often even densely wooded; abundantly watered by the
tributaries of the Alabama, Conecuh, and other rivers; abounding in immense tracts of ungathered Indian corn, and unpacked cotton; but with
scarcely a village, homestead, or hut within sight. As we approached
Montgomery, however, the country became clearer, more elevated, and
broken, and towns more frequent, retaining at the same time the evidences of that great fertility which had been observable the whole way.[16]

15. Corsan may have taken one of the Confederate transports *Henry J. King, James Battle,* or
William H. Young, but it is more likely he was on the Alabama River packet *Jeff Davis* or *Virginia.*
The riverboats left Mobile at 4:00 P.M. on Wednesday with stops on the waterway. Corsan exaggerated the number of troops on board the steamboat; hundreds would have been a more accurate
description. Silverstone, *Warships,* 236–37; Mobile *Register and Advertiser,* October 22, 1862.

16. The water journey covered just over 330 miles and lasted three to four days. The Montgomery to Greenville railway jaunt was forty-three miles (Thomas, *Appleton's Railway Guide,* 247; *Appleton's, 1857,* 290; Mobile *Register and Advertiser,* October 22, 1862). The Tombigbee and Alabama
Rivers flow south to form the Mobile River; the Coneich (Conecuh) runs southwest to Florida
(*Columbia Lippincott Gazetteer,* 441; Harder, *Place Names,* 5, 117; *OM Atlas,* CXXXV-A).

The position of Montgomery is commanding and picturesque in the extreme, standing, as it does, on the bosom of several bold hills, which might almost be called mountains, sloping down to the beautiful Alabama River. It is an important town, of 6,000 inhabitants; a great depôt for cotton, corn, tobacco, and rice; the seat of the State Legislature of Alabama, and adorned with some imposing buildings. The view from the dome of the State House, on a fine day, is very grand and very extensive; and looking, as I did when there, on a vast panorama of swelling hills and plains, mostly covered with ripe corn, wheat, and cotton; the woods vivid with every autumnal tint, farmhouses and negroes' huts nestling among them, and the noble river winding across the view—anything finer, or more pleasing, I think I never saw.[17]

The streets, as usual in Southern cities of this class, are wide, unmacadamized, ankle-deep in sand, and usually lined with trees.[18] Altogether, the place had the air of a comfortable quiet country-town. The fatigue and discomfort incurred on the run from Mobile had been as great as before experienced, and the rush for bed and supper on the hotels at Montgomery as frantic, and as difficult to satisfy. Ten of us slept, hot and dusty as we were, in our clothes, each on a mattress, on the floor of a small parlour, and were very thankful for it. As usual, there were not more than half cars sufficient to take the troops and passengers which the boat from Mobile had brought up; and sick, wounded, convalescent, women, children, citizens, officers, and soldiers were all crammed and piled into or upon passenger cars, freight-cars, trucks, cattle-cars, or, in fact, anything that had wheels and would run. All the food which we had been able to procure for sixteen hours, was just what the negroes hawked round the cars at the depôts, during the few moments we

17. Montgomery, the state's capital, had 8,843 peacetime residents. It had served as the first capital of the Confederacy before the government shifted to Richmond, which was a larger city and thought to be closer to the events "that would decide the fate of the young nation" (Emory M. Thomas, *The Confederate State of Richmond: A Biography of the Capital* [Austin, 1971], 15); Dept. of Interior, *Population, 1860*, 9; William Warren Rogers, Jr., " 'In Defense of Our Sacred Cause': Rabbi James K. Gutheim in Confederate Montgomery," *Journal of Confederate History*, VII (1991), 115. Another autumn visitor noted about Montgomery that "a great demand exists here for residences, the applicants being mostly refugees from above and below, and the prices being a matter of minor consideration" (Jones, "A Confederate Soldier Visits Montgomery," 101).

18. "John Loudon McAdam (1756–1836) invented and gave his name to a method of surfacing road known as *macadamizing*. The method utilized the weight of normal road traffic to crush layers of small broken stones of fairly uniform size into the road surface" (Cyril Leslie Beechine, *A Dictionary of Eponyms* [Oxford, Eng., 1988], 120). Thus, an unmacadamized road is rugged and full of ruts (*OED*, XIX, 109).

stopped, such as apples, molasses, cake, cracked corn, baked sweet potatoes, &c. The crowd, heat, dust, jolting, hunger, and thirst put the healthy out of temper, and taxed the sick sorely.

I spent an hour or two listening to the debates of the State Legislature at Montgomery, which was in session. The greatest order, moderation, and despatch were manifested in discussing the questions before the House—such as "compensation for crops destroyed and negroes stolen by the enemy," &c. The Government of President Lincoln was never referred to except as a foreign Government, nor that of President Davis but as the only legal Government in the Confederate States. If names and dates could have been changed, it would have been very easy to believe that I was listening to the debates of some State Legislature at the time when the colonies were in rebellion against Great Britain. The same complaints of attempted tyranny, the same fervent and confident invocations of the blessing of God on the cause of right and liberty against wrong and slavery, and the same fixed resolve to conquer or perish, were the burden of the speeches I listened to in Montgomery, as I read in history they were of other speeches eighty odd years ago.

The SS *Marion,* which carried Corsan from New York to New Orleans
in October, 1862
Courtesy of the Mariners' Museum, Newport News, Va.

Major General Benjamin F. Butler, commander of the Union forces
in New Orleans
Courtesy of the Mariners' Museum, Newport News, Va.

Contemporary engraving of the port of Charleston
Courtesy of the Mariners' Museum, Newport News, Va.

Sketch of Richmond that appeared in the May 21, 1862, issue of the
Illustrated London News. Such images may have inspired Corsan to visit the
Confederate capital.
Courtesy of the Mariners' Museum, Newport News, Va.

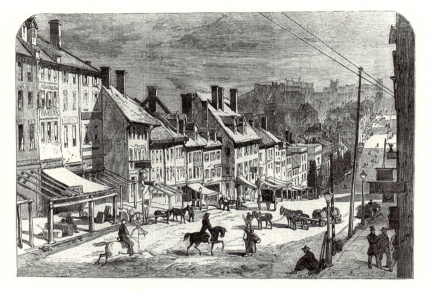

High Street in Richmond, as shown in the *Illustrated London News.*
Courtesy of the Mariners' Museum, Newport News, Va.

FIVE

Through the Deep South to Charleston

*L*eaving Montgomery, I then proceeded, viâ *Opelika, West Point, La* Grange, Atalanta, Augusta, and Hamburgh, to Charleston, crossing the States of Alabama, Georgia, and South Carolina, by the Montgomery and West Point, Atalanta and La Grange, Georgia and South Carolina rail-roads.[1] That portion of Alabama, and the whole of Georgia, through which these lines ran, struck me as being a very fine fertile country. As a rule, it was elevated and uneven, made up either of bold swelling hills, or a rolling prairie-like country, with abundance of fine timber (chiefly oak, hickory, cedar, and pine), a good deal of strong rich soil, immense crops of Indian corn, wheat, and vegetables, and a very considerable quantity of cotton, neat thriving villages and farm-houses, at very short distances, and abundance of fine streams.

West Point, Atalanta, and Augusta, especially, were plainly places of great and growing importance, the two latter being places with 13,000 and 18,000 inhabitants respectively; important railway centres, great de-pôts of cotton, corn, and other produce, and the thriving seats of the infant manufactories of the Confederacy, in iron, cotton, wool, and wood.[2]

1. The Montgomery and West Point Railroad went through Mount Meigs, Cliett's, Chorter's, Cowles's, Franklin, Chehaw, Notasulga, Lochepoga, Opelika, and Rough and Ready and stopped at West Point on the Georgia border. This section of the journey covered eighty-eight miles. From there, the Atlanta (Atalanta) and West Point Railroad headed northeast for eighty-seven miles. Some of the stations on this route included Long Cane, La Grange, Palmetto, and East Point (Thomas, *Appleton's Railway Guide,* 243).

2. Atlanta's antebellum population was 8,843, with almost half that number being slaves. DeKalb and Fulton Counties and Atlanta supported industries that were critical to victory. The Gate City rolling mill was in the same class as the Tredegar works in Richmond. Other assets included a railroad shop, a tannery, two flour mills, four machine and engine builders, and manu-facturers of metal wares. Like other cities, the population swelled during the war with laborers,

The rivers which we crossed, the Chattahoochie and the Savannah especially, besides many tributaries of the Coosa, Appalachicola, Altamaha, &c., were very noble streams, with abundant water-power, waiting to be used and turned to profit. Nothing can prevent very important manufacturing interests from growing up in the interior of these States, where the raw material and water-power are so abundant and so close at hand. In fact, this movement has commenced already, and Augusta really begins to look like a little Lowell at least.[3]

The ride through South Carolina was not by any means so picturesque, owing to the fact that the railway runs through the least fertile part of the State. Commencing at Hamburgh, its course lies through one long succession of arid, sterile sandhills, and plains covered with pines and thick undergrowth, and then through a low swampy stretch of morasses, pine-barrens, and forests, from the branches of whose trees hang long festoons of a funereal looking moss—altogether the most gloomy, God-forsaken country the eye ever rested upon.

We arrived at length in world-renowned Charleston, at daybreak one cold morning, and were driven rapidly, through the silent deserted streets, to that most comfortable house, the "Charleston Hotel," hungry, sore, sleepy, and dirty. A clean bed, quiet house, bath, shampoo, and good breakfast, however, soon set all that right, and about mid-day I strolled out into the hot sunny day, to see how the "cradle of Secession" looked, talked, and acted.[4]

---

refugees, and soldiers (Dept. of Interior, *Population, 1860,* 74; Dew, *Ironmaker to the Confederacy,* 87; Dept. of Interior, *Manufactures, 1860,* 68). In 1860, Augusta had 12,493 people, with only a quarter being bondsmen. War industries such as Augusta Powder Works, its railroad lines, and its position on the head of the Savannah River made it another important city. See Current, ed., *Encycl. of the Confederacy,* III, 1245; Dew, *Ironmaker to the Confederacy,* 125; *Columbia Lippincott Gazetteer,* 122; Larry J. Daniel and Riley W. Gunter, *Confederate Cannon Foundries* (Union City, Tenn., 1977), 62.

3. The Chattahoochee (Chattahoochie) forms a stretch of the border between Georgia and Alabama; it runs generally south to help make the Apalachicola (Appalachicola) River. The Altamaha is formed from the Oconee and Ocomulgee Rivers and rolls to the Atlantic Ocean on the Georgia coast. The Coosa, a stream in Alabama and Georgia, merges with the Tallapoosa to make the Alabama River (*OM Atlas,* CXXXV-A; Harder, *Place Names,* 12, 17, 95, 120; *Columbia Lippincott Gazetteer,* 53, 82, 378, 446).

In 1859, Lowell, Massachusetts, on the Merrimack River, was home to twelve cotton or wool manufacturers with about 372,000 spindles and thirteen thousand women and men employees. The South had nothing to compare with this dynamo (Homans and Homans, *Cyclopedia of Commerce,* 1288–89).

4. Charleston, with over forty thousand residences, was one of the largest cities in the South. The area's industries were timber, turpentine, boat building, flour mills, and machinery and railroad

I had been already astonished at the number of Jewish-looking faces which I had met on the stairs, in the halls and parlours of the hotel, and at breakfast. Fully one-half the large number of guests in the house seemed as if they had just stepped out of Houndsditch, and reminded me of what a friend in Mobile said, that "I should meet more Jews in Charleston than I could see in Jerusalem."[5] They all seemed absorbed in the study of the auctioneers' pamphlets, and the long advertisements of sales which half filled the papers. I found these sales were all of goods which had run the blockade, and the quantity seemed very large, and very varied. On issuing from the cool hotel into the bright, hot street, I saw the large store of Chamberlain, Miller, & Co., the auctioneers, opposite, crammed with my Hebrew friends, and a large sale of foreign goods going on.[6] It continued the whole day, and when I retired, near midnight, the place was lighted up, and buyers still paying for their purchases and receiving their invoices. The quantity and variety of goods sold was very great, including medicines, scents, soaps, tea, coffee, cocoa, chocolate, all sorts of spices, enough drugs to stock I know not how many apothecaries' shops, wines, spirits, hardware, all kinds of dry-goods and smallwares, boots, shoes, hats, bonnets, crinolines—in short, nearly every imaginable necessary or luxury usually imported from abroad by the South.[7] The prices obtained (for cash) seemed to me very large, such as:—

---

car production (Roller and Twyman, eds., *Encycl. of Southern History,* 196–97; Dept. of Interior, *Population, 1860,* 452; Dept. of Interior, *Manufactures, 1860,* 553). The Charleston Hotel on Meeting Street was described as "among the most conspicuous" of the city's hotels and a "particularly good" specimen of Charleston architecture (*Appleton's, 1857,* 249, 252).

5. In Charleston, a "very small community of Sephardic Jews that had been in the port since the turn of the [eighteenth] century had been augmented in the 1740s by Jewish immigrants from London and Amsterdam who knew the indigo trade" (Walter J. Fraser, Jr., *Charleston! Charleston!: The History of a Southern City* [Columbia, S.C., 1989], 82). "Jews, many of them Poles and Germans (the so-called Ashkenazim) who escaped from persecution, began to arrive in London in considerable numbers after the 1750s. . . . They set up house and shop in humble quarters in Whitechapel, Houndsditch, Mile End or Petticoat Lane" (George Rudé, *Hanoverian London, 1714–1808* [London, 1971], 7). Many of these individuals were in the garment business. The neighborhood of Houndsditch got its name supposedly because the sector was a "filthy place, full of dead dogs," many of them in an open grave (Walter Thornbury, *Old and New London: A Narrative of Its History, Its People and Its Places* [London, n.d.], II, 163–65). What Corsan did not see was the ten to twelve thousand southern Jews in Confederate uniforms who supported the cause, as did most Jewish citizens in the region (Current, ed., *Encycl. of the Confederacy,* II, 845; Rogers, "Rabbi Gutheim in Montgomery," 113, 114).

6. The dry goods store of Chamberlain, Miler [Miller] & Co. was on Meeting Street (*Directory of the City of Charleston, to Which Is Added a Business Directory* [Charleston, 1860], 51).

7. The city's newspapers confirmed both the "quantity and variety" of goods offered for sale. Other imported luxury items not mentioned by Corsan were kid gloves, gold braid for uniforms, and black silk (Charleston *Daily Courier,* November 1, 3, 1862).

Sulphate of Quinine	18	dollars per	ounce.
″ Morphia	30	″ ″	″
Chloroform	13	″ per	pound.
Calomel	9	″ ″	″
Pulv. Turkey Opium	40	″ ″	″
Pins	10	dollars per	packet.
Matches	14	″ ″	gross.
Tooth-brushes	17	″ ″	dozen.
Port	29	″ ″	″
Brandy	20 to 70	″ ″	″
Champagne	55	″ ″	″
Rye Whiskey	37	″ ″	″
Needles	3.50	″ ″	M.
Note-paper	7.50	″ ″	ream.
Hair-brushes	13	″ ″	dozen.
Felt Hats	14	″	each.
Socks	11	″ per	dozen.
Woollen Shirts	33	″ ″	″
Cotton and Linen Shirts	75	″ ″	″
Boots (good)	40	″ ″	pair.
Shoes for negroes	25	″ ″	″
Envelopes	12	″ ″	M.

&c. &c. &c.[8]

Of course the above prices were in Confederate currency, and exchange was about 200 per cent. premium. Still, judging from the quality

8. Sulphate of morphia is "a salt formed by saturating morphia with sulphuric acid, evaporating, and crystallizing . . ." (Dunglison, *Medical Science,* 572). The normal dose was an eighth to a quarter of a grain. Opium is made from inspissated juice of the poppy flower; at that time its many varieties included the Turkey, Smyrna, and East Indian, "of which the first is the best." It could be a stimulant in small doses and a narcotic in large. "Turkey opium is in flattish, rounded masses of half a pound to two pounds in weight, covered externally with the seed vessels. . . . The texture is soft; the color is pale brown; the odor is strong and narcotic, and the taste acrid" (Griffith, *Universal Formulary,* 295). Sadly, "with few effective therapeutic techniques, physicians and their patients appreciated the analgesic and tranquilizing properties of opium" (Hallock, "Lethal and Debilitating," 60).

By examining the antebellum prices for medicines, the wartime prices, and the quantities run through the blockade for Chamberlain, Miler & Co., one can better understand Corsan's excitement. The exchange he quoted would mean that a dollar in gold would be worth two dollars in Confederate currency. Also bear in mind that a private in the army earned eleven dollars a month, so one can see that profits were great.

of the goods, some one netted an enormous profit.[9] It was the practice, I found, among the houses who had run goods in, to offer the whole shipment first to the Government at the regulation prices of the day, that is, at the list of prices which Government had, by the usual printed announcement of the week, offered to give for certain goods needed by the department.[10]

Medicine	Antebellum Price	Wartime Price	Price Increase	Blockade Importation	Gross Sales
Sulphate of quinine	$2.00/oz .	$18.00/oz.	900%	24 cases (2,400 ozs.)	$4,320
Sulphate of morphia	$4.75/oz.	$18.00/oz.	630%	1 case (150 ozs.)	$2,700
Chloroform	$1.60/lb.	$13.00/lb.	813%	1 case (50 lbs.)	$ 650
Calomel	$1.40/lb.	$ 9.00/lb.	560%	5 cases (560 lbs.)	$5,040
Gum opium	$9.50/lb.	$40.00/lb.	420%	2 cases (2,400 oz.)	$4,320

Note that the antebellum price for opium is for Smyrna gum. (George Griffenhagen to Benjamin H. Trask, October 14, 1992, quoting from "August 1857 Price Current and Catalogue of Matthews, Levering & Co., Wholesale Druggist ... St. Louis, Missouri," editor's files; Charleston *Daily Courier,* November 1, 1862).

The prices found in Bullock and Crenshaw, *Catalogue of Drugs, Pharmaceutical Preparations ... Offered to Physicians* (Philadelphia, May, 1860) are comparable to the wholesale drugs offered by the St. Louis establishment. Traditionally, wholesalers sold drugs to pharmacists under the avoirdupois system, but druggists distributed them to patients under the troy apothecaries' system; under the avoirdupois system a pound contains sixteen ounces, whereas under the apothecaries' system it contains only twelve. A troy pound is .373 kilograms, while an avoirdupois pound is .454 kilograms (Michael A. Ermilio to Benjamin H. Trask, February 24, 26, 1993; editor's files).

9. As the war continued, prices climbed and resentment of the middlemen did, too. Southerners did not seem to resent, however, the ships' masters, owners, and crews, who also became wealthy on the blockade trade. In the summer of 1862, one South Carolinian complained in her diary: "Three vessels have run the blockade during the last fortnight, but prices are getting more exorbitant, even at auction, the Jews outbidding all others and setting up a quantity of little shops. Toothbrushes at $2 each" (John F. Marszalek, ed., *The Diary of Miss Emma Holmes, 1861–1866* [Baton Rouge, 1979], 192). Also see Fraser, *Charleston,* 262. John Milton, the governor of Florida, complained to the secretary of war that cotton and naval stores should not be exported, as they were often captured or sent to Havana and then sent north. Also, the goods imported were northern made and "realized heavy profits by the most villainous and treacherous arts of traffic" (*OR,* Ser. IV, Vol. I, 1173).

10. At this point, the government had not become very active in blockade running or the businesses it supplied. As a result, precious cargo space would just as likely be used for silk, formal civilian clothing, or celebratory libations as for much-needed weapons and pharmaceuticals. Thus,

There is no doubt that the Confederate Government has been very materially strengthened in its earlier history by this self-denial and liberality of such firms as Fraser & Co., who in turn, in all probability, have received considerable assistance in their enterprises, and have been enabled to realize, it is said, enormous fortunes.[11] I was told, for instance, of a very large lot of strong army shoes being sold by a house to the Confederate Government at fifteen or sixteen dollars per pair, which could have been sold outside easily at twenty to thirty dollars per pair.[12] These shoes, it was said, went to Bragg's army in Kentucky, and really enabled his men to accomplish the long and rapid marches which characterised that arduous though indecisive campaign. I saw instances of similar liberality in smaller matters fifty times with my own eyes while in the Confederacy; and there can be no doubt that what with the open-handed patriotism of the merchants and manufacturers, the unwillingness of officers and men to draw a fraction of pay if they can avoid it, and the freedom of Government purchases and transactions from the rapacity of contractors and all kinds of swindling go-betweens, the war is not costing the Confederate Government five dollars where it is costing the Federal Government twenty at least.

The rule seems to be, about the export of cotton, that no one is permitted to take cotton or any produce *out* of the Confederacy who has not previously brought a cargo of merchandize *in;* and the vessel only which brings the goods in is allowed to be filled with produce.[13] This really

---

the war effort was not being fully supported by this vital means of supply. See *OR,* Ser. IV, Vol. I, 1173; Current, ed., *Encycl. of the Confederacy,* I, 182–83. Another consideration regarding the influx of luxury goods was that "as the blockade tightened between 1861 and 1865, the relative cost of luxury imports fell in relation to other Southern imports." Consequently, the blockade "contributed to the demise of the Confederacy through both general economic degradation and the untoward impact that it had on morale due to the luxury-biased composition of imports it helped to create" (Ekelund and Thornton, "Union Blockade," 891, 890).

11. The shipping and banking house of John Fraser & Co., with a subsidiary, Fraser, Trenholm & Co., in Liverpool, served as the Confederate government's depository in England. The firm kept accounts, converted currency, handled specie, provided credit, and took part "in all foreign aspects of Confederate finance" (Faust, ed., *HTIE-CW,* 286). Also see Todd, *Confederate Finance,* 176–78.

12. In the summer of 1863, a Virginia commission set the price of army shoes at ten dollars a pair; a similar commission in the Palmetto State that fall was willing to pay eight dollars a pair (*OR,* Ser. IV, Vol. II, 653, 837).

13. Judah P. Benjamin, the Confederate secretary of war early in the conflict, explained the reasoning for his country's position on the matter. "I know no stronger test of good faith than when parties run the blockade into our ports with cargoes adapted for our needs. But when vessels enter in ballast for the purpose of taking out cargoes of naval stores or cotton, both much needed by the enemy, I have felt justified as regarding such cases with great suspicion as prima facie collusive and fraudulent" (*OR,* Ser. IV, Vol. I, 814).

limits the possible export of cotton very much, but I cannot say that it is not equitable. Speculation in cotton, tobacco, and indeed every kind of produce, had run to a great height. Before I left the Confederacy, I was told that cotton could not be purchased in Charleston under twenty-five or even thirty cents per pound.[14] There seemed to be no secresy maintained in Charleston about the vessels expected in or going out. Blockade-running was looked upon as a legitimate and patriotic pursuit. One evening, three steamers were to start, but some change in the wind determined the captains to postpone the trial for twenty-four hours. This fact, the reasons, and the intended attempt next evening, were discussed *vivâ voce* in one of the parlours of the Charleston Hotel, by parties implicated, before twenty or thirty guests.[15]

The truth is, that the business caused by these sales of blockade-goods formed almost the whole business of the city. It was a very large trade, filled the hotels with strangers, and employed many porters, draymen, and other labourers. The regular resident merchants had, I found, sold out their stocks long ago, closed their stores, invested their money in plantations, cotton, scrip, gold, or sterling exchange, removed their families into the interior, and remained behind watching events. Meeting-house Street,[16] King Street, Hayne Street, East Bay, &c.—bustling places in times of peace—were now little more than rows of closed stores, and looked very much as if a perpetual Sunday or holiday prevailed. Still, I could hear of no house which had not done well. The answer to every inquiry was, "Smith, Jones, & Co.? Oh, they sold out their stock and closed up twelve months ago. They made piles of money. They're as rich as Jews. I suppose they could pay every cent they owe twenty times over."

I took good care to ask the question, often enough, whether the Charleston people considered themselves absolved from paying their European and Northern debts? but the notion that they would ever be repudiated was scouted universally. "We will never have it said that we

---

14. The Collector's Office of Charleston reported that from October 1 to December 31, 1862, seven vessels had entered the harbor and thirteen had cleared with 10,220 bales (4,655,364 lbs.) of mostly upland cotton valued at $954,000, which would make the average pound worth twenty-one cents (*OR,* Ser. IV, Vol. II, 562).

15. Blockade running was a big business. The Importing and Exporting Company of South Carolina, whose stockholders included such notable citizens as William Bee, Theodore P. Jervey, William P. Ravenel, and Benjamin Mordeci, "was one of the most successful." Fraser, *Charleston,* 261; Ekelund and Thornton, "Union Blockade," 895.

16. Meeting-house Street is referred to more often as Meeting Street. See *Directory of the City of Charleston,* 51; *Appleton's, 1857,* map between 248–49; Fraser, *Charleston,* 254.

owe the Yankee one cent when we can once get a chance to pay him," they said. "We will pay him and let him go. No more trading, however, between us. We don't want ever to see New York or Boston again our-selves; and if any Yankee comes peddling his trash here, woe be to him or those that encourage him! No, no! we will send our cotton, tobacco, naval stores, &c. direct to Europe, and buy all we want from Europe. If you can't send us exactly what we *do* want at first, as well as the Yankee did, we will put up with what you *can* send until you get into our ways. We never will trade with the North again!"

In a commercial sense Charleston is, for the present, out of business. The shows of goods in the drapers', hosiers', and fancy goods' shops in fashionable King Street are simply ridiculous; but as the ladies and most of the women of the city have gone up the country, to stay till the war is over, it does not much matter. Charleston is, in fact, populated only by the troops and their hangers-on, the Jews and other visitors attending the auction sales, and the families and negroes who cater for the first-named classes.[17]

Most of the fine residences are closed or left in the hands of servants, and I was assured, on authority which I could not doubt, that means were already prepared to fire, blow up, and otherwise totally destroy the city, if there was even a *chance* of its falling into the enemy's hands.[18] With this catastrophe in view, I was told that families had removed all their plate and valuables, the Bank their specie, the lawyers and officials their papers, and everybody who had them their wives and children. In spite of these precautions, however, the conviction was universal that Charleston could not be taken, by any plan or force, seaward or landward. Every creek and inlet was defended; all the forts cased outside with iron; line within line of powerful earth-works heavily armed; at least five pow-erful iron-clad rams, carrying large guns, besides a little fleet of smaller vessels, ready to run out; the channels obstructed and fitted with torpe-does; new masked shore and water-batteries ready on all sides, and a powerful army close at hand, all under the tried skill of General Beau-

---

17. Not all of Charleston's blue bloods left the city. "Many of the city's female elite continued to appear in expensive clothes despite the increasing effectiveness of the Union blockade, which drove up prices and scarcities" (Fraser, *Charleston,* 257).

18. In a secret session, a "convention of the people" of South Carolina, it was decided that "Charleston should be defended at any cost of life or property, and that in their deliberate judgement they would prefer a repulse of the enemy with the city in ruins to an evacuation or surrender on any terms whatever" (*OR,* Ser. IV, Vol. II, 136).

regard.[19] I had partly forgotten to state, that all the way from Montgomery to Branchville, in South Carolina, where the line continues northeast to Wilmington and Richmond, we had passed large bodies of men, at intervals, in the woods, evidently waiting orders to concentrate east or west, as might be most needful. All these bodies of men, constituting no doubt a formidable army, could in a day or two rush down on Charleston, Mobile, or Savannah, and crush any force that could land.

The ruins of the disastrous fire of 1861 remained, untouched apparently, since the flames were extinguished, and gave a most melancholy appearance to the city.[20] Commencing opposite the market, on the north side of Meeting-house Street, and just past the same market on the south side, everything was cleared away up to the "Mills' House" on both sides—churches, Hibernian Hall, and everything else—and almost as far south as East Bay, and north as the railroad. Such a complete gutting I never saw; the very heart of the city seemed burnt out; and I scarcely dare venture to estimate how many acres of blackened ruins there were. In spite of this, the people of Charleston seemed cheerful and confident; no spark of fear or notion of submission or reunion evidently entered their minds.

The negroes, too, seemed just as contented and jolly as ever. I was told that those of their colour who had been seduced or taken into the Federal lines at Port Royal, Beaufort, &c. had brought back such tales of starvation, beating, and hard work, as to make those who never left rather conceited.[21]

19. Beauregard, a professional soldier with engineering experience, was the "Hero of Sumter" and returned to Charleston as commander of the defenses of South Carolina and Georgia (Boatner, *Civil War Dictionary,* 54–55). For a better understanding of the fortifications around the harbor, see Warren Ripley, ed., *Siege Train: The Journal of a Confederate Artilleryman in the Defense of Charleston* (Columbia, S.C., 1986).

20. The inferno raged the evening of December 11, 1861, and "burned over 540 acres and 575 private homes ... numerous businesses and public buildings, and five churches. The property losses ranged between $5 million and $8 million" (Fraser, *Charleston,* 254).

21. While some blacks were mistreated, thousands of slaves still fled the region to gain their freedom, enlist in the army, and earn an education. See Willie Lee Rose, *Rehearsal for Reconstruction: The Port Royal Experiment* (New York, 1964).

SIX

Across the Carolinas to Richmond

*A*fter *a few pleasant days at Charleston I left for Richmond,* viâ Florence, Wilmington, Goldsboro', Weldon, and Petersburgh.[1] There is, probably, no equal distance in the whole United States less interesting or more devoid of beauty than that between Charleston and Petersburgh. So long as we were in South Carolina, or, at all events, until we had crossed the Great and Little Pedee Rivers, the land was evidently productive, though flat, densely wooded, and uninteresting; but when we entered North Carolina the prospect was depressing. Low swampy levels, intersected with turbid streams, were followed by long stretches of poor, sandy, monotonous country, covered with pitch pines, and destitute apparently of inhabitants. To crown all, we plunged into the region of the Dismal Swamp, a most doleful country, covered with cypress, pine, juniper, and oak.[2] Escaping at last into Virginia, the character of the country improved in every respect, rapidly as we neared Petersburgh, and ended ultimately in the rich, elevated, picturesque country round Richmond.

As we approached the boundaries of North Carolina, from Charleston, we began to notice that, instead of cotton being piled up in every direction wherever we stopped, resin, &c. appeared to take its place. All along the

---

1. The North Eastern Railroad would take Corsan the 108 miles from Charleston to Florence. A less likely, though possible, route would have been for him to backtrack to Branchville, then take the train to Florence; however, the former would have been the more direct route. On the Wilmington and Manchester Railroad, Corsan rode 107 miles from South Carolina to the Old North State's only major port—Wilmington (Thomas, *Appleton's Railway Guide,* 237, 238; *OM Atlas,* CXXXV-A).

2. The Pee Dee (Pedee) Rivers take their names from a local Indian tribe. The Great Dismal Swamp covers the far eastern boundary of Virginia and North Carolina, not the two Carolinas; however, the term *dismal* can be used to describe any swampy area (Harder, *Place Names,* 147, 416).

line through North Carolina, at every stopping place, this valuable staple was piled in thousands on thousands of barrels, apparently belonging to, or cared for by, nobody, hoops off, staves loose, and the resin melted by the hot sun into enormous masses, and plainly left to take care of itself until the war is over. We saw, also, very large lots of cotton; for the uplands of the interior of North Carolina are very fertile, and she is by no means the sterile, poor, deserted State which the traveller would take her to be, who knew nothing but what he saw from a railway car window.[3]

At Florence, in South Carolina, we joined the stream of troops and stores again, setting North, out of which we had dropped when diverging to Charleston. From what I could learn, the men were mostly returning from furlough, to join the armies in North Carolina and Virginia. The trains were immense, and, as usual, crammed inside and outside with the most unmilitary-looking set of men that could be imagined (except as regards their bright rifles and well-kept accoutrements), full of health, good humour, and enthusiasm, and all bent on fighting. Everybody asked everybody else such questions as, "Can you tell me where the —th Georgia is now?" "Is Lee at Culpepper?" "Do you know where Longstreet's division is?" and so on. The men told fearful tales of what they had suffered for want of shoes, blankets, medicines, and tents, in the snow, frost, and sleet, of the winter campaign of 1861–62, in Virginia and North Carolina; and when we met the first snow at Goldsboro', the wish was universal, that either the winter was over, or the war at an end.[4]

It certainly did seem such a demand on the patriotism and endurance of a people, as never was made before, to call out those men, born in and accustomed to the sunny South, and ask them to freeze on watch, or march through the long, cold, wet, or snowy nights and days of a Virginia winter. They were warmly clothed in homespun, woven thick, had mostly woollen shirts, good shoes, and over-coat or blanket, or both. But

3. North Carolinians harvested $5,356,000 worth of tar gum, spirits of turpentine, and resin before the war from the "resinous juices" of pine trees. The products were used in naval stores, solvents, paints, printing, and as an illuminant (Roller and Twyman, eds., *Encycl. of Southern History,* 884).

4. Culpeper (Culpepper) County is located northwest of Richmond in Virginia and was both camp and battleground for much of the war. The two opposing armies moved through the county before the battle of Fredericksburg. James Longstreet (1821–1904) commanded the First Corps of the Army of Northern Virginia under Robert E. Lee (Faust, ed., *HTIE-CW,* 444–45). There was a heavy snowfall during the fall and winter of 1861–62. A resident of Richmond lamented about the same time Corsan arrived that "we had quite a snow-storm day before yesterday and it is still very cold" (Katharine M. Jones, *Ladies of Richmond: Confederate Capital* [Indianapolis, 1962], 144).

clothes and shoes soon wear out, or are lost in the slush and mud of a winter campaign; and a man needs many blankets to keep off rheumatism if he has to lie down to sleep on the wet ground and finds himself frozen fast in the morning; and this is what many a thousand men have had to endure and are enduring this present bitter winter. Still, I could detect no grumbling, "funking," or shadow of intention to give in until they had what they called their "independence." It made my heart bleed to hear them talk through the long nights about the dear ones they had left behind, the little local interests of their villages, the untimely ends of friends and friends' families, their small plans frustrated, ambitions curbed, loves nipped in the bud, their little worlds, in fact seen, perhaps, for the last time for ever by many a brave loving heart! No one knows through what a sea of tears, trouble, and blood, war can drag a nation, until he realizes the fact that every unit of the tens of thousands he sees reported as killed, wounded, or missing, was the hope, head, heart, of some little unknown company, which lost its all when it lost him!

At Wilmington, on Cape Fear River, the yellow fever had been raging most violently, and had not ceased when we were there though the frosts had set in, which hitherto had usually checked the disease. Out of a population of 10,000, about 1,000 died very soon, very many of them negroes.[5]

There was evidently an impression that the Federal generals and naval commanders intended mischief in North Carolina, either at Wilmington, up the Cape Fear River; at Goldsboro', up the railroad; at Weldon, up the Roanoke River; or from Suffolk, up the James River again. If any of the first three attacks were successful, of course *one* of the trunk lines,

---

5. Wilmington's prewar population was 9,552 residents (about half were African Americans). Certainly some left during the war, but there was a boost from the army and naval personnel in the area. The small port had become vital to the Confederates because of its role as a blockade runner's harbor (Dept. of Interior, *Population, 1860,* 357). With so much shipping coming to the port, the chance of plague was a real risk. Apparently, the steamer *Kate* from Nassau brought yellow fever to the city in the summer, and the subsequent epidemic raged until November. It is estimated that 500 to 650 people died, and the population dropped to 4,000. Even when Corsan arrived, cases of yellow fever were still being reported, but by mid-November the newspaper rejoiced that "our streets begin to look lively once more" (*Daily Journal,* November 4, 11, 1862). See John G. Barrett, *The Civil War in North Carolina* (Chapel Hill, N.C., 1963), 259; Alan D. Watson, *Wilmington: Port of North Carolina* (Columbia, S.C., 1992), 86.

Corsan's remark concerning the high numbers of African Americans who perished is odd because blacks "proved remarkably resistant to ravages of yellow fever, which paid regular epidemic visits to the coastal cities. Thus it was the Southern whites who dominated the death rolls" (Randall M. Miller and John David Smith, eds., *Dictionary of Afro-American Slavery* [New York, 1988], 308).

connecting Virginia with the South, would be severed, but only one. Still, much loss of time and extra labour would be caused, and an evidently heavy force was being concentrated in North Carolina, to check any attack.

We were "laid over," one whole dreary night, at that most wretched of all wretched places, Weldon; for what reason no one could tell.[6] The only amusement I could find was to watch a benevolent-looking old gentleman, spectacles on nose, and adorned with a white cravat, looking very much like a rural dean in fact, who was ticking off, in his pocket-book, by the aid of a hand-lamp and a "buck nigger," a lot of twenty-one slaves, which he had purchased that afternoon for 25,000 dollars—a good price, everybody said. It seems these unfortunates were the property of an "estate which had to be closed," and our old friend had bought the lot, so that Pompey and Juno only really changed masters;[7] and, unless the face of the new master told a great lie, there was a great probability that they had gained by the change. There they stood, however, stolid, muscular "field-hands;" giggling slim "yellow gals," evidently house servants or ladies' maids; "Aunties" of twenty to thirty stone weight, whose forte was among pots and pans; little ebony infants, with crisp curly wool, protruding lips, bright rolling eyes, and no doubt long heels, like their parents, if one could have seen them, though only a few months old;— there they stood, excited, happy in view of change, proud of being noticed, and in no way sensible of any injury or degradation.

Leaving Weldon we arrived at length, however, at Petersburgh, in Virginia, twenty-two miles south of Richmond, and after being detained, not unwillingly, in that thriving, hospitable, and really important city, fully half a day, we saw late the same night the lights of Richmond twinkling on the opposite side of the James River, as we slowly crossed the railroad bridge, tired, cold, hungry, and very dirty.[8]

6. The Wilmington and Weldon Railroad ran due north for 162 miles; the layover Corsan experienced was quite common. Later, the governor of North Carolina, "in a cooperative mood, transferred ten cars originally promised from the transportation of state supplies to the use of the Confederate government in hauling food and forage out of eastern North Carolina" (Richard D. Goff, *Confederate Supply* [Durham, N.C., 1969], 108).

7. *Buck* is a derogatory word for "a strong young black man" (Henderickson, *Whistlin' Dixie,* 41). The reference to "Pompey and Juno" harks back to the old habit of naming slaves after ancient Roman and Greek figures. In the colonial English Caribbean, "classical tags were also thought amusing: Dido and Venus for women, Pompey, Nero, Scipio for men. All of this suggests the ambiguous status of the black man" (Richard S. Dunn, *Sugar and Slaves: The Rise of the Planter Class in the English West Indies, 1624–1713* [New York, 1973], 252).

8. Weldon, in northern Halifax County, was sixty-four miles from Petersburg (Petersburgh),

The railway communication between Petersburgh and Richmond was, I found, in the same unsatisfactory state that it had been for years. Passengers from the South are turned out of the cars on the outskirts of Petersburgh, furthest from Richmond, and are left to find their way, through the city, across the Appomattox River, to the Richmond depôt, with their baggage, as well as they can. In our case, an immense train, full of troops and civilians, including sick, wounded, and females, were deposited, about seven A.M. on a bitterly cold Sunday morning, and left to take care of themselves until about five P.M. when a train was put on to take them the remaining twenty-two miles, which were accomplished in about three hours. Of course the inevitable Provost-Marshal must be visited, and a pass obtained, "to leave Petersburgh and visit Richmond." I have forgotten to state prominently that these passes are the great hindrances to Southern travel. Without the Provost-Marshal's, or some "pass," no one can move about any road, river, or railroad—no, not even from county to county. The entrances to the steam-boats, the toll-gates, and the doors of the cars are blocked by armed sentinels, who will let no one enter or pass without the necessary voucher. They do their duty civilly, I must admit, but most rigorously, showing favour or excuse to no one, high or low.

Petersburgh is, as I have said, a thriving place.[9] I visited it often while at Richmond, and may as well say now what I have to say about it. As most people know, it stands on the Appomattox River, nine miles from City Point on the James River, and twenty-two miles from Richmond. It has about 18,000 or 19,000 inhabitants, is a great tobacco depôt, has many flour, grist, and saw-mills, some iron-works, and an important commercial connexion generally. It is built chiefly of brick, has one long, main, business-street, no public building of much consequence or beauty, many streets of pleasant and even elegant private residences, and, above all, an enterprising, well-to-do, hospitable population. There, as elsewhere, one-half to two-thirds of the business men have "sold out" and "realized," which means that they have made their fortunes and put it where it is safe.

The stores are mostly closed or cleared out; the streets filled with

Virginia, which was twenty-two miles south of Richmond on the Richmond, Fredericksburg and Potomac Railroad (Thomas, *Appleton's Railway Guide,* 232).

9. Petersburg, in Prince George County, had an antebellum population of 18,266. It was a railroad hub, manufacturing town, and strategic link in the defense of the Confederate capital (Dept. of Interior, *Population, 1860,* 519).

crowds of grey-vestured soldiers with blankets, knapsacks, and rifles; the river obstructed, and everything ready for the enemy if he comes. Children go to school, however; families visit each other; churches and Sunday-schools go on; and the whole machinery of social life moves as though "the war" was on the other side of the globe. Except the passing troops and hospitals reminded one of the change, the Petersburgh of to-day is very much the Petersburgh of two years ago.

SEVEN

Observations of the Confederate Capital

*W*hen, at length, we arrived in Richmond, and had to turn out into the dark muddy enclosure which answers the purpose of a station there, a scene of indescribable confusion ensued. Most of our passengers were soldiers, and wanted to know how they were to reach their regiment, when they were to start, and which way. Nobody seemed to know what was to be done, except go to the Provost-Marshal, or the Secretary-of-War, or some other official whose whereabouts nobody knew.

A few companies of soldiers at length arrived, were drawn across the entrance to the depôt, and orders given to permit no one but civilians to leave. I took advantage of this permission, mounted on the top of one of half a dozen omnibuses whose negro conductors had been yelling "Spottiswoode House!"—"Exchange Hotel!"—"Dis way for de Planters' Hotel omnibus, gemmen!" &c. for the last ten minutes, and plunged, at the imminent risk of being flung, as from a catapult, into some second-story window from the jolting seat, into the pitchy darkness and atrociously-paved streets of hilly and now famous Richmond.[1]

I have said the streets were pitch-dark. It seems that the gas-retorts were out of order, and labour was so much needed for more urgent tasks that they could be but slowly repaired. Hence, from sheer mismanage-

---

1. The Exchange Hotel and Ballard House were on the corner of Franklin and 14th Streets. John Ballard and his brother were the proprietors. The Spotswood Hotel (Spottswoode House) served as President Davis' quarters before his permanent residence was ready. It was on Main Street, and such attractive features as its classic iron façade attracted the city's key social and political figures. All told, there were seventeen established hotels in the city. Thomas, *Richmond,* 44; Richard M. Lee, *General Lee's City: An Illustrated Guide to the Historic Sites of Confederate Richmond* (McLean, Va., 1987), 81, 140, 148; W. Eugene Ferslew, comp., *Second Annual Directory for the City of Richmond to Which Is Added a Business Directory for 1860* (Richmond, *ca.* 1860), 93.

ment, a large city, filled with soldiers and strangers, at a critical and exciting season, was left in darkness during the long winter nights. The consequences might easily be anticipated; rows, burglaries, even assassinations, were frequent; and the streets after nightfall, in spite of the fact that all bar-rooms were closed and no liquor permitted to be sold, were really dangerous to solitary foot-passengers.[2] The Richmond people asserted that all this disorder was owing to the fact that Baltimore had discharged her tainted population, male and female, upon them; and that the "plug-uglies," "dead-rabbits," "shoulder-hitters," gamblers and sharpers, and a hundred other classes of villains for whom the hangman had sighed for many a long year, unable to bear the martial-law of the Federal Government, had emigrated to Richmond. I believe this was about the truth.[3]

The population of Richmond, in ordinary times, is set down as somewhere between 38,000 and 40,000. It is said that double that number of people now cluster in and about it. It stands at the head of navigation on the James River, about 150 miles from its mouth, and fifty to sixty miles above City Point, where the Appomattox enters the James River.[4] The

---

2. By December the street lights were still inoperable and promises to have the city illuminated "by the next dark of the moon" were greeted with skepticism (Richmond *Enquirer,* December 4, 1862). Confederate officials forbade importing more than six thousand gallons of liquor into the city, and none of it could be sold to uniformed servicemen. Virginia's General Assembly later passed an even stronger law for the commonwealth requiring distillers to obtain permission before production, to have it inspected to meet standards, to pay fees, and then to manufacture spirits "for medical, hospital, chemical and manufacturing purposes" only. *Acts of the General Assembly of the State of Virginia, Passed at Called Session, 1862, in the Eighty-Seventh Year of the Commonwealth* (Richmond, 1862), 17; Thomas, *Richmond,* 82, 83, 106–107.

3. On November 22, 1862, Union secretary of war Edwin M. Stanton released most of the political prisoners held in the North. Among these were Marylanders retained at Fort Lafayette and Fort Warren in Massachusetts—politicians and "troublemakers" with prosouthern tendencies. Some of the rebel sympathizers found their way to Richmond but were evidently not welcomed with open arms. Faust, ed., *HTIE-CW,* 275; Bowman, ed., *Civil War Almanac,* 120; Richmond *Enquirer,* December 12, 16, 1862.

The Plug-Uglies were one of the earliest criminal gangs in the United States, originating in the Five Points district in New York City. They were usually tall men who wore "plug hats which they stuffed with leather and wool scraps and pulled down over their ears to serve as helmets" (Jay Robert Nash, *Encyclopedia of World Crime: Criminal Justice, Criminology, and Law Enforcement* [Wilmette, Ill., 1989–90], III, 2476). The name became synonymous with hoodlums and was often used by Richmonders to describe rough Marylanders and other "undesirables" in the capital (Thomas, *Richmond,* 83, 86). The rival gang of the Plug-Uglies was the Dead Rabbits. Roaming the Lower East Side, these Irish and Welsh thugs, robbers, and pickpockets went into battle with a dead hare impaled on a spear as their banner (Nash, *Encycl. of World Crime,* II, 889).

4. Richmond's peacetime population of 38,000 would grow to over 100,000 before the war

position of the city is very commanding and picturesque, being built on and around (it is said) seven bold, elevated hills, on either side of a creek, called Shockoe Creek, which enters the north shore of the James River. The streets run almost parallel and at right angles with the river, are mostly hilly, some extremely so, and are paved with that most detestable of all pavements—boulders. The houses are almost exclusively of brick; very many streets of well-built and even elegant private residences vouch for the wealth and refinement of their inhabitants; and there are about twenty-five churches of various denominations.[5]

On the opposite side of the James River there is a considerable suburb, called Manchester, and all along both shores were flour, tobacco, and cotton-mills, iron-works, cartridge-factories, foundries, small-arms works, &c. grinding, spinning, puffing, and thumping, night and day, as hard as an exhaustless water and steam-power could drive them.[6]

Having met in Richmond representatives from all classes and every State in the Confederacy, I have deferred until now referring to the language and opinions held and uttered on the topics of the day by the people generally. Before doing this, however, I will endeavour in a few words to describe how Richmond looked when I was there.

The military situation of the Confederacy, to begin with, was this— General Bragg, in the West, after leading a powerful army within arm's-length almost of Louisville in Kentucky, and raising high hopes that he would take the city, free the State from the enemy, and transfer the war to Ohio, had suddenly fallen back before General Buell, fought an in-

---

ended. Richmond was the capital and nerve center of the Confederate government, the most important manufacturing city, a railroad crossroads, an arsenal, and the site of the largest hospital in North America. Roller and Twyman, eds., *Encycl. of Southern History,* 1058; Dept. of Interior, *Population, 1860,* 519; see also Lee, *General Lee's City.*

The distance from Richmond to the mouth of the James River (Hampton Roads) is actually closer to eighty miles, and from City Point the distance is twenty-five miles.

5. Most of the congregations in the area were Baptist and Methodist, but there were also Union, Episcopalian, Presbyterian, Lutheran, and Universalist churches, as well as a Friends meeting place and Jewish temples (U.S. Department of the Interior, *Statistics of the United States, in 1860 ...* [Washington, D.C., 1866], 481–84).

6. Manchester, named for the great industrial city in England, was then in Chesterfield County and linked to Richmond by Mayo's Bridge. Before the war, the county's manufacturers included five blacksmith shops, two boot and shoe producers, seven cooperages, six flour and meal mills, two tobacco centers, four wagon- and cartwrights, ten lumber mills, a locomotive shop, four bituminous coal mines, and a plant for making iron castings (Dept. of Interior, *Manufactures, 1860,* 610; James Hagemann, *The Heritage of Virginia: The Story of Place Names in the Old Dominion* [Norfolk, Va., 1986], 149).

decisive battle at Perryville, and evacuated Kentucky, carrying with him an enormous amount of stores, cattle, horses, and spoil generally.[7]

Of course his conduct and plans were criticised severely. Some affirmed that the Kentuckians did not respond with sufficient promptitude and assist to expel the invader, hence they were left to their fate; others, that Bragg went only to get, what he had got, supplies. No one, however, talked of deposing him, or said a word against his ability, honour, or patriotism. It seemed as if the people, having once given their confidence, would not withdraw it.

General "Stonewall" Jackson was at Winchester, at the mouth of the valley of Virginia; General Lee at Culpepper; and General McClellan at or about Warrenton. It was known that an enormous naval and military expedition was fitting out under General Banks at the North, and the grand question of the day was—"Where will the expedition land?" A few thought it was intended for Charleston, Savannah, or Mobile, but the majority considered it certain that an advance from Suffolk, up the James River, and on to Richmond, *viâ* Petersburgh, was intended.[8]

To check any such advance, I was told that from 4,000 to 6,000 negroes had been for a long time at work constructing a series of powerful earthworks, commanding completely the Norfolk and Petersburgh Railway, the Petersburgh and City Point Railway, and the line from Petersburgh to Richmond. These works were about completed, and heavily armed, when I was there. In my frequent trips along these lines, and rides in the neighbourhood, I found neat and very extensive works at every creek, hill, or position of any kind, at distances from ten to thirty miles round Richmond; while in and near the city a very heavy body of troops was kept, ready to dash down to the assistance of the army in the field towards Suffolk.

There can be no doubt that the inaction of the Federal generals has enabled the Confederate Government to make Richmond inaccessible. On every side towards Fredericksburgh, to the south and southeast, on the James River, towards the peninsula, and round to the Pamunkey, works and obstructions of a most formidable nature abound; such, in

---

7. From Brantville, Kentucky, General Braxton Bragg (1817–1876) reported he had captured over thirty pieces of artillery, seventeen thousand small arms, and roughly two million cartridges (Boatner, *Civil War Dictionary,* 78). For his complete report, see *OR,* XV, 1093–94.

8. General Nathaniel Prentiss Banks (1816–1894) actually took his expedition up the Mississippi River to assist General U. S. Grant's effort to capture Vicksburg (Boatner, *Civil War Dictionary,* 42, 684–85).

fact, as to set free the great bulk of the army to operate in the field, and crush the baffled foe on the slightest check.[9]

Richmond is the safest place in the Confederacy, and the Southern people know it well. When I was there, it was a very busy place. Its streets and hotels were literally crammed with soldiers, officers, and civilians, of all ranks, connected with Government business. Trains of quartermasters' waggons, bodies of Federal prisoners, ambulances with sick and wounded, mounted aides-de-camp, or masses of determined, though rough-looking Confederate troops, trailed through the streets incessantly.

Most of the Government offices were in and about Bank Street, on the south side of Capitol Square—once a quiet, retired locality, which never dreamed of ever being the scene of such turmoil and anxiety as it now is. The Mechanics' Institution, which faces down Bank Street, a substantially-built, but small and modest, brick edifice, never thoroughly finished inside, has been taken for the accommodation of the war, naval, and other departments.[10] There, in small, plain, unfurnished rooms, whose virgin walls never knew paper or whitewash, on whose woodwork no extravagant painter ever exhibited his skill, whose floors are innocent of carpet or any other covering, a small staff of civil, intelligent clerks, at little common desks, with a very small show of stationery, despatch with marvellous celerity all the multifarious business connected with the administration of an army of half a million of men, at least.

The Secretary of War occupied what was once, I suppose, a Committee-room, rather better furnished, with which his clerks' office communicated, the door guarded only by a lad.[11] In and out of that door streamed, for six hours daily, all sorts of people, on all kinds of business,

9. The permanent units guarding Petersburg and Richmond were militia forces made up of old men, young boys, clerks, partially disabled veterans, and factory and shipyard workers (Lee A. Wallace, Jr., *A Guide to Virginia Military Organizations, 1861–1865* [Lynchburg, Va., 1986], 234–37, 258–62). The Pamunkey River "joins the Mattaponi at West Point to form the York" (Hagemann, *Heritage of Virginia,* 187).

10. The Mechanics' Hall (Institution), situated on 9th Street between Main and Franklin Streets, was headquarters for a number of government offices, such as the lighthouse bureau of the Treasury Department; superintendent of public printing; commandant of the Confederate States Marine Corps; and ordnance and the adjutant and inspector general's office of the Confederate army. Much of the building burned during the great fire that swept the city during its evacuation. Lee, *General Lee's City,* 127–28; V & C, *The City Intelligencer; or Stranger's Guide* (Richmond, 1862), 23.

11. Until November 15, 1862, George W. Randolph held the post of secretary of war. The acting secretary for a few days was General Gustavus W. Smith before James A. Seddon assumed the position (Faust, ed., *HTIE-CW,* 614, 665, 696).

the most trivial and patent, or the most momentous and delicate. Those who had to wait their turns lounged about, smoking, chewing, laughing, talking, or bullying the poor lad who kept the door of the temple of Janus.[12] In one corner of the noisy, crowded room sat Judge Campbell, and perhaps a brigadier-general whose name is a household word, arguing some knotty point at a shabby second-hand desk.[13] In another corner, some paymaster or quartermaster perhaps was energetically endeavouring to explain to his colonel or major-general how apparent discrepancies in his accounts could be explained; and elsewhere, soldiers were trying to get a furlough from some officer—women to get a pass to visit son, husband, or brother, who was sick or wounded—or a hundred other questions were being discussed, as freely and with as little reserve as if no listener was within five miles.

Into the midst of this crowd, every now and then, would dash a courier, booted and spurred, splashed with mud from head to foot, and evidently at the end of a long, anxious ride. A whisper to the lad at the door, and into the sacred presence he is ushered at once. In a few moments he is out and off again. No unexpected news, no plan disconcerted, no hesitation about what is to be done, evidently.

If I described the appearance of any other Confederate Government office during business hours, it would resemble the above very closely. Departments and offices which in other countries are lodged in palaces, served by armies of gentlemen with independent means, and as effectually shut out from the gaze of the vulgar herd as the Grand Lama of Thibet, by mahogany doors, green-baize doors, and all other wooden contrivances, animate and inanimate, are here thrust into garrets, *ci-devant* class-rooms, back and front bed-rooms, or, in fact, any hole or corner which anybody will lend or rent, and may be invaded at any moment by anybody who thinks he has business, and will take the trouble of climbing the stairs and pushing forward. The idea seems to be, that this great task of winning their independence is everybody's business, nearest everybody's heart, and one about which no mystery or secresy is necessary among themselves, where treason is not possible.

12. Janus was the "god of good beginnings" and good endings. His temple doors were only closed in times of peace and therefore were very rarely shut during the days of the great Roman Empire (Edith Hamilton, *Mythology* [Boston, 1942], 51).

13. John Archibald Campbell (1811–1889) had served as an associate justice of the U.S. Supreme Court before taking the position of assistant secretary of war (Roller and Twyman, eds., *Encycl. of Southern History,* 162; Edward Younger, ed., *Inside the Confederate Government: The Diary of Robert Garlick Hill Kean* [New York, 1957], 32).

As for the machinery by which the departments are managed, so that the grand ends are gained, at little cost, and without peculation, neither Government nor people care how cheap and simple it is. They promise themselves, in the future, to give their Government a home worthy of the country it governs; and, until they can do that, they are content to see their clerks sit on cane-bottomed chairs, at shabby desks, use home-made ink, very bad pens, and brown paper envelopes, write despatches on copy-book paper, and never dream of sealing-wax, stamps as big as saucers, or miles of broad red tape.

Strange to say, the people of Richmond are, I am told, not at all anxious that the seat of Government should be fixed in their city ultimately. They have a notion that it will alter the character of the people, bring to the place a vast number of idle and vicious visitors, and, in short, change Richmond from a cozy, quiet country town to a busy, restless metropolis. But at Richmond, I hope and believe, the Government will eventually settle. In fact, the locality for the public buildings is nearly decided; and somewhere about the north-east side of the Capitol Square, on the hill-top, a noble position, is spoken of.

The hospitals of Richmond are among the most depressing sights which the city presents. They are all clean, and well supplied; but their number attests loudly to the terrible ravages which the war has made. Richmond is, probably, one of the most healthy cities on the continent; and hence a large proportion of the sick is sent here. Not only are the tobacco factories, warehouses, poor-houses, hotels, and even some churches, occupied as hospitals, but many of the large dry-goods stores in Main Street have also been given up to Government for the same purpose; and as the stranger walks past them, after the gas is lit, he can see rows of neatly-furnished iron bedsteads all down the long floors, each occupied by a pale, anxious face, entering on another of their long, watch-ful nights, of which he has known or may know so many.[14]

The women of Virginia are, however, indefatigable in their attentions on these poor fellows. Many ladies have private hospitals of their own, into which they admit as many only as they can personally superintend: and the amount of voluntary assistance which the congregations of the

14. All told, during the war there may have been about one hundred hospitals in Richmond, including those structures used for wounded and sick prisoners in emergencies. The *City Intelligencer* lists forty-four hospitals active during Corsan's stay (*City Intelligencer*, 16; Robert W. Waitt, Jr., *Confederate Military Hospitals in Richmond* [1964]; rpr. Richmond, Va., 1979], 4–18). Those hospitals on Main Street would have included Robertson and General Hospital No. 5 (Lee, *General Lee's City*, 124; *City Intelligencer*, 16).

churches, the Sunday-school children, and, in fact, every class of the population gives, is something amazing and very honourable.[15]

It should be said, that there never has been, and is not now, any distinction shown between friend and foe among the sick and wounded. Eye-witnesses assure me that all along, during those terrible days in June and July 1861 [*sic*], when McClellan and his 150,000 men were within five to ten miles of the city, and when the railway-cars, ambulances, country-waggons, and litters, were pouring in thousands of wounded men daily, from the bloody "seven days' " fight, no distinction was shown between friend and enemy.[16] The hot coffee, iced water, lemonade, food, and other happily-selected luxuries, which every family daily prepared, and sent or took down to the depôts, were indifferently distributed to the man most in need. Every church was stripped of its carpets, cushions, and hassocks, to make pillows and mattresses, and have never been replaced; ladies laboured like Hood's poor sewing-girl,[17] making lint, bandages, splinters; and the gentlemen and boys with their own hands lifted the fainting heads, eased the shattered limb, moistened the parched throat, or fed the craving mouth. But in all this, I am assured, Federal and Confederate fared alike.

The prisons of Richmond certainly are discreditable places. The celebrated "Libby," like all its fellows, seems to me to have been originally

---

15. Sally Louisa Tompkins (1833–1916) operated the most famous hospital run by a woman. She earned a glowing reputation for returning soldiers to the field. To ensure that her house of mercy stayed open when other private operations were directed to close, President Davis granted her a commission. Tompkins' date of rank was September 9, 1861; she was a "captain in the cavalry, unassigned" (Faust, ed., *HTIE-CW*, 757).

16. Corsan has exaggerated the size of McClellan's active force; the Army of the Potomac was closer to 100,000 fit soldiers. Also, the Seven Days' battles occurred in 1862, not in 1861 (Stephen W. Sears, *To the Gates of Richmond: The Peninsula Campaign* [New York, 1992], 256).

17. Thomas Hood's (1799–1845) poem "Song of the Shirt" first appeared in the December, 1843, issue of *Punch* and sang the plight of British garment workers. It moved thousands to tears, inspired numerous paintings, and is still famous today. The opening stanza goes:

> With fingers weary and worn,
> With eyelids heavy and red,
> A woman sat in unwomanly rags,
> Plying her needle and thread—
> Stitch! Stitch! Stitch!
> In poverty, hunger and dirt,
> And still with a voice of dolorous pitch
> She sang the "Song of the Shirt"!

Christina Walkley, *The Ghost in the Looking Glass* (London, 1981), 133; *DNB*, XXVII, 270–72.

either dwelling-houses, schoolrooms, or a tobacco factory.[18] Crowds of unshaven, filthy, scowling vagabonds, with their heads, and even bodies, thrust out of the windows at every storey, up to the roof, chaff or spit on any unlucky passenger on the footpath beneath, or swear and bully the Confederate sentinels, who, with loaded rifles, pace backwards and forwards in the street, vigilant and impassable. Very short work is made of them, however, if they become unruly or try to escape. I was passing a prison one day, when a sentinel was warning a Federal prisoner, at a fourth-storey window, to cease spitting on the pavement, and telling him if he persisted he would shoot him.[19] It seems that the prisoner, who was a bad fellow, took no notice, but repeated his offence; upon which, without a moment's hesitation, the sentinel warned him thrice, and shot him dead. The man, it seems, did his duty only, and was of course at once acquitted; and the prison was very orderly afterwards. The Federal soldiers complain, I am told, of the crowding and filth of these prisons. I am inclined to think they are justified in this complaint, for they are discreditable places.

I was very much struck with the absence of excitement or apprehension exhibited by the people of Richmond in many little things. During the three weeks which I spent there, I never heard of an evening edition of any of the newspapers, much more "extras" issued every few hours, as in New York or New Orleans.[20] Although the grand advance on Fredericksburgh, the flight of its population, the partial bombardment of that city, the removal of McClellan,[21] the opening of the Federal Congress, and the issue of President Lincoln's important Message, besides a hun-

18. Libby Prison, on the corner of 20th and Cary Streets, formerly housed L. Libby and Son, Ship Chandlers and Grocers, before it became an overcrowded prison. The three-story, red-brick complex was "more than 300 feet in length [and] appeared to be one warehouse with separate entrances and identical interior design" (Sandra V. Parker, *Richmond's Civil War Prisons* [Lynchburg, Va., 1990], 9). Other prisons were Castles Thunder, Lightning, and Godwin; Smith and McCrudy's Warehouse; and Palmer's Factory. See Lee, *General Lee's City,* 109–11; *City Intelligencer,* 19.

19. The prison guards established a "dead-line." If an inmate positioned himself in front of a door or window, he was often shot. "Several prisoners were killed or wounded when they thoughtlessly violated the rule" (Parker, *Richmond's Civil War Prisons,* 12); Thomas, *Richmond,* 62.

20. Because of paper and other shortages, newspaper editors in Richmond may have been unable to print "extras." And at this point in the conflict, Richmonders had seen rebel armies in the Old Dominion defeat Union forces under Generals McClellan, McDowell, Pope, Banks, Fremont, and Butler. As a consequence, the citizens had developed confidence in their own legions.

21. On November 5, 1862, Lincoln relieved McClellan of his command and replaced him with General Ambrose E. Burnside. A Richmond paper bragged: "The Northern journals received at this office late last night confirm the whole rumour of McClellan's removal and disgrace" (*Daily Richmond Examiner,* November 15, 1862); *OR,* XIX, Part 2, p. 545.

dred other important events, transpired, people seemed content to wait for their morning paper, which, when it did come, told what it had to tell in as few and as modest words as possible, and without "sensation" headings of any kind. A small half-sheet left no room for display, and that was the size of most of the papers. The editors of these prints seemed to delight, I thought, in putting the worst side of the Confederate cause outside, especially the clever, sparkling *Examiner,* many of whose leading articles would compare favourably for force, point, wit, and directness, with our London *Times* or *Saturday Review.* The army was "barefooted, ragged, and without tents;" the enemy was "overmatching us in the West;" or some other such startling assertions, kept the public and the departments incessantly alive like a succession of blisters.[22]

The absence of exaggeration, the evident intention to anticipate evil and overstate dangers, and the merciless manner in which the President, his Cabinet, his Generals, and indeed everybody who deserved it, were castigated by the newspapers of Richmond, and the unmistakeable ability which conducted them all, amazed me, when I considered their position. But nothing that could be said could provoke a reply from the reticent President and his advisers. I was told that things were put right, or looked into, without any fuss, and nothing said. If that was so, and I believe it to be true in the main, I scarcely know whether most to admire the courage and patriotism of the critic, or the wisdom of the rulers, who had sense to see when they were wrong, and get as quickly as possible into the right track.[23]

It is almost unnecessary to say that the merchants of Richmond were, like all their brethren in the Confederate States, put to great straits for goods to sell. Most of their stocks had been sold out long ago, and the proceeds, which were very large, invested. The stocks of the smaller cities, like Petersburgh, Fredericksburgh, Raleigh, &c., had then been bought up and re-sold, and the stores that were open presented a most hetero-

---

22. At the time of Corsan's visit, the four dailies were the Richmond *Daily Whig,* Richmond *Daily Examiner, Daily Richmond Enquirer,* and *Daily Dispatch.* The *Enquirer* tended to defend President Davis, while the *Whig* was a constant critic (Thomas, *Richmond,* 17–19; Ferslew, *Richmond Directory,* 32, 58–59).

23. Actually, Davis was very sensitive to criticism of himself, his family, or his military appointees. As a result, he was often slow to replace his appointees who were in positions beyond their abilities. On the other hand, the Confederate states' cabinet endured the rotation of fourteen secretaries in six different departments. (Faust, ed., *HTIE-CW,* 102; Clement Eaton, *Jefferson Davis* [New York, 1977], 272–73).

geneous collection of odds and ends of old shop-keepers. Of course the prices for all kinds of foreign goods were very high, such as—

English refined iron	8	cents	per pound.
Cast-steel	2	dollars	" "
Cut nails	60	"	" keg.
Scotch pig-iron	200	"	" ton.
Scrap cast-iron	3	cents	" pound.
Plain black velvet bonnets	80 to 90	dollars	each.
Boots	40	dollars	per pair.
Shoes	20	"	" "
Shoes for negroes	16	"	" "
Tea	15	"	" pound.
Coffee	3	"	" "
Unbleached calicos	80	cents	" yard.
Bleached "	1 dol.	75	cents "
Kid gloves	3	dollars	per pair.
Over-coats, of black cloth	75 to 100	"	each.
Suit of black cloth	150	"	

&c. &c. &c.

Provisions, too, were dear, partly owing to the rush of visitors and partly to the lines being blocked by military stores. For instance—

Flour	20 to 25	dollars	per barrel.
Butter	2	"	" pound.
Beef	40	cents	" "
Chickens	1 dollar	25	cents each.
Potatoes (Irish)	3 dols.	50	" bushel.
Eggs	1	dollar	per dozen.
Bacon	75	cents	per pound.
Mutton	50	"	" "
Turkeys	3 to 4	dols.	each.
Milk	25	cents	per quart.
Wood	20	dols.	per cord.
Coal	10	"	per ton.
Salt	50	cents	" pound.
Candles	1 dol.	75 cents	per pound.[24]

and so on.

---

24. Corsan's report on prices is confirmed by newspaper accounts. With Christmas just a few

Richmond differed, however, very much from many other Confederate cities I visited, in the respect that she is the seat of large and active manufactories of various kinds, which employ a vast number of people, whose presence in the streets, hurrying to and from their work in crowds, with the mark of occupation on them, make one fancy almost that they are in Birmingham and Manchester again.[25] Flour-mills, saw-mills, tobacco-factories, powder-works, cartridge-manufactories, foundries for cannon, rolling-mills, sword, bayonet, rifle, and revolver factories, locomotive and ocean-steamer engine factories, and the ship-yards, where the iron-clad rams have been built and are building, employ an immense number of white men, women, girls, and boys, keep thousands of families in comfort, and give to the streets near, and on the river, on both banks, a most animated appearance.[26] Sales of negroes go on at auction, just as usual, below "Ballard's Hotel," and high prices for them, as indeed all other "property," are obtained. There is nothing, however, either less or more offensive in this business than there used to be; it is a hateful trade, and one which I hope the South herself will soon stop.[27]

The "Exchange Hotel," which cost, when new, 118,000 dollars, was sold at auction, when I was in Richmond, for 101,000 dollars—a good

weeks away, related celebratory foods found their way to market. The auction prices fell briefly when interest shifted to the events before the battle of Fredericksburg. Lard sold for sixty-five to seventy-five cents per pound; ducks and chickens (dressed) were $1.00 to $1.50 each; beef and mutton were thirty-seven and a half to fifty cents a pound; pork was fifty cents a pound; turkeys sold for $3.50 to $10.00 each; butter was $1.75 to $2.00 a pound; eggs were $1.00 to $1.25 a dozen; superfine flour sold from $18 to $25 a barrel (196 lbs.); superior black tea was $9.25 a pound; molasses was $4.50 a gallon; sugar was eighty-one to eighty-five cents a pound; and salt was sixty to ninety cents a pound (*Daily Richmond Examiner*, December 12, 13, 15, 25, 1862; *OR*, Ser. IV, II, 836).

25. Manchester was the most important manufacturing city in England; it produced cloth, chemicals, and iron. Coal fields were nearby, as was access to American and European markets that facilitated industry (W. G. Blackie, ed., *Imperial Gazetteer*, II, 280, 283). Birmingham, England milled firearms and iron and steel hardware for export (*ibid.*, I, 412).

26. Near Rocketts Landing, the headwaters of the James River, the navy established two ship-yards; however, neither facility mass-produced ocean-going steam engines (Hagemann, *Heritage of Virginia*, 214; Lee, *General Lee's City*, 96–97).

27. Antebellum Richmond had fifteen "Negro Traders," many of them based east of the capitol, between Franklin and Broad, in the area around 15th and 16th Streets. At the end of 1862, the market showed "considerable activity" (*Daily Examiner*, November 22, 1862). The brisk trade was attributed to masters selling their slaves to avoid their capture by advancing Union brigades. A mother and her seven children were sold for $5,100; another mother and her four youngsters went for $2,880. A male farmhand was purchased for $1,010, and $600 bought a laundress (Ferslew, *Richmond Directory*, 27–28; *Daily Examiner*, November 29, 1862). For a slave's perspective of the auction arena near the capitol, see the interview with Patience M. Avery in Charles L. Perdue, Jr., et al., eds., *Weevils in the Wheat: Interviews with Virginia Ex-Slaves* (Charlottesville, Va., 1992), 14–16.

price, considering its situation, size, and the times.[28] But as I had been charged at the hotel, up to the time of its close, five dollars per day—and that, too, with the poorest bill of fare I ever saw in the whole Confederacy—I think the purchasers would make money if they reopen it, and can get people to pay the same sum, in sufficient numbers, for eating which would cost as little.

Except as regards the new floating population which the Government has brought with it, Richmond itself, though hungry fleets and enormous armies *were* prowling within a three hours' run by railway, thirsting for its ruin, and eighteen millions of foes in the North *did* long and pray for its destruction—still Richmond itself went on as placidly as if in the very centre of peace and security. The streets on a Sunday morning were as quiet, the stores as religiously closed, everybody as scrupulously adorned in their "go-to-meetin' " clothes, and business as completely laid aside as in pious Glasgow itself.

As at home in dear Old England, fathers of families, who rose with the cock every other day in the week, snored away until that biped had begun to think about dinner. No one could get a letter into or out of the Post-office; and a lame or sick man could ride neither in cab, omnibus, nor horse-car.

At the appointed hour, a score or more church-bells would tinkle; the familiar processions of prim 'pas and 'mas would appear, with Mary Anns and Johnnies following hard and close to the chosen edifice; then the long lines of Sunday-school children; behind them more Mary Anns and Johnnies of advanced years, inaugurating, or preparing to complete a flirtation; then, as at home, the bells would cease, and two hours of perfect silence be followed by the well-known rush home to a warm fire and a Sunday dinner.[29]

Such was the picture that Richmond presented to the eye of the traveller in November and December, 1862!

28. Ballard transferred some of the fixtures and furniture of the Exchange Hotel to improve the Ballard House before an auction of the hotel's holdings. The *Examiner* recounted that the furnishings reaped between sixty and seventy thousand dollars (*Daily Richmond Examiner,* November 26–29, 1862).

29. One of the church bells Corsan heard may have been from the First Baptist Church. Parishioners had decided to give their bronze bell to the cause to be recast into cannon; however, one of the flock's members negotiated a deal with the government whereby gold was provided in place of the bell (Lee, *General Lee's City,* 67).

EIGHT

Confederate Battlefields and Leaders

I *had an opportunity, while at Richmond, of going over the celebrated* battlefields which were the scene of the utter overthrow of the Federal army under General McClellan, in June and July, 1861, when he was attempting to take the city. Beginning with the fight at Mechanicsville, where General "Stonewall" Jackson fell so unexpectedly on the Federal extreme right, and ending with that of Malvern Hill, when nothing but the presence of gunboats saved the Northern army from complete an-nihilation, these "seven days' fighting" present a series of defeats inflicted on an enemy, probably succeeding each other more rapidly, and of a more crushing character, than can be found elsewhere in history.[1]

On the 25th of June, the Federal troops were a short five miles from Richmond at several points. The rattle of their file-firing, and the boom of their cannon, could be heard, all day and night long, in every room of every house of the city. With a good glass, from some points in Richmond, the flags and even the masses of the enemy could be seen. All day long, balloons hung in the air, observing the apparently doomed city;[2] all night long, the shells could be distinctly seen bursting in the air, and seemingly

---

1. Corsan mistakenly believed that the Seven Days' battles he describes here took place in 1861; they actually began June 25, 1862, only a few months before his visit, at Oak Grove (also called King's School-House, French's Field, and the Orchard). See Faust, ed., *HTIE-CW,* 195–200; E. B. Long with Barbara Long, *The Civil War Day by Day: An Almanac, 1861–1865* (New York, 1971), 230–31.

2. On June 27, 1862, Confederates inflated one, and perhaps their only, balloon at Richmond Gas Works near the corner of 17th and Cary Streets. Teamsters carted the balloon to a train at the York River Railroad Depot on Dock near 22nd Street, which then took it to the CSS *Teaser* (*Teazer*) at the Rocketts shipyard. The gunboat steamed down the James River in order to launch the balloon nearer the enemy (Current, ed., *Encycl. of the Confederacy,* I, 125; Faust, ed., *HTIE-CW,* 36; *City Intelligencer,* 22; Lee, *General Lee's City,* 108).

about to descend into the streets; while not unfrequently, the shouts of the attacking columns could be heard even faintly. Every road, and the fields alongside of them, were lined with eager troops going out to the front, or wearied columns returning for rest and food, intermixed with ambulances, litters, and fifty other contrivances, for carrying in wounded and sick as easily as possible.

In one short week, where was the foe which pressed the city so closely? Why, huddled together in a swamp—a defeated, terrified, demoralized mob—twenty miles away at least, powerless for further injury, and needing consummate skill, and the greatest haste, to save them from death, from disease, or annihilation by their triumphant foes!

Leaving Richmond, one fine morning, by the Mechanicsville Turnpike, we passed over some four miles of what was once a very tolerable road, through a fine, rolling, well-cultivated country. So completely, however, had it been cut up by the incessant passage of artillery, stores, and troops, for a year and a half, that it was getting into very bad condition.

About a mile from Mechanicsville—which is really only a hamlet of perhaps a dozen wooden houses—we had to cross the celebrated Chickahominy swamp and river, on a kind of corduroy road and bridge, in very bad order.[3] The river here is not over fifteen or twenty yards wide, and quite shallow; but with the swamp, supposing the bridge and road to be removed, it would form a serious impediment to the passage of artillery and troops. On this side of Richmond every elevation and wood is crowned with or conceals earthworks and heavy batteries. The city is naturally strong here, but no pains have been spared to make her defences very formidable.

Approaching Mechanicsville traces are soon seen, even yet, after seventeen months have elapsed, of the desperate fight which took place there on June 26th, 1861 [sic]. The houses are riddled with rifle-balls and of course deserted, fences torn up, the by-roads strewed with castaway accoutrements, and the woods and fields dotted over with thousands of mounds, where the dead lie buried. Turning to the right, we continued on towards Ellerson's Mill, where the Federal troops made a stand on June 27th, and were again driven back, with heavy loss on both sides.[4]

---

3. The "corduroy road," or Mechanicsville Turnpike, runs north-northeast for about five miles from Richmond to Mechanicsville. The battle of June 26 was also known as the battle of Beaver Dam Creek and Ellerson's Mill (Sears, *Peninsula Campaign*, 198; Long and Long, *Civil War Day by Day*, 230).

4. "A mile east of Mechanicsville, Beaver Dam Creek wends its sluggish way southward to the

The country through which the Federal army was retreating may be briefly described as a fine, rolling, farming country, tolerably well cleared, but with many dense woods still left, and traversed by small streams running into the Chickahominy River, through swamps at the bottom of deep ravines. The Federal troops made their several stands on these streams, putting them and the swamps they run through between themselves and the pursuing foe, cutting down or blowing up the bridges, and crowning the opposite height with batteries and riflepits.

Briefly described, this was the character of most of the localities of the battles on the 26th, 27th, 28th, and 29th of June, called respectively the Battles of Ellerson's Mill, Gaine's Mill, Gaine's Farm, Coal Harbour, and Savage's Station.[5] All along the country-roads leading over these districts traces of the fights could be seen. The residences were all or nearly all deserted, many partially burnt—all showing evidences of the use of artillery or small-arms; and every trace of gates, fences, stacks, cattle, and all the usual abundance of the Virginian farmer's homestead gone, stolen, or wantonly destroyed, as the case might be. Here and there on the edges of the woods, hastily-constructed earthworks could be seen, and round them hundreds of mounds, showing where the struggles had occurred. Skeletons of horses and mules; fragments of clothing, knapsacks, or broken artillery waggons; hundreds of trees hurriedly cut down, and formed into rude abbatis across some contested piece of ground;[6] gaps in the woods, dismembered or fallen timber, showing where the shell had burst, or the grape and round-shot had ploughed through;—all these and a thousand other little evidences remained even yet, in spite of the sun, wind, and rain of eighteen months, to show how desperate had been the resistance, and how furious and relentless the pursuit.

About Gaine's Mill, Gaine's Farm, and Coal Harbour,[7] the traces of

---

Chickahominy through a rather small but sharp ravine. Where the Cold Harbor road crossed the creek, Dr. Ellerson had constructed a millrace and a gristmill" (Joseph P. Cullen, *The Peninsula Campaign 1862: McClellan and Lee Struggle for Richmond* [New York, 1973], 86). Also see Sears, *Peninsula Campaign*, 202.

5. The battle of June 27 is more commonly known as the battle of Gaines' Mill. The following day, clashes occurred at Garnett's and Golding's farms and along the York River Railroad. On June 29, the battle of Savage's Station took place with skirmishes on the James River Road near Willis' Church and engagements at the Peach Orchard (Allen's Farm) near Fair Oaks and Cold Harbor (Sears, *Peninsula Campaign*, 231, 273; Long and Long, *Civil War Day by Day*, 231–33).

6. An *abatis* is "an arrangement of felled trees, with branches facing outward from the defending position to impede the charging enemy" (Faust, ed., *HTIE-CW*, 1).

7. Cold Harbor (Coal Harbour) may have been a remote stop providing a place to rest but no heat to travelers (Hagemann, *Heritage of Virginia*, 57). A local tradition states that the name may originally have been "Cool Arbor," referring to a pleasant place to rest.

desperate fighting were especially evident in the immense number of fresh-looking graves. An attempt had plainly been made here to bury the Confederate soldiers carefully; but as the number of dead was very great, the heat intense, the enemy still showing a bold front, though retreating, and the men to do the burying very few, what had been done was done only in a very rude way. The woods were filled with graves surrounded by extemporized railings of felled trees, covered with boughs, and occasionally a wooden shingle was stuck in the grave, bearing the names of the dozen men, probably, whose remains reposed under the rude but friendly defence. The vast mass of the dead, however, had been interred just where they fell. Perhaps ten or a dozen bodies had apparently been dragged together and heaped up in their uniform, and then the loose sandy earth around them had been shovelled over the pile to the depth of perhaps one or two feet, and trampled down. In course of time the rain or animals, or both, had washed away or removed a good deal of this covering; and when I was there, thousands of these piles of bodies could be seen, with the feet protruding at one side of the mound, the hands at another, and the head at a third perhaps, with the trousers, shoes, and jackets covering the bare bones as in life, and altogether presenting as sad and as disgusting a sight as the eye could well rest upon.

As might be expected, the final removal of the Federal army from the neighbourhood had tempted the owners and occupiers of farms to commence agricultural operations again; and in a very short time, all traces of war will doubtless be finally erased by the hand of industry. Would that Time could, as certainly and easily, smooth out from the memories of the poor sufferers by this unhappy struggle the wounds and sorrows incident to it, as he can remove from their fields and cities the evidences of the actual struggle! But it is a fact so melancholy that we scarcely dare think of it—that, end as the war may, it has bequeathed to the survivors such a heritage of suffering, broken hopes, and bitter passions, as to make the return of the feelings of the past between South and North in the nature of things impossible. They may cease to fight; but a river of crimson blood, spilt in anger, flows between the happy past and the doubtful future. It will be enough to expect that widows and orphans, on both sides, should be at peace with each other: too many wrongs are unavenged to make it reasonable that they should be asked to call each other brothers and sisters these fifty years.

It seems to me that most people, both in the North and in Europe, overlook or underestimate the changes of feeling which rapidly succeed each other in a community at war. There was a time, no doubt, up to which the struggle on the part of the Southern people had been carried on mainly as a political matter; and if proper guarantees had been offered by the North at that time, great numbers in the South would have been satisfied with a victory on paper. But when the struggle has been prolonged and aggravated, until there is scarcely a family in the South which has not lost one or more of its number; and when, from Republican and Democrat, merchant and professional man, parson and lawyer—in fact, from all at the North which presumes to speak for the North, the cry has been, "First submit, and then we will say what we will do," the time for thinking of submission is past for ever. Accordingly, this war has become a war for independence—a war to save their soil from confiscation, and themselves and their families from poverty and insult. It is no use telling the South that the North is not thirsting for their blood, and wish only for the "Union as it was": they point to a hundred "orders" and "proclamations," followed by such atrocities as convince them, as their President lately said, "that they had better submit to a Government of hyænas, than to that in power at Washington."[8]

The women, especially, feel their position most keenly, and burn with an unquenchable thirst for revenge and victory. It was a common saying among the men I travelled with, returning from furlough to the armies in the field: "I should have preferred staying another week with the old people, but the girls give a fellow no peace. They won't let a man capable of carrying and handling a rifle stay round home. If he can walk he must be off." And that is, I believe, the fact: the South will owe her independence eventually very much to the fiery enthusiasm of her own daughters.[9] It is this feature of the national feeling which makes the vigorous conscription in force at the South tolerable and effective: so that [if] a man is under arms he is all right, and he will never be troubled unless really wanted.

8. Corsan's remarks about prevailing opinions in the South are generally sound. Many southerners did not rally to the Confederate cause until after Lincoln called for seventy-five thousand volunteers from states loyal to the Union to invade the South. Additional evidence that the rebels compared their cause to that of the earlier American War for Independence is that the Confederacy claimed thirteen states, like the original English colonies, and Jefferson Davis did not become president officially until February 22, 1862, George Washington's birthday. Washington also graced the obverse side of the Confederate seal. Finally, "most Confederates did not think of themselves as fighting for slavery but for independence" (Gabor S. Boritt, ed. *Why the Confederacy Lost* [New York, 1992], 33). Also see Hagemann, *Heritage of Virginia*, 208.

9. "Southern women were among the most ardent advocates of secession" (Bell Irvin Wiley, *Confederate Women* [Westport, Conn, 1975], 140). But the war brought to women "unsettling and occasionally terrifying change" (Rable, *Civil Wars*, 51).

The Government has also issued very carefully-constructed and elaborate orders, allotting to each department of agriculture, commercial or professional callings in every district, a sufficient number of exempts to prevent the wheels of society from standing still. Thus one member of each firm, carrying on a business necessary to society, is exempt; a sufficient number of artisans, labourers, and clerks, to do the needful work for any locality, are free, and so on: so that while the whole male population may be said to be under arms, and occasional instances of hardship and oppression occur, still the example and fate of all around reconcile the least war-like to his lot, and soon make a soldier of him. Towards skulks, deserters, or cowards, no mercy whatever is shown: death, and that quickly carried into effect, is the only punishment considered effective.[10]

I was surprised to find so little interest taken in the question, as to whether England and France would interfere or offer mediation in their quarrel. Though the newspapers invariably published every scrap of news bearing on this point, they always accompanied it by some sneering paragraph or article, ridiculing the idea that Europe cared more for them than her own ease, and urging on the South dependence on themselves and their own swords only for ultimate victory. There was a time, about the end of 1861, when their chief reliance was evidently on foreign intervention: and the universal opinion was, that but for this fallacious hope, which induced them to make no more sacrifice or preparation than seemed then needful, they would never have lost Kentucky, or suffered the reverses at New Orleans.[11]

Though everybody asked, "What does England intend to do?" everybody usually answered their own question in some such fashion as this: "We never expected England to interfere, and do not now expect her. We quite understand the policy of the Government of such a country as England. Yours is a rich aristocratic country, and you can afford to keep

10. Actually, deserters faced a range of punishments, from fines to reduction in rank, confinement to the camp stockade, hard labor, subsistence on bread and water, imprisonment, carrying a placard labeled *deserter*, wearing a ball and chain, and dishonorable discharge. Thus, "the frequency and degree of army punishment also depended in great part on the whims of the commanding officer" (Robertson, *Soldiers Blue and Gray*, 132 [quote], 131–37).

11. In reality, Corsan's own text shows how much southerners yearned for European involvement when he wrote that "the newspapers invariably published every scrap of news bearing this point." If the Confederacy was to earn its independence like the original thirteen colonies, European intervention was critical. "Even limited European power, thrown effectively into the scale against the North, could have rendered the Southern cause successful" (David Donald, ed., *Why the North Won the Civil War* [New York, 1971], 55).

the poor caused by the Cotton Famine for twenty years, if necessary, if at the end of that time you shall have made yourselves independent of the world for cotton, and such discredit has been thrown on republican institutions by our ruin, as to render their rise for another century impossible. We believe the *people* of England is [*sic*] with us: but your aristocracy, which hates a democracy; your capitalists, who hold United States and Northern Stocks; your Manchester men, who are making money out of their stocks of manufactured and raw cotton; your Sheffield men, who are selling steel to the Northern Government; your Birmingham men, who are selling rifles, swords, and bayonets; your Huddersfield, Leeds, &c. men, who are selling shoddy clothes; and your shipowners, into whose hands our *Alabamas,* &c. are throwing all the carrying-trade of the world—all these classes, who are all-powerful in England, are against us, and want the war to go on. But we shall win nevertheless, and some of your greedy people won't make much in the long run, either, by their conduct." [12]

These, I believe, are the genuine sentiments of the mass of the leading men in the South, though they acknowledge with deep gratitude the sympathy of the masses in England, and the help which British merchants have given them in many ways. Perhaps the strongest feeling in the South is that directed against the naturalization of foreigners as citizens. To the influx at the North of uneducated masses, saturated with political fallacies and crotchets, who at once acquired the power of voting and, consequently, great weight in the State—to this chiefly do Southern people attribute the steady deterioration in political virtue which, they say, has

---

12. "British attitudes toward the South and Southern attitudes toward Britain were based on mutually beneficial economics and were characterized by a spirit of friendliness and even admiration" (Current, ed., *Encycl. of the Confederacy,* II, 711). English liberals, reformers, abolitionists, and factory laborers did support the Union, however, more so than the elite who held political power in Great Britain (Donald, ed., *Why the North Won,* 65–66).

Along with Manchester and Birmingham, Sheffield, Leeds, and Huddersfield were great manufacturing centers. Huddersfield, in Yorkshire, produced "plain and fancy woollens" and some cotton goods; the woolens were traded in America and Germany. Leeds, also in York, produced silk goods, woolens, leather, glass, oils, mustard, and earthenware. At Sheffield, Corsan's hometown, workers turned Swedish iron into "knives, scissors, razors, edge-tools, files, and reaping-instruments." It is interesting that Corsan made no mention of his association with Sheffield at this point. Blackie, ed., *Imperial Gazetteer,* I, 1242, II, 156, 905.

Shoddy was "an inferior wool cloth used in the manufacture of Federal soldiers' uniforms early in the war; shoddy was of such poor quality that clothing literally fell apart within weeks of being issued. *Shoddy* quickly became the word used to describe any inferior government equipment" (Faust, ed., *HTIE-CW,* 685).

been going on at the North for years. The Confederate Constitution provides no means by which a foreigner can become a citizen; and the intention undoubtedly is, to make it possible only after a very considerable residence, or the presence of actual property.[13] In very many ways the Confederate Government promises to oppose pure democracy, and the whole people seem of one mind about it.

Supposing that the South gains her independence, and becomes an united people, with a strong Government, it seems to me that the bitter hatred to the Yankees is likely to lead to stupendous changes in the commercial relations of the Southern States and Europe generally. Persons on whose knowledge reliance can be placed, estimate that the South formerly purchased from the North from 250,000,000 to 400,000,000 dollars' worth of goods, which could have been more cheaply purchased direct from Europe, and which nothing but protection-tariffs forced them to buy from the North.[14] This amount would consist partly of imported goods, but mainly of the products of New England and Pennsylvania, which Protection had fostered, and would be made up of clothing, boots and shoes, medicines, luxuries of all kinds, hardware, crockery, and, in fact, every imaginable kind of manufactured goods—for the South made

13. In 1861, civilians could become citizens by establishing "five years of continued residence in one or more of the Confederate States." The declaration of intention had to be made at least two years before admission to citizenship. The candidate was required to renounce his previous allegiance and to swear to support the constitution of the Confederate states, no mention being made of the state constitution. Foreigners in the Confederate military service needed only to take an oath supporting the Confederacy and its laws, to renounce allegiance to other sovereigns or governments, and to support the constitution of the state in which the individual expected to reside as a citizen (William M. Robinson, Jr., *Justice in Gray: A History of the Judicial System of the Confederate States of America* [Cambridge, Mass., 1941], 177–79).

14. The North-South economic ties remained strong even during the war, with all its geographical, military, moral, and social obstacles. "The sudden disruption of normal commercial relationships in a closely integrated economy created enormous pressures to trade through the military lines. Of particular concern was cotton." It seems likely that trade would have resumed after the war if the South had achieved its independence (Ludwell H. Johnson III, "Trading with the Enemy: Some New Lincoln Documents," *Manuscripts,* XXXIX [Winter, 1987], 29).

A paradox in the South's patriarchal society was that, unlike northern industrialists and their workers, southern planters saw virtue in taking care of their workers (*i.e.,* slaves) from cradle to grave, but they supported free trade and did not want to shelter manufacturing and its laborers with protective tariffs (James L. Huston, *The Panic of 1857 and the Coming of the Civil War* [Baton Rouge, 1987], 66–67). At least one southern industrialist, Daniel Pratt, based his manufacturing plan on paternalism; however, his models were New England firms, not southern plantations (Martin T. Olliff, "Life and Work in a Progressive Cotton Community: Prattville, Alabama, 1846–1860," *Agricultural History,* LXVIII [Spring, 1994], 151–61).

nothing herself.[15] I consider it much underestimated. Now, whatever other result may flow out of peace, that there will be no protection-tariffs and no navigation-laws at the South is certain; and England, France, and Germany will, for the first time, have full and free play at a trade from three to five times greater than that done thus far with the whole continent before.

I do not believe that a hostile tariff will ever be set up against the North, nor do I think any one European country will be able to make a better treaty of commerce than any other (though very many people are in favour of giving France advantages, on account of her effort to stop the war); but the unlimited capital, cheap labour, skill and industry of Europe, will undoubtedly wrest from New England and Pennsylvania, in fair fight, the great bulk of the Southern trade. Intelligent Southern men are very fond of pointing out the immeasurably superior position in which the Confederate States will stand, for buying European goods and paying off her debt, over the North, in consequence of their having absolute control of the bulk of the exportable produce of the continent, which alone makes a real basis for exchange.

Taking the year 1856 for instance, the declared value of the cotton, rice, sugar, tobacco, and naval stores *alone* exported, which all came from the South, was about 146,000,000 dollars, out of the total 218,000,000 dollars of agricultural products exported from the whole United States, (which, exclusive of gold, constitutes five-sixths of the total exports of the country) of the residue of which, no doubt, Southern wheat, wood, Indian corn, flour, &c. formed no inconsiderable part. It is, therefore, evident that the South has a reserve of exportable wealth, which, with peace and a moderately economical and prudent Government, will render her a formidable rival of the North as a purchaser in any market.[16]

15. On March 15, 1861, no doubt to raise revenue, the South imposed "an *ad valorem* duty of fifteen percent" on imported "coal, cheese, iron in blooms, pigs, bars, bolts and slabs, and on all iron in a less manufactured state; also on railroad rails, spikes, fishing plates, and chairs used in the construction of railroads; paper of all sorts and all manufacturers of wood, unmanufactured, of all sorts" (Matthews, *Statutes of the Confederate States,* 69). Two months later, Congress established a five to twenty-five *"percentum ad valorem"* on six different schedules. A seventh schedule specifically exempted books, maps, charts, teaching aids, gold and silver bullion, rags, fertilizers, livestock, garden seeds, paving stones, arms and lead for making projectiles, dredging equipment, coffee, and coins and copper imported by the mint (*ibid.,* 127–36).

16. Cotton's export value for the fiscal year ending 1856 was $128,382,351 (for 2,991,175 bales). The refined sugar export value was $360,444; molasses, $154,630; snuff and tobacco, $1,829,207; rice, $2,390,233; and linseed oil and spirits of turpentine, $896,238. The total for these exports was $134,013,103, with an overall domestic produce value of $310,586,330. Note that Corsan's figure of

The great question is, whether the South is not eating rapidly into her wealth by this war. It is stated, by the Secretary of the Confederate Treasury, that the Confederate Debt on July 1st, 1863, will be 846,598,875 dollars. So much is being borne by the people themselves in the way of expense, and the Southern statements have thus far been so near the truth, that we may safely accept the above as about the truth.[17] Supposing the war to be over by the autumn of 1863, and the debt to be 1,000,000,000 dollars, the question is, whether twelve millions of people—with the exportable produce of nearly three years stored up (which, at present prices in Europe, would bring possibly 3,000,000,000 dollars), and the resources for producing these exportable staples alluded to, can grapple with this debt, which, if funded at, say, six per cent. interest, would call for about 12,000,000 pounds sterling per annum?[18] There is no doubt that it would be a load for an agricultural people to bear; but I believe the

---

$218 million is for "agricultural products exported." The coin and bullion export was just $45,745,485; however, the country imported only approximately one-ninth of that amount (Treasury Dept., *Finances, 1856*, 83, 85, 99, 116; *Finances, 1862*, 223).

In 1860, southern states—including Virginia, present-day West Virginia, North Carolina, South Carolina, Maryland, Tennessee, Kentucky, Arkansas, Missouri, Louisiana, Texas, Alabama, and Mississippi—produced 48,177,892 bushels of wheat out of 173,104,924 grown throughout the states and territories. The South's output accounted for 28 percent of the total crop. Concerning Indian corn, the region grew 350,971,940 bushels out of 838,792,740 bushels total, which was 42 percent of the whole. (U.S. Department of the Interior, *Agriculture of the United States in 1860; Compiled from the Original Returns of the Eighth Census* [Washington, D.C., 1864], 184–85).

17. The figure $846,598,875 for the Confederate debt appears to be relatively correct for this time frame. I could not find Corsan's source for this number or if he believed it was the debt for the central government only or for all government levels. It appears to apply only to the Confederate government.

One secondary source concludes that $500 million "is a conservative estimate of the amount of indebtedness incurred to this time" (William West Bradbeer, *Confederate and Southern State Currency* [Mt. Vernon, N.Y., 1915], 23). A second source reports, "By January 1, 1863, the debt equaled $605.8 million. . . . The debt expanded geometrically during 1863. Total indebtedness by January, 1864, came to $1,340 million" (Current, ed., *Encycl. of the Confederacy*, II, 462). And a third source estimates the actual debt for the period ending October, 1863, to be $156.2 million (Douglas B. Ball, *Financial Failure and Confederate Defeat* [Urbana, Ill., 1991], 288). The great discrepancies may result from the combination of local and state government debts with the Confederate debt in some cases and not in others. "They accounted for slightly more than $87 million of the South's public indebtedness in 1860. Most of them suspended interest payments during the war years, and these overdue obligations boosted their debts to more than $111 million by 1865" (Roller and Twyman, eds., *Encycl. of Southern History*, 337).

18. While Corsan's projected figures are moot, estimates of the debt after Appomattox range from $700 million to $2 billion. *Boatner, Civil War Dictionary*, 170; Roller and Twyman, eds., *Encycl. of Southern History*, 337.

resources of the country are so immense, and the market for all she can grow so certain, that, with good management, there would be no great difficulty. However, all that is in the future, both as to how many people will unite to pay the debt, and what the amount of the debt will be.

A vast field will open in the Confederate States, when peace is declared, for the profitable use of their wealth at home, in the construction of railways, roads, canals, and the erection of hotels, stores, and buildings generally. The South is sadly deficient in all these things, in spite of the appearance of the maps; and as her mineral wealth especially is developed, a large increase in her carrying power must be had. It is not very likely that the South will very soon become a great shipbuilding country, as skilled labour must remain well paid for so very many years; though what the effect of high wages may be, in attracting the artisans of the North and of Europe, it is hard to say. Very likely, large numbers will throw over their sentimental objections to slavery, if ten or twenty shillings per day, and plenty of work, is shaken in their faces.[19] I believe that for steady temperate artisans, of all kinds, there will be a great opening in the South, and especially in Virginia, when peace is declared.

The great want of the South is white people, and especially white people who know how to work and will work. The negroes are in their proper place in the fields, where the white man cannot work with that sustained and certain energy which is necessary to obtain the crops which the South produces. Without negro labour, the South must relapse into a desert. No white man can pick cotton, or do any other outdoor work, with the sun pouring down his rays on his head at the rate of 130 degrees of Fahrenheit; but a negro can and does, and prefers heat to shade.[20] The white man can work as many hours in the shade, earn good wages, and live long; but he cannot take the negro's place, nor can the negro take his.

19. At twenty shillings to a pound, the wage would be between $2.32 and $4.63 in U.S. currency of the time (*OED*, XV, 263).

20. The belief was that slaves could withstand heat much better than whites and "that blacks were uniquely and inherently capable of agricultural labor in tropical climates" (Miller and Smith, eds., *Dictionary of Slavery*, 615). Some credibility for this conclusion is found in studies that show blacks acclimatize to heat more quickly than whites do and "discharge smaller amounts of sodium chloride and other vital body salts," thus being less susceptible to heat stroke. However, these differences based on race are not large (Todd L. Savitt, *Medicine and Slavery: The Diseases and Health Care of Blacks in Antebellum Virginia* [Urbana, Ill., 1978], 39–41).

Certainly slaves did not prefer sun to shade, and 130°F is not an average temperature for the region. From 1931 to 1960, the record high temperature in St. Louis was 115°, in Montgomery it was 107°, and in Little Rock, 108° (Hilliard, *Southern Agriculture Atlas*, 15).

Before entering the Confederate States, I had heard a great deal about the state of terrified obedience into which the peaceably-inclined inhabitants of the South had been coerced by the President, his Cabinet, Generals, and advisers. The rebellion, in fact, had been represented to me as a conspiracy, cleverly planned, its secrets well kept, and sprung so suddenly on the people as to take them by surprise. Once in the saddle, it was said, with the power of raising an army, making paper-money, and generally performing the functions of Government, it was not difficult for the rebellious faction to overawe or bribe the whole population.

I was at great trouble to ascertain whether this was the notion the Southern people had themselves—whether there was any restiveness under the new yoke, and in what personal estimation the leaders of the rebellion were actually held. Though the evils which the war has inflicted on all classes have been, and now are, terrible and innumerable, and though bitter regrets and longings for peace are even very general, I am bound in truth to say, that I never met one person who blamed his leaders for what they had done, or would have undone their work if he could.[21] Everybody held the same opinion, that, sooner or later, the split must have come, and that, come when it would, it must have been followed by intense suffering to multitudes; hence, that it might as well be borne by this as by any other generation. The only regret was, that it had not come sooner, when there was less to destroy, and fewer people to bear it. As for the feeling, personally, towards the members of the Confederate Government and their Generals, it amounted almost to idolatry. Whatever the President said must be obeyed, without comment, grumbling, or question.[22]

While I was in Richmond, Mr. Randolph suddenly resigned his post as Secretary of War, owing, it was said, to "differences of opinion" between himself and the President. Without the slightest forewarning, a high-spirited gentleman, who had filled his difficult position with honour and consummate skill, was, in fact, dismissed, privily, without fuss, and without the slightest trouble from his numerous and powerful friends. The newspapers had nothing to say about it, and in private society the

---

21. The Richmond newspapers, however, and diaries of Robert G. H. Kean and John B. Jones, both clerks in the War Department, are filled with second-guessing and comments; possibly, southerners tried to put up a united front when they discussed affairs with Corsan, a foreigner. See John B. Jones, *A Rebel War Clerk's Diary at the Confederate States Capital,* ed. Howard Swiggett (1866; rpr. New York, 1935), and Younger, ed., *Kean Diary.*

22. For an illustrated look at southern hero worshipping before and after the war, see Mark E. Neely, Jr., *et al., The Confederate Image: Prints of the Lost Cause* (Chapel Hill, N.C., 1987).

only remark was: "I suppose the President knows best what he is doing. We have given him our confidence, and thus far he has never abused it. Besides, this is not a time for allowing personal quarrels to interfere with the action of the Government. We have all too much to do and think about just now. When the war is over, it will be time enough to straighten all these matters out properly."[23]

Beyond any doubt, President Davis sways at this moment a more unquestioned and absolute power than any other ruler in the civilized world; and it is to his honour, that no public act can thus far be pointed at, which has had any other than a national object, to be gained at the least possible cost of liberty, treasure, and blood. Whatever the enemies of the leaders of this rebellion can say against their acts up to the time when Secession occurred, it is undeniable that since that time their conduct has been disinterested, pure, and self-devoted. They give their sons and relatives to the sword like the meanest white man in the Confederacy; their plantations, houses, and stock are destroyed like those of any other citizen; and they neither draw enormous salaries, nor meddle in contracts to reimburse themselves. They seem to look more to the success of their cause than anything else.

The President can be seen, any weekday, walking quietly down to his office, at from nine to ten o'clock each day, from his residence in Twelfth Street, in Richmond, like any other lawyer or merchant in the city, unattended, plainly dressed, and accessible to any passer-by who wishes to speak to him. On Sunday, he and his family, as well as all the other members of the Cabinet, walk, without parade of any kind, to their respective places of worship, exciting no more notice than any other inhabitant.[24]

Those who are in the habit of seeing the President regularly, say that they can tell from his looks whether things are going well with the State

23. Because Davis immersed himself in military affairs, G. W. Randolph became "a mere clerk" and was not allowed to fill the role of secretary of war as one might expect (Younger, ed., *Kean Diary*, 30). The *Daily Richmond Examiner* (November 17, 1862) lamented upon Randolph's resignation that "in some respects he was regarded with more confidence than any other member of the present Cabinet." When given the chance, Randolph "demonstrated considerable organizational ability" (Roller and Twyman, eds., *Encycl. of Southern History*, 1026).

24. Davis lived in the "Confederate White House" on 12th and Clay Streets. The Confederate Congress made specific arrangements for the president's quarters, and a congressional committee was "authorized to lease a furnished mansion" (Matthews, *Statutes of the Confederate States*, 93). The house is now part of the Museum of the Confederacy complex. His office was on the third floor in the old U.S. Customs House on Main between 10th and 11th Streets. From 11:00 A.M. to noon the chief executive kept office hours (*City Intelligencer*, 1; Lee, *General Lee's City*, 126).

or not. When the news arrived that General Burnside had marched on Fredericksburgh, it is said, his looks were particularly lively. He saw at a glance the fearful mistake the Federal General had made, and no doubt, in his mind's eye, traced every successive disaster which has ruined the Federal cause in Virginia for ever. Occasionally, he disappears suddenly for a few days; and it is then known that he is gone to consult personally with some General at headquarters in the field.

Now and then, Generals Lee, Longstreet, "Stonewall" Jackson, or some commander from the West, will be met paying a flying visit to the President, at his residence, coming, without any staff or attendance, into town, probably in the afternoon, and departing early next morning. The mutual reliance and unity of purpose existing between the President, his Cabinet, and the Generals in the field, combined with the profound secrecy in which all their plans are wrapped, and the fact that they *do their own work themselves,* and not by deputy or correspondence, account, to a great extent, in my opinion, for the marvellous success of the Confederate armies.

A great deal has been said about the religious character of many of the Confederate Generals. Inquiries, in Richmond and elsewhere, confirmed the reports I had heard on this subject. It was asserted positively, that at least Generals Lee, Longstreet, Johnson [*sic*], and "Stonewall" Jackson were men of decided religious opinions, and members of Churches.[25] General Jackson's character in this respect was [a] matter of notoriety. In many respects, the tales about him reminded one more of Cromwell, or some old Covenanter.[26] The same silent, brooding self-

25. For a discussion of Lee's religious principles, see Emory M. Thomas, "God and General Lee," *Anglican and Episcopal History,* LX (March, 1991), 15–24. In a broader sense, "as evangelical Protestantism engaged the nineteenth-century South, it increasingly provided white southerners of all social classes with a vocabulary for interpreting their world" (Edward R. Crowther, "Holy Honor: Sacred and Secular in the Old South," *Journal of Southern History,* LVIII [November, 1992], 619).

26. A Covenanter upheld the Scottish National Covenant of 1638 and the Solemn League and Covenant; both declarations supported Presbyterianism and objected to the religious position of the English Crown. Oliver Cromwell (1599–1658) headed the parliamentary troops in the English civil war and had Charles I beheaded. He was the Lord Protector and Lord Great Chamberlain of England and was devoted to the Calvinist cause. The comparisons between Jackson and Cromwell have often been made by scholar and soldier alike. James I. Robertson, Jr., describes the general after his rise to fame as "this Cromwellian Confederate idol" and before the war as a "colorless graduate of West Point, inconspicuous in the Mexican War and well-nigh forgotten with the coming of peace" (James I. Robertson, Jr., *The Stonewall Brigade* [Baton Rouge, 1963], 7); Frank E. Vandiver, *Mighty Stonewall* (New York, 1967), 331–33. Longstreet and Johnston did not have the same traditional religious outlook as Jackson and Lee. Early in 1862, three of Longstreet's children died of

reliance—the same iron will—the same tenacity of purpose—the same rapid, unwearied prosecution of a plan laid down—all surrounded and tinged by the same almost fanatical mingling of incessant devotions with arduous duties—seem to distinguish the Confederate General that distinguished the "Praise-God-Barebones," or the poor hunted Nonconformist of precious memory.

I was told by the colonel of an artillery regiment, who happened to be encamped in Northern Virginia last summer close to General Jackson's headquarters, that the personal piety of that General, as evidenced by his actions, had not been at all exaggerated. It seems that my friend's tent was so pitched that, from its rear, he commanded a view of the corner of a field, surrounded by a wood, which was not far from Jackson's own tent, but which could be seen by no other persons than those either in my friend's tent or in that of General Jackson himself. Twice a day, for weeks (my friend said), rain or shine, he saw Jackson slip away to this secluded place—unseen, as he believed—and seat himself upon the small fence which bounded the field. There he would remain, often for an hour, with his hands clasped, face turned upwards, convulsed with emotion, the tears streaming down his face, deep in the performance of secret and agonizing prayer. Nothing can be said that can increase the value of this evidence as proving the sincerity of the man.[27]

It is possible that such Generals may be beaten, if opposed to superior numbers and skill, of course; but what chance equal forces and ability can have against an army led by such a man as the above incident proves General Jackson to be, I cannot imagine. Such heroism will inflame even cowards, and it falls on the fiery and reckless Southern soldiers like a spark on gunpowder. They may be annihilated, but the force does not exist on earth that can subdue them.

While endeavouring to make our way to the Potomac from Richmond, we met the bulk of General "Stonewall" Jackson's army, on its way to Hanover Junction—a place about twenty-five miles north of Richmond,

---

scarlet fever in Richmond. Longstreet "was a changed man" and was possibly jaded by the tragedy (Donald Bridgman Sanger and Thomas Robson Hay, *James Longstreet* [Baton Rouge, 1952], 36). Johnston was not even baptized until May, 1864, when Lieutenant General Leonidas Polk, "the fighting bishop," performed the rite (Craig L. Symonds, *Joseph E. Johnston: A Civil War Biography* [New York, 1992], 290).

27. Jackson, a devout Presbyterian, prayed openly in deep and tremulous tones. His religious leanings were known throughout the Army of Northern Virginia (Vandiver, *Mighty Stonewall*, 331–33).

and possibly thirty miles south of Fredericksburgh.[28] This was early in
December, when General Burnside, with the Federal army, was encamped on the north bank of the Rappahannock, opposite to Fredericksburgh, and was expected to bombard that city, and cross, on his way
to Richmond, any day.[29]

General Jackson's forces were, it seems, being withdrawn from the
Shenandoah Valley (where he had been for some time encamped, between Winchester and Strasburgh), and posted, in divisions, at various
points on the railway between Staunton and Hanover Junction; so that
they could be concentrated with equal rapidity either in the Valley of the
Shenandoah again, or on Fredericksburgh, or pushed through Richmond
itself down towards Suffolk.[30]

We met them all along the railway between Hanover Junction and
Staunton, in great numbers—at Louisa Court-house, Gordonsville, Charlottesville, &c.: a hardy, active-looking set of men, evidently used to rough
lodging and fare, but full of enthusiasm and anxiety for a fight. I noticed
comparatively few very young men among them. They looked like troops
that had served in several campaigns, and knew their duty. Of course
they were clad, shod, and armed just like all the other Confederate troops
I ever saw: no attempt at uniform, either in hats, clothes, or anything
else; but the same dingy homespun dress, nondescript caps, strong shoes,
unshaven, unwashed, uncombed heads and faces, and the same bright
rifles and bayonets I had seen all through the South.

I was told by one of the quartermasters, that all the tales we had heard
about the army being in want of shoes, blankets, and tents, had, for a
long time, been either totally false or gross exaggerations. He said the
men were very wasteful and careless, and would often march great distances, and go about for a long time, in fair weather, without shoes, even

28. "A rough triangle in which some of the most severe fighting of the war was to take place
was formed by the Orange & Alexandria, the Richmond, Fredericksburg & Potomac, and the section
of the Virginia Central between Hanover Junction and Gordonsville" (Johnston, *Virginia Railroads*,
5). The junction is located north of the capital in Hanover County (*OM Atlas*, 23, No. 3).

29. On November, 27, 1862, General Burnside reluctantly accepted command of the Army of
the Potomac. Early the following year, Lincoln relieved him of the command after his setback at
the battle at Fredericksburg and his inability to maneuver around the Confederates (Faust, ed.,
HTIE-CW, 96–98).

30. "When Lee moved east with Longstreet's Corps, he had permitted Jackson to remain behind
in the Shenandoah, where his well-known proficiency in independent service might be used to
threaten the flank of any Yank thrusts beyond the Blue Ridge and where he could directly oppose
an invasion west of the mountains" (Vandiver, *Mighty Stonewall*, 417). Strasburg (Strasburgh) is just
south of Winchester.

when they had them. I saw numbers of men myself with bare feet, and their shoes slung over their knapsacks; and can quite understand how a Federal prisoner, accustomed to all the abundance of the Northern army, or even a civilian from Richmond not accustomed to seeing an army at all, would run away with an impression that such troops were in the greatest extremity of want and destitution.[31]

It must be borne in mind always, however, that while the mass of the Southern army is drawn from the agricultural classes—accustomed from boyhood to hunting and shooting in swamps and forests, and consequently needing less than troops more daintily bred—a very large proportion of the Federal troops, and nearly all the Federal officers, are taken from classes used to the comforts of city-life, and even from sedentary occupations.[32] In our own country, the food and lodging which would kill a lawyer's-clerk in a month would make a navigator fat, and fit for any work which lungs and muscles could do. The Southern army owes much of its success to the superior aptitude of the Southern men for camping out, riding, and handling a gun.[33] They have become true soldiers sooner; and an advantage thus once gained can never be wrested from the possessor. General Jackson's men, certainly, looked as if they could march any distance, live on anything they could catch, sleep just when night overtook them, and fight when called upon.

When in the Valley of the Shenandoah, I was told, by the inhabitants

31. "A more serious criticism of the war effort up to early 1863 does not involve the efficiency or the sources of the supply policies. Rather, it concerns the fact that the Confederate administration continued its essentially negative habit of formulating policy by reacting to circumstances instead of planning ahead" (Goff, *Confederate Supply,* 125).

32. Confederate horsemen did hold the edge over their counterparts for the first two years, but by the middle of the war, fresh leadership and training made the Union troopers equal to the rebel cavalrymen. Even though overall the South's military prowess and tradition have been overplayed as an advantage, boasting did pay dividends. Southerners "were viewed as fearsome fighters, products of a healthy outdoors rural environment, whereas the Northeast of the pallid, urban-dwelling factory worker produced only debilitated martial qualities in its citizenry" (R. Don Higginbotham, "The Martial Spirit in the Antebellum South: Some Further Speculation in a National Context," *Journal of Southern History,* LVIII [February, 1992], 6, 5, 12). McMurry, *Two Great Rebel Armies,* 47–50.

33. The dark side of white male southerners' ability to hold their own on the battlefield is that it was based on a "fondness" for violence. Many Confederate officers settled differences with their peers on the dueling field. This tendency dates back at least to the time of the American Revolution. "Connecticut soldiers threatened to leave the front if they were forced to serve alongside those from Virginia because of the cruelty of the fights among the latter." Furthermore, the violence in the South "is of a particular kind. It has meant primarily lethal violence, or violence that is cruel and abrupt, designed to punish" (Wilson and Ferris, eds., *Encycl. of Southern Culture,* 1473); Roller and Twyman, eds., *Encycl. of Southern History,* 1274.

of the little places through which the turnpike from Winchester to Staunton runs, that Jackson had marched up the valley with 60,000 infantry, 10,000 cavalry, and a heavy force of artillery. I am inclined to think that this was an exaggeration; but the number of men we saw was very great, certainly two-thirds of that stated.[34] It seemed that General Jackson himself never halted in any of the towns through which he passed, but, with his staff, pushed through at a smart trot, dressed in a long military cloak, trousers stuffed into his jackboots, his head adorned with a general's hat and feathers, and riding a magnificent horse—good-humouredly acknowledging the cheers, blessings, and good wishes of the poor frightened people he met, by all of whom he was regarded as little less than an unconquerable deliverer.[35]

The march up the valley to Staunton, where the railway commences, was said to have been performed very rapidly. The distance is about ninety miles, and, I was told, occupied the advanced division about three to four days only—the General and his staff riding on ahead, and choosing personally the camping-ground for the division which followed first after him. General Jackson is said to be very particular about his men having their food at regular intervals, and a proper amount of rest in a proper place. I was told that there was not a man in his army without shoes and blankets, and that the whole of the force had an ample supply of tents and stores, &c.

34. Jackson's Second Corps of the Army of Northern Virginia numbered about thirty-thousand infantrymen (Faust, ed., *HTIE-CW*, 287).

35. Corsan has bestowed the flashy characteristics of General J. E. B. Stuart on Jackson. In reality, Stonewall wore a stained kepi without insignia and "had a shabby, nondescript air" (Vandiver, *Mighty Stonewall,* 295). His most famous mount, Little Sorrel, "was a plebeian-looking little beast, not a chestnut; he was stocky and well-made, round-barrelled, close-coupled, excellent legs and feet, not fourteen hands high, of boundless endurance" (Henry Kyd Douglas, *I Rode with Stonewall* [Chapel Hill, N.C., 1940], 206). Also see Robertson, *Stonewall Brigade,* 23, 40. Corsan was correct in that the general did wear jackboots for his very large feet and did have a nice coat. In September, 1862, Stuart had given Jackson "a new shiny coat, gleaming with brass buttons," from a Richmond tailor. It fit smoothly and created a stir among his soldiers (Vandiver, *Mighty Stonewall,* 409).

Corsan's praise of Jackson was typical for both traveler and citizen. At times Jackson was mobbed and gave away autographs and buttons to his enchanted public. It should be noted that "considerable attention was given to Jackson after his Valley army was merged as a corps into Lee's force in late June 1862. Lee's success in the Seven Days did not establish him as the South's supreme hero. Press coverage during these months more often concentrated on Jackson's activities, and some newspapers seldom mentioned Lee's name. In fact, Jackson was often credited with the victory in the Seven Days, despite his actual poor showing. His slowness at Mechanicsville and in the White Oak Swamp was not criticized until after the war" (Thomas L. Connelly, *The Marble Man: Robert E. Lee and His Image in American Society* [Baton Rouge, 1977], 18).

I could not account for the very correct notions which even the common soldiers of Jackson's army, with whom I conversed, seemed to have formed of the impending fight at Fredericksburgh, in which they hoped to take a part. They all seemed confident that General Burnside had made a grand mistake in moving on that city, and foretold the disaster which followed on the 13th, 14th, and 15th December most accurately. "We shall let them cross the river," said one man, "and punish them heavily in doing it. But the fight will be at the heights; and it will be our fault if they ever cross the river again." There can be no doubt that the dense fog, under cover of which General Burnside withdrew his army from the south side of the Rappahannock, alone saved it from annihilation.[36]

36. The fog Corsan mentioned had lifted by the time Burnside's men began their retreat at Fredericksburg; it was Union batteries, not fog, that checked the Confederates (Faust, ed., *HITE-CW,* 289).

NINE

Attitudes and Monetary Affairs

*S*ince my return from the Confederate States, I have often been asked
whether there is any reason to suppose that the South would come back
to the Union on any terms whatever. My decided opinion is that they
would not. Of course, that opinion is based upon a comparatively limited
intercourse with the people of the South; but I never heard an individual,
of all the classes I talked with, who ever permitted such a notion apparently even to enter his mind.

Judging by what I saw and heard, I am confident that any terms of
peace, of which the first clause is not the complete and unconditional
acknowledgment of the independence of the South, will be rejected by
the Government at Richmond with contempt.[1] In that view, any trans-
ference of power, in the Federal States, from the Republican to the Democratic Party (supposing the Democratic not to be a Peace Party), will be
utterly without effect in the struggle. It was a common remark, among
the officers and civilians all over the South: "If President Lincoln would
give us a clean sheet of paper, and allow us to write ourselves the terms
on which we would go back, we would not return. We wish to have
nothing more to do with the North. Let them leave our soil, and we will
be content; but so long as a foot of Southern soil is polluted with the
presence of the Yankee, we will make no peace."

I was in Richmond, in November, when the news arrived of the great

---

1. Confederate and Union officials did meet on board a ship very late in the war. On February
3, 1865, Confederate vice-president Alexander H. Stephens and two other officials met with Lincoln
and Union secretary of state William H. Seward on the *River Queen* in Hampton Roads. Among
the topics discussed were joint military action against Mexican and French activities in North America, an armistice, and under what terms the southern states would return to the Union. "The
conference ended with nothing accomplished" (Faust, ed., *HTIE-CW*, 336).

Democratic victories in the New York, Pennsylvania, &c. elections. Like most other foreigners, I was inclined to think that this might presage such a change in the political condition as to make peace possible. To my surprise, however, no one there seemed to take much notice of it; and the universal opinion was that, as regards themselves, it was news of very little consequence. The feeling against the Democratic Party at the North seemed very bitter. The uncompromising manner in which that party, after the fall of Fort Sumter, had supported the Republicans in attempting to coerce and subdue their old friends at the South, seemed to have sunk very deeply into the Southern mind. "We have less to hope for from the Democratic than from the Republican Party," they said. "If the Democrats gain power, they will probably carry on the war more sensibly than the Abolitionists, though with no more success. This will, however, serve to delude the population of the North into continuing the war, which will, of course, only entail more misery, and end in but one way. It would be better for us if the Abolitionists could be permitted to do their very worst, and let the people of the North and the world see how cold-blooded, selfish, and utterly without principle they are, as we know well; and then they would be hooted out of power for ever, and peace made in sheer desperation."

Subsequent events have shown that these views were very just. Beyond any doubt, the leaders of the rebellion are fully advised of the hopes and plans of the various parties at the North; but, like a wild beast at bay in a corner, they see the strength of their position, and refuse to be coaxed out of their stronghold by those who have failed to get them out by force.

It is mere waste of time and words for the Northern people to concoct "compromises" which, in *their* opinion, they think the South will or ought to accept. All such phrases as "an erring sister," and so on, are only laughed at in the South. The North has only two alternatives before her—either to crush the South, or let her go free. Any intermediate course is out of the question, at present, evidently. Whether she can do the first or not, time will show. Certainly, the South is not impressed with the idea that there is the faintest chance of her being subjugated. On the contrary, every success which the North has gained is either shown by their papers to be so utterly fruitless as neither to advance the Northern cause nor injure that of the South in the slightest degree, or else is explained to have been accompanied by such corresponding loss of men, materials, and spirit to the North, as to be almost tantamount to a Confederate victory.

Not a day passes, either, without numbers of small successes being

reported as gained by scouting parties, pickets, or bodies of cavalry over
the Federals, of which nothing is ever heard at the North, but which
seem to keep the Southern troops in high spirits.

It is a fact worth knowing, that in the South there is no notion whatever about the war except that they are, have been, and will continue to
be victorious. People in that frame of mind are not inclined to give in;
and in my opinion, the South must be overrun, and every hamlet held
by Northern soldiers, before there would be any perceptible change from
this state of feeling.[2]

The question of boundary-lines will, I think, be ultimately a very
difficult one to settle. The bulk of the people I conversed with look upon
the whole of the Slave States as "theirs," and would regard a peace as
disgraceful which left any one of them joined to the North. A boundary-
line drawn in accordance with *their* views would, of course, include both
[sic] Missouri, Maryland, and Delaware, to say nothing of Kentucky and
Tennessee. Most thinking men have however, I imagine, made up their
minds that Missouri, Maryland, and Delaware will go with the North
when peace is made: not that they doubt which way the populations of
these States would lean, if permitted; but they see clearly that, if the West
and East hold together, the terms of peace would be too ignominious to
be accepted if the surrender of all the five States was insisted upon. About
giving up Kentucky and Tennessee, however, I am sure there is no difference of opinion. The Richmond Government will continue the struggle until those two States are evacuated beyond any doubt, as well as all
points occupied on the seacoast, New Orleans of course included.[3]

The feeling in many States on the invasion of their soil runs very high,
and, but for the influential restraint of the President and his Cabinet, the
"black flag" would certainly have been hoisted long ago.[4]

---

2. Such a violent storm, which Corsan thought would be needed to subjugate the South, was
stirred in Federal generals like William T. Sherman, U. S. Grant, and Philip H. Sheridan. To better
understand this devastating momentum found in the North and South, see Charles Royster, *The
Destructive War: William Tecumseh Sherman, Stonewall Jackson, and the Americans* (New York, 1991).

3. Corsan has touched upon slippery issues: where is the South, where is the Confederacy, and
what is a slave state? Even though they were under Union control, both Maryland and Delaware
allowed slavery within their borders just before the war. The Confederacy did not claim Delaware,
but it did recognize Maryland, Kentucky, and Missouri as part of its alliance. The division even
split states when, in 1863, the western counties of Virginia (with few slaves) left the Old Dominion
to form West Virginia. Add to this nearly four million blacks who were southerners but who
certainly did not support the Confederacy. See Faust, ed., *HTIE-CW*, 816–17; Roller and Twyman,
eds., *Encycl. of Southern History*, 346, 1113; Boritt, *Why the Confederacy Lost*, 13.

4. "A flag of black cloth, used with some reference to death or deadly purpose, e.g., as a sign
that no quarter will be given or asked" (*OED*, II, 246).

The soldiers and officers with whom I conversed, to a man declared that, so long as prisoners were taken, the war must go on. There is no terror in imprisonment for a certain class of troops.

The only currency in the South is the "Confederate States' Treasury Note," for from one dollar upwards. Small-change is provided, by City and State issues, for five, ten, twenty-five, and fifty cents. In the early months of the Confederacy, I am told that the currency was in a most wretched condition—all sorts of personal and Corporation "promises to pay," or "shin-plasters," being afloat.[5]

Up to the date of Secession, the currency of the South has been very largely metallic, or the issue of their own Bank. The first disturbances, of course, drove both these means of exchange out of circulation: hence, until the Confederate Government had arranged a currency of its own, and the various Cities and States had consented to issue small notes, transactions of all kinds were almost brought to a standstill, for want of a medium by which sales could be effected.[6] For a long time this state of things produced great distress, among the planters and farmers especially. No matter what amount of cotton, tobacco, or sugar a man had, he could not exchange it for what he wanted conveniently; so that while some sections of the country had abundance of food, for instance, others were nearly starving.[7]

---

5. Corsan was correct. The Confederate currency system was a mess. The law specifically allowed for the exchange of British, French, Spanish, Mexican, and United States coinage. Along with notes issued by states, cities, and banks, privately printed shinplasters and tokens circulated. The situation was poor before the war and grew worse. And like many problems with the young alliance, its leaders reacted to conditions rather than forging long-term policy. Finally, it should be remembered that by 1864 the central government did distribute notes for fifty cents, one dollar, and two dollars. Matthews, *Statutes of the Confederate States*, 62–63; James F. Morgan, *Graybacks and Gold: Confederate Monetary Policy* (Pensacola, Fla., 1985), 4–5, 39, 41; Ball, *Financial Failure and Confederate Defeat*, 189–91.

6. The antebellum South had relatively little gold, and much of that would find its way overseas or to the North to pay debts. The region's wealth was its slaves and land, not bullion or specie. Added to this was an uneven Federal system that minted a limited number of coins and "a few short-term Treasury notes in times of dire necessity." Citizens had to be content with loosely enforced state banking laws and notes that "varied greatly, depending largely upon the integrity and reputation of the bankers who issued them" (American Numismatic Association, *Selections from the Numismatist* [Racine, Wisc., 1960], 195).

7. Corsan has touched upon two problems: the overworked rail system that could not move produce from one state to the next and the currency failure. The South had the agricultural means to feed itself but lacked the transportation requirements and financial medium to supply foodstuffs to the workers of growing urban areas. See Current, ed., *Encycl. of the Confederacy*, II, 595; Hilliard, *Hog Meat and Hoe Cake*, 233–35.

The first important measure by which the Government contrived to relieve this deadlock was an arrangement with each owner of produce (not perishable), who chose to avail himself of the plan, to pledge his cotton, or whatever it was, to the Confederate Government, in consideration of a loan, in Confederate treasury-notes, to the extent of one-half its market value last before the breaking out of the war (I believe), bearing interest. In some such way as this the Confederate Government money began to get into circulation, purchases and sales became possible, speculation began to revive: and during the greater part of the past twelve or fifteen months, the Southern people have enjoyed a state of commercial activity not known there for very many years.[8]

By the above means, and subsequently by direct purchase, the Confederate Government became, towards the end of 1862, the actual holder of a very large quantity of cotton; and if the war goes on long enough, the probability is that, in time, the bulk of the cotton in the Southern States will be controlled by the Confederate Government. If so, any lingering impatience on the part of the owners of cotton that the war should end, in order that they might sell their stock, would be removed, and the people of the South would become even more an unit than they now are on the question of continuing the war until their end is fully gained.

Speaking of the currency of the Confederate States, reminds me of the intense feeling created by the discovery that spurious Confederate notes were being regularly printed in the Northern cities, and sold in large lots, at mere nominal prices, to the Federal troops in the field. They were sold again of course, or paid away for provisions, &c., by the men in Kentucky, Tennessee, Virginia, &c.; and hence, at one time, a very serious amount of bad Confederate paper-money was in circulation on the frontier. It never, however, seemed to reach the interior: I never saw a single note in circulation. Nothing infuriated the Confederate soldiers more than the discovery of this "bogus" currency on the persons of their prisoners:[9] and

8. At this point in the conflict, investors could expect a profit for their speculative efforts. As mentioned, cotton growers, railroad officials, and owners of blockade-runner ships all had the chance to make a profit early in the war. However, as the tide turned against the Confederacy and inflation soared, the opportunity to make a real profit and avoid the oncoming Union army became harder and harder for the southern entrepreneur. In the spring of 1862, cotton production fell to 150,000 bales in the South (Owsley, *King Cotton Diplomacy,* 361; Woodman, *King Cotton,* 209).

9. Corsan highlighted the word *bogus* because it was an American expression. The *OED* shows that it may have first appeared early in the century in an Ohio newspaper, in reference to "an apparatus for coining false money." Further study shows that it has connections to the English word *bogey,* another name for the devil (*OED,* II, 360).

many a poor Northerner has had to pay with his health, and even life, for the mean fraud which the New York or Philadelphia printer profited by. At one time it was actually proposed that any Yankee found with bad money on him should be instantly put to death without further trial![10]

When I arrived at Philadelphia, after leaving the Confederate States, among the first things I noticed, on leaving the depôt, were boys hawking spurious Confederate notes for sale about the streets: " 'Ere's a whole sheet of rebel-notes for a dime! From one dollar to a thousand! only one dime!" The engraver and printer had done their work too well on these counterfeits to exactly deceive an eye used to the rude productions actually in use at the South. The safety of the Confederate notes seems, at present, to depend more on their inimitably bad execution than anything else. Be that as it may, however, counterfeit Confederate money is regularly produced, advertised, and sold at the North;[11] and this is reckoned by the Southerners as one of the most powerful evidences in existence of the determination of the North to ruin them, if possible. Northern people, generally, have never seen the matter in this light, I am sure, and have no idea how it has counted against them in the minds of the Southerners.

10. Originally, the Confederacy adopted the relevant United States laws for counterfeiting. This, however, did not deter the mass production of "unofficial" Confederate, state, and local notes. In a tirade about these bills, a Richmond paper lamented that "thousands of them are in circulation wherever the graceless and professional swindlers have set their feet within the limits of Virginia" (Richmond *Examiner,* December 30, 1862). By the fall of 1862, Confederate lawmakers believed that the large-scale counterfeiting operation was a Federal plot to undermine the new nation's fiscal stability. This prompted the stronger act that required the death penalty for those caught even passing bogus notes.

At high noon on August 22, 1862, "John Richardson, *alias* John Richards, *alias* Louis Napoleon" was hanged in Virginia for counterfeiting treasury notes (Robinson, *Justice in Gray,* 206, 184, 204). Richardson was the only perpetrator to be executed for this crime. To undermine counterfeiters' efforts, the government changed treasury issues and design (Current, ed., *Encycl. of the Confederacy,* I, 421).

11. Entrepreneurs in New York and Philadelphia did make facsimiles of southern notes. It should be noted, however, that many southern notes were not engraved on metal plates; therefore, they were much easier to forge. In the City of Brotherly Love, Samuel C. Upham produced notes under great public demand as curiosities and for those heading south who needed quick cash. As the northern public still clamored for more, Upham obtained plates from the New York firm of Haney & Hilton. Upham printed his notes with the word *fac-simile* on the edge; nevertheless, those wanting to use the money for currency in the South could just trim *fac-simile* from the note. According to Upham, he charged a penny a note regardless of its face value. During the time this side business flourished, from March, 1862, to August, 1863, Upham generated fifteen million dollars' worth of bogus currency, from shinplasters to one-hundred-dollar notes, for souvenir seekers and adventurous travelers. See Matthews, *Statutes of the Confederate States,* 62–63; *Daily Richmond Examiner,* November 15, 1862; P. H. Chase, *Paper Money of the Confederate States of America and Cross Index to Types* (Philadelphia, 1947), 95–98.

While I was in Richmond, exchange on London and gold ranged from 225 to 250 per cent. The rate has risen since to 350 per cent, and may go higher. About the same time exchange was from 130 to 160 per cent only in New York, and inferences very favourable, I am told, to the power and resources of the North were drawn from a comparison of these figures.[12] In effect, however, the positions of the two sections of the country are essentially different. At the North the importing of war material [*sic*], merchandise, colonial produce, American Stocks, &c. and exporting of produce, gold, and manufactures goes on much as ever, though no doubt on a more limited scale. The making and sale of bills of course is involved in all this, and anything like a monopoly of the supply of either exchange or the precious metals, is impossible. There is the old competition between a hundred different drawers of bills on a steamer-day in New York, as to who can sell most exchange, and the usual rush by purchasers from one office to another, to ascertain which house asks the lowest rate. All this keeps the price of gold and exchange down to just that point when the inflation of the currency begins to operate, and, as a rule, probably rather under than over that point. At the South there are, to begin with, no drawers of bills, except those few far-seeing people who, in anticipation of trouble after the November elections in 1860, had for many months before been sending cotton, tobacco, exchange, gold, stock, or in fact any valuable property, easily realizable, to England. While the blockade continues, of course any further exports are almost impossible, and consequently no new exchange can be created. What chance any person would have of inducing people who had so invested property for their own and their family's safe support, end how the struggle might, to draw bills against that property and sell them, any one may easily guess. I met with numbers of persons in this position, and am confident that scarcely any premium would tempt them to disturb their invest-

12. At the time of Corsan's visit, brokers bought gold at $1.90 to $2.00 for each Confederate dollar and offered gold at $2.25 a paper dollar. Silver was purchased at $1.80 by brokers and sold for $2.10 in notes. About the time of the battle of Fredericksburg, there was little activity in the market on these metals. Eventually, inflation soared and the value of southern paper money crashed. In Augusta, Georgia, just before the final surrender, an officer paid "$2,700 for a coat, vest, and pair of trousers; $700 for two weeks' board; $6,000 for the purchase of $60 gold; $1,700 for an ounce of sulphate quinine" (Boatner, *Civil War Dictionary*, 170–71). Also see *Daily Richmond Examiner*, November 24, December 1, 15, 1862. It is not clear to me what Corsan means by "on London." This may be a misprint, or he may be referring to British sterling. At that time, an English pound or sovereign (new and average), after a deduction of "one-half of one per cent," was worth about $4.83. The silver shilling (new and average) was valued at about twenty-three cents (Treasury Dept., *Finances, 1862*, 74–77).

ments. At any rate, the price asked would be about in the same proportion to the real value of the bill, as the sum which a retired millionaire would demand for the mansion he had just built and finished to his liking; which in fact would very likely amount to saying in other words that he would not sell at any price which any sane man would give.

Then again, all the State legislatures in the South have passed what are called "stay" laws; that is, acts forbidding the payment of any debt during the continuance of the war to either Northern or foreign creditor. This takes out of the market all the regular demand, which would be influenced to purchase or let it alone by the price asked, and leaves only what are called "blockade-runners," (whose profits have been so enormous, that the rate they pay for exchange really does not much matter,) to compete for the limited quantity of gold, and the few bills which from time to time weak or wavering holders are willing to part with.

The thousands of Jews and Gentiles who regularly trade between Baltimore, Washington, and Richmond, of course know it is of no use taking Confederate paper to either of the two first-named places to purchase goods with. If they take anything, it must be "greenback," gold, or good exchange. To get these indispensables, they will pay any rate which is demanded, and charge it in the prices they get in return.

Those gentlemen again, who so obligingly run cargoes of goods from London and Liverpool, and pocket from one to two thousand per cent. profit, of course do not care whether bills cost 250 or 500 per cent., so that they can be had at all, and the proceeds of their sales remitted home.

The fact then is, that exchange and gold are high in Richmond—first because, while few or no new bills can be created on account of the blockade, those who either hold gold or are in a position to draw against property in Europe have a complete monopoly of the supply; and secondly, because the only purchasers for gold or exchange are those who having realized enormous profits are not much concerned about the price they have to pay to get their remittances home. I believe that a very large amount of gold is hoarded by individuals, and stored away in safe places on account of Banks and other Corporations in the South. This is stated to be the case, and I have the best of reasons for believing it to be true.[13]

13. The myths of hidden riches have continued to the present. The Confederate treasury, Richmond banks, and rebel concerns overseas all had stashes of gold; some can be traced, some cannot. Nonetheless, with paper money almost valueless at war's end, it is likely that most gold and silver would have been spent on survival.

TEN

Trying to Leave Richmond

I *frequently while in Richmond met with the "rebel" of by-gone days,* John Mitchell.[1] The South does not possess in my opinion a firmer or more disinterested friend than he. Leaving his wife and daughters in Paris, he and his two or three sons have successively made their way into the Confederacy, and (the sons at any rate) have taken an active part in the conflict. One son has been wounded, the others are in the field, and all are said to be brave soldiers.[2] Mr. Mitchell himself has only very

---

1. John Mitchel (1815–1875) was an Irish nationalist born at Camnish, County Londonderry. He issued a weekly newspaper, the *United Irishman,* that "openly incited his fellow-countrymen to rebellion," and he was arrested by British authorities and sentenced to exile in prison ships and colonies for fourteen years. He spent time off Bermuda in a hulk, in a ship anchored in Simon's Bay, Cape of Good Hope, and on Van Diemen's Land, Australia. From Australia, he escaped to San Francisco. In 1854, he initiated an antiabolitionist New York paper called the *Citizen,* and for two years published at Knoxville and Washington, D.C., the *Southern Citizen.* Just before the war, he went to Paris. In September, 1862, Mitchel returned to New York, then managed to get through the lines to Richmond, where he worked first for the *Examiner* and later for the *Enquirer.* He was described as "an honest, but hopelessly unpractical man," and "his whole mind was warped by his implacable hatred of England." Tall and gaunt, with piercing gray eyes, he was a loving family man, "incisive speaker, [and] forcible writer." Given Mitchel's background and characteristics, it is no surprise that Corsan was taken with him (*DNB,* XXXVIII, 58–60).

2. Mitchel's poor eyesight would not allow him to fight for the Confederacy, but his sons "wore the gray." Captain John C. Mitchel, Jr., an artillery officer with an engineering background, served in the Charleston defenses. On July 30, 1864, while Charleston was under attack, an artillery round mortally wounded Mitchel. After three agonizing hours, he died; his comrades buried him in a nearby cemetery. See Ella Lonn, *Foreigners in the Confederacy* (1940; rpr. Gloucester, Mass., 1965), 242–44; Claudine Rhett, "Sketch of John C. Mitchel of Ireland, Killed Whilst in Command of Fort Sumter," *Southern Historical Society Papers,* X (1882), 268–72; *DNB,* XXXVIII, 59–60.

William and James Mitchel enlisted as privates in the First Virginia Infantry. William became a color-bearer and fell at Gettysburg. James apparently rose to the rank of captain and joined General John Brown Gordon's staff. He survived the war but lost an arm in battle. Lee A. Wallace, Jr., *1st*

recently arrived from France, *via* the North, and had twice during the trip been, he told me, in imminent peril; first, in Southampton, where he was compelled unexpectedly to land from the Bremen steamer and remain ashore, disguised, for many hours, the easy prey of any inhabitant or detective with a long memory, who with a word could have consigned him to the banishment and prison he had escaped from; and, secondly, when escaping from Washington, through Maryland and across the Potomac, to Richmond.

Altogether, the anxiety and privation through which he had passed has told seriously on his health; but he consoled himself with being the only Irishman of his "rebel" compeers, who, having decided to take a side at all in the American question, has taken that consistent with logic and the traditions of their class and country. He believed that, if the North succeeded in subjugating the South, a fatal blow would be dealt to true liberty on the American continent, and that it was really doubtful whether the slavery which would be imposed on the South, or the insolent and unbridled pride, which such a result would foster in the North, would lead to most waste of blood and treasure in the end, and keep peace longest from the distracted country.

I am not inclined to think that his estimate and opinion of the Government of Great Britain is calculated to inspire the Southern mind with much love of, or respect for, England and her policy. He believes Great Britain to be wholly and solely governed by, and for the benefit of, the two aristocracies of blood and money; that the masses and intellect of the nation, while amused with a *seeming* power in the State, have really no effect on the current of national policy; and that at all times and under all circumstances, the course which Great Britain will take may be predicated without doubt, if only her *interest* can be ascertained. It is not without profit that a thinking man learns the real opinion of even an unfriendly foreigner. There is more truth in Mr. Mitchell's estimate than is pleasant for some people to hear.

Having, at length, completed my business in the Confederate States, and being anxious to return to Europe, I made application, in proper form, to the Assistant Secretary of War (General Gustavus W. Smith) for a pass to leave Richmond by the flag-of-truce boat, which, once or twice a week, came up from Fortress Monroe to City Point with paroled

---

Virginia Infantry (Lynchburg, Va., 1984), 107; Charles T. Loehr, *Of The Old First Virginia Infantry Regiment, Army of Northern Virginia* (1884; rpr. Dayton, Ohio, 1978), 78; Lonn, *Foreigners in the Confederacy*, 155n; William Dillon, *Life of John Mitchell [sic]* (London, 1888), II, 173.

Confederate prisoners, and received paroled Federal prisoners in return.[3] Excepting Vicksburgh, City Point was the only place of regular exchange established.

To my surprise, the pass was refused, on the ground that Secretary Randolph (who had just resigned the post of Secretary of War, and whose successor was not appointed) had issued a peremptory order that no person was to be permitted to leave the Confederacy, on any pretence whatever. This, it seems, was a retaliatory order to one which the Federal authorities had issued, ordering that the flag-of-truce boat (which was a Federal vessel) was not to be used to convey passengers of any kind, except Consuls, to or from City Point. It was alleged that the boat had been extensively used by Confederate ladies, Jews, and speculators generally, who were in the habit of regularly going to Washington, and even Baltimore, from Richmond, taking letters and papers, and bringing back information, medicines, or, in fact, anything they could smuggle through.

No doubt it was to some extent true, and no doubt each side suffered. In my opinion, however, it would have been wiser on the part of the Federals to have set the information gained against the information given, and considered twice before inflicting the inconvenience and misery they did on innocent third-parties, by suddenly stopping the use of the truce-boat.

This act had not the slightest effect on the supply of Northern newspapers, letters, and news. The full files of the *New York Herald,* and several Washington, Baltimore, and Philadelphia papers, could be seen, two or three days old, at any of the news-rooms in Richmond; and numbers of persons came in from, and went out to, Washington and Baltimore every day I was in the city.[4]

---

3. On July 22, 1862, Confederate general Daniel Harvey Hill and Union general John A. Dix signed an agreement whereby prisoners would be exchanged at Vicksburg in the West and City Point in the East. The document laid out nine articles, which determined the exchange of civilians, militiamen, privateers, and military and naval personnel (Boatner, *Civil War Dictionary,* 270; *OR,* Ser. IV, Vol. 4, 266–68).

Fort Monroe, at the tip of the Virginia peninsula, guarded Hampton Roads and remained in Federal hands throughout the war. It served as a staging area for the Peninsula Campaign and the assault on Norfolk, as well as a hub for prisoner exchanges. City Point (now Hopewell in Henrico County) was seven miles east of Petersburg on the James River; this spot was also known as Aiken's Landing in the exchange of prisoners (Faust, ed., *HTIE-CW,* 141; *OR,* Ser. II, Vol. IV, 971–72).

4. Newspaper editors of the period did not have the advantages of news services to tap for national events. Instead, they would acquire papers from other parts of the country, borrow the text, and cite their sources. For an example of how this information became military intelligence, see the dispatch of November 17, 1862, from Jefferson Davis to Lieutenant General T. H. Holmes of the Trans-Mississippi Department, *OR,* Ser. II, Vol. IV, 946.

As for early information about the plans and councils of the Federal Generals, it was well known in Richmond that General Lee had full information of General Burnside's intended march on Fredericksburgh as soon as that fatal step was decided upon, and, as every one now knows, was quietly encamped with his army a few miles south of the Rappahannock, near Fredericksburgh, when, towards the end of November, General Burnside, believing the Confederate commander to be outmarched, and left certainly as far off as Culpepper, sent across the river to demand the surrender of the city.[5]

To return, however, to my own case: I found myself really in a predicament. The British Consul—having, as he told me, really no position before the Confederate Government—could give me no help; and there was nothing for it but to pester the various departments with my case until, for the sake of peace and quietness, they let me go.[6] After ten or twelve days' petitioning, talking, and using my friends, and being passed from Provost-Marshal to Acting Secretary of War, Acting Secretary of War to Commissioner for Exchange of Prisoners, then back again, I eventually succeeded in obtaining a hearing from Judge Campbell, who kindly examined my case, and, after some delay, obtained from Mr. Seddon, who had accepted office as Secretary of War, a pass to go by the truce-boat.[7]

Accordingly I went down, one fine Sunday morning, by rail, to City Point, with about 450 paroled Federal soldiers, officers, sailors, and civilians. The men seemed to me in very bad spirits, or else they reserved their good temper until out of my sight. I never saw a cheerful face or

5. Actually, Burnside had surprised Lee with his quick move to Fredericksburg. It was the delay in crossing the Rappahannock River that proved to be the Union general's downfall. As he waited at Falmouth, Lee shifted his divisions south of Burnside's grand divisions and waited for the bluecoats to try to break his strong defenses. Charge after charge failed to dislodge the rebels, and the Yankees fell back across the river (Faust, ed., *HTIE-CW*, 288–90).

6. The British consul to the Confederacy in Richmond was George Moore. British Lieutenant Colonel Arthur James Lyon Fremantle's famed travel account in the spring of 1863 reported, "Moore had always been considered a good friend to the Southern cause, and had got into the mess which caused his removal entirely by his want of tact and discretion" (Fremantle, *Three Months in the Southern States,* 215). Also see *OR,* Ser. II, Vol. IV, 800, 991; John J. Mayo, ed., *The Mercantile Navy List and Annual Appendage to the Commercial Code of Signals for All Nations* (London, 1863), 272.

7. In the spring of 1862, Colonel John G. Porter assumed the responsibilities of provost marshal in Richmond (Thomas, *Richmond,* 81). Robert Ould (1820–1881) had served as assistant secretary of war for about three months before taking charge of the Bureau of Exchange of Prisoners. After the war, he resumed his practice as an attorney (Thomas, *Richmond,* 102; Sifakis, *Who Was Who in the Confederacy,* 213).

heard a laugh all the way down. It appeared that they had found out that an order had been issued from head-quarters at Washington to put all paroled prisoners into camps of instruction, as soon as they arrived from the South; so that, after being taken prisoners in fight, lying in a filthy prison, and then getting at liberty, they saw no chance of a run home, but only the certainty of drill and work again.[8]

They were guarded by about fifty Confederate soldiers with loaded rifles, and made no complaints that I heard of their fare at Richmond, or general treatment. But, indeed, they said very little—kept close together as they walked, like a mob, from the Richmond cars at Petersburgh, across the bridge to the City Point cars—never looked at the crowd of women, boys, and negroes, who ran staring alongside of them— and noticed still less the long line of quizzing or scowling citizens at Petersburgh, who had strolled down, after their Sunday dinner, to see them start. Not a word of insult was uttered on one side, or retort on the other. Every order of the Confederate officer was quietly obeyed; but I could not help feeling the truth of what several of my friends said, that the whole scene, brother prisoners in the hands of brothers, was a disgrace to the age and country.

Among the prisoners was an unlucky wight in the ridiculous costume of a Zouave, or, as the boys called him, "a red-legged devil." The hatred and contempt of the Confederate soldiers towards these military mountebanks is such that they never spare one, if they can avoid it. A good many fingers itched towards the poor fellow who went down that day.[9]

8. This menagerie of people took the South Side Railroad to City Point. The most likely date was December 7, 1862, because it was a Sunday and Corsan does not mention the Battle of Fredericksburg, which took place the following weekend (Johnston, *Virginia Railroads*, 3, 6). Corsan makes two sharp observations. The Federal authorities did dispatch former prisoners to camps of instruction, one of which was located in Annapolis, and this did cause trouble. A soldier complained to the U.S. secretary of war about the behavior of parolees at the Maryland detention center. Their vices were "drunkenness, fighting, burglary, robbery, gambling, &c." (*OR*, Ser. II, Vol. IV, 727, 345, 569–71).

On December 3, 1862, Lieutenant Colonel William H. Ludlow, agent for exchange of prisoners at Fort Monroe, asked Robert Ould if he would permit the landing of mostly women and children at City Point in a few days. There is no mention of Jews. However, the prejudice had grown so great across the country against suspected Jewish entrepreneurs trading in the South that General U. S. Grant outlawed all Jews in the Department of Tennessee. Lincoln repealed this order. In Virginia "the atmosphere in Richmond against all Jews...grew worse as the impact of the war unsettled the economy" (Eli N. Evans, *Judah P. Benjamin: The Jewish Confederate* [New York, 1988], 200). Also see *OR*, Ser. I, Vol. XVII, Part 2, p. 424; Ser. II, Vol. V, 19–21.

9. Early in the contest, some Confederate and Union units donned Zouave garb, and the

After some delay, we reached the boat at City Point, and the process of passing the prisoners on board commenced, preceded by a little chaffing on the part of the Confederate officers about the balance against the Federals in prisoners. It seemed that the Confederates had returned about 21,000 men more than the Federals, and that the boat which was taking about four hundred and fifty men away only brought nine up.

"Never mind," said the dandy Federal officer, whose neat uniform, bright buttons, gold lace, and clean boots, positively dazzled the eyes of any one accustomed for many weeks to the dingy, unshorn, muddy heroes who stood by; "wait a bit: we will bring you an army, some day!"

"Very likely you will," retorted his tormentor; "but your folks will come first, and the army will follow after!"

After some considerable delay, the men were all told off, and marched on board the boat. I then presented myself, produced my British passport, explained my name, business, and position, showed my Confederate pass, and was very curtly *refused,* with expressions as to my being an Englishman which it is no use repeating. It was useless arguing the matter; the Federal officer was in a bad temper, had orders under which he could shelter himself, and wanted to be off.[10] He did not like his task, evidently, and felt that his spite might be safely shown against a harmless foreigner; so there was nothing for it but to return with my "butternut" friends to Richmond, with my tail figuratively between my legs, which I did with as good a grace as possible.

On reflection, it was pretty plain that, unless I helped myself, I was a prisoner for an indefinite period; so I resolved to run the Confederate and Federal lines somewhere on the Upper Potomac. In a few days I found several other persons in a similar predicament to my own, and, after careful inquiry, we started on our novel trip. Many personal and

---

southern government even created a regiment of Zouaves. The uniforms were modeled after those of French soldiers in Algeria and were characterized by "white leggings, red baggy pants, a blue sash, a dark blue vest . . . and a red fez" (Faust, ed., *HTIE-CW,* 850). Though the Confederate companies could not hope to maintain this standard of dress, some northern Zouaves still wore the romantic outfit late in the war (Robertson, *Soldiers Blue and Gray,* 16; Matthews, *Statutes of the Confederate States,* 99).

10. On November 5, the Union assistant secretary of war warned Major General John A. Dix at Fort Monroe that "several women intend to leave Richmond soon to obtain supplies or to quarter themselves and their families on their friends in the North while their husbands and sons are fighting in the rebel armies." That same day, Dix assured his superior, "I have given positive orders to let no one come from Aiken's Landing with the flag-of-truce boats except released prisoners" (*OR,* Ser. II, Vol. IV, 688). This helps to explain why Corsan could not get passage on the boat to Fort Monroe.

political reasons combine to prevent my stating exactly by what route we
escaped from the Confederacy; and I can, therefore, only add that, after
an exciting and interesting week or ten days' travel, we got from Richmond into Maryland, and were at liberty to go where we pleased.

ELEVEN

A Circuitous Route Home

*I*n the course of the attempts our party made to get into Maryland, we had to go over many of the counties of Northern Virginia and the whole length of the Valley of the Shenandoah River. For nearly two years this district had been incessantly occupied by armies, marching and counter-marching; and a vast deal of desperate fighting has occurred here. It was not to be expected, of course, that all this could occur without a very great destruction of property; but I was surprised to see really so little evidence of the war in the open country itself as I did.

As we approached the Potomac, either east or west of the Green Mountains, when within perhaps forty or fifty miles of the Federal lines, of course such towns as Winchester, Romney, Leesburgh, &c. were almost wholly deserted; and the surrounding country showed painful evidence of the work that had been going on. But it was not until we had passed, say Strasburgh, or Front Royal, in the Virginia Valley, or Culpepper on the east side of the Green Mountains, that the face of the country, the towns, roads, fences, &c. were materially altered from what they were in time of peace. South of the points named, farming operations seemed to be going on much as before; the fences and homesteads were in tolerable order; and the roads, though much cut up by the constant passage of artillery and stores, were still far from being bad roads.[1]

---

1. The logical route for Corsan, in order to pass through or by all the towns mentioned, would have been on the Virginia Central Railroad through Charlottesville and Gordonsville to Staunton, then along the Shenandoah Valley to Harrisonburg, Woodstock, and Strasburg. For part of this leg he could have used the Manassas Gap Railroad; this same line went to Front Royal, and roads connected Front Royal to Winchester. Then he would have headed almost due west to Romney (now in West Virginia) (*OM Atlas*, CXXXVI–CXXXVII). It is not clear where or if he went through Culpeper County and Leesburg. Corsan may have woven some location names into his text pur-

Excepting when troops were passing through them, the towns were certainly dull enough; the stores being almost universally closed for want of goods to sell; the young men mostly off to the war, and the streets left to women, children, negroes, elderly citizens, or those whom the conscript law necessarily exempted from service. Such towns as Gordonsville, Charlottesville, Staunton, Harrisonburgh, Woodstock, &c. seemed to be taking a long Sunday nap. One might look up or down the long streets of some of these places for a quarter of an hour and not see a human being. If such a thing as a square of soap, a box of matches, a spool of cotton, or a pin or needle were wanted, every shop in the place would have to be visited, and the solitary salesman or principal sent for from the hotel, or roused out of a nap, to say that "he hadn't the article, and didn't believe it could be got in town at any price."[2]

Still, the machinery of society was moving, though not very glibly. At Woodstock, for instance, what we should call "Petty Sessions" were being held, under the presidency of as grave, intelligent, and responsible-looking magistrates and jurymen as any agricultural county in England could produce. Certainly, the temple in which Justice held her court would have been all the better for a little paint, whitewash, and window-glass; and the proceedings might have been more impressively conducted than they were. For instance, everybody chewed tobacco, and expectorated, from the chairman down to the prisoner, with a vigour and unanimity which I never saw elsewhere, even in America. The jurymen, witnesses, lawyers, plaintiffs, prisoners, officers, and even spectators, seemed to take an equal interest in two immense stoves, which stood inside the railing of the Court. They put their feet on them, spat on them, poked them up, or put in enormous logs of wood incessantly, no matter what was going on. I defy any man either to have told juryman from counsel, witness from tipstaff, or spectator from prisoner, by position, bearing, or dress.

When my friend, a Confederate officer, and I entered, some one pres-

---

posefully to deceive the reader as to his exact route. Nevertheless, at Romney he may have found water transportation down the Potomac River but had to disembark before reaching Washington, D.C., which he did at Leesburg. At Leesburg, he could have taken the Alexandria, Loudoun and Hampshire Railroad to Alexandria and headed north to cross the Potomac, or journeyed down the Potomac by boat. Some of these options would have been very difficult without clearance from Federal provost marshals (Johnston, *Virginia Railroads,* 47).

   2. Gordonsville in Orange County is the crossroads for the Virginia Central and Orange and Alexandria Railroads. Corsan could have disembarked here to journey north into Culpeper County; however, he would have needed eventually to head south to reach Charlottesville (Johnston, *Virginia Railroads,* 47).

ent was being tried for stealing a horse. Of course we did as everybody else did, that is, pushed up to one of the stoves, looked intently at it for a moment, poked it up, and then asked a gentleman with a large beard, who sat by, with his hands in his pockets and his feet on the stove, chewing and spitting like the rest, how the case was likely to go? He expressed a very decided opinion that the prosecutor's case "hadn't a leg to stand on." In the course of a short time, however, the jury decided differently, and the chairman condemned the "prisoner at the bar" (for whom I had been looking) to six months' imprisonment. Whereupon another gentleman, who had just put a log into the opposite stove, walked across to where our bearded friend sat, and quietly suggested that "they'd better clear out." I was then informed that the two gentlemen who were retiring, in amicable conversation, were, respectively, the prisoner in the case just concluded, and the officer of the Court; and I could account at once for the strong opinion of the gentleman with whom I had been chatting as to the chance of the prosecutor. However, in this, as in all other cases, no doubt substantial justice is done, for an hour afterwards our bearded friend could be seen gloomily looking out of a heavily-barred window in the lock-up, safe enough no doubt.

The stage-coaches were running through all this district, and post and telegraphs in full and regular operation. As we approached the frontier, however, all this was changed. Gradually every vestige of fencing disappeared, as far as the eye could reach. At short intervals, a heap of scorched stones and bricks told where a homestead once stood; the open fields were covered with the Indian cornstalks standing, among which the cattle of a bivouacking army had been turned, to eat the cobs off as they listed; bridges were blown up; commanding eminences crowned with hastily-constructed earthworks, or rifle-pits; the roads lined with the skeletons or putrifying carcases of horses or mules, either killed by round-shot or broken down under excessive work; and large tracts of grass-fields, or thin woods, strewed with the remains of camp-fires, scattered fire-wood and fodder, abandoned kettles, boots, blankets, bones, and all the refuse of an army on the move, evidences where immense numbers of men had been quartered, eating up the country round.

Such houses as did remain standing along the roads were either deserted or apparently barricaded; and occasionally a frightened woman, with two or three scared-looking children, all pinched and meanly clad, would peep round the corner of the house at the passer-by, and run in, if noticed, like frightened hares. Towns like Winchester and Leesburgh presented a most deserted and forlorn appearance.[3] Being occupied alternately by the advanced posts of the Federal and Confederate armies, they were the scenes of desperate hand-to-hand cavalry fights in their streets nearly every day. Of course every store, house, or hotel was closed, and kept closed against almost any entreaty; the streets were as deserted as a city of the dead; and if a traveller rode into the town, it was only by looking behind him, and catching sight of the women and men peeping after him, out of entries and upper windows, that he could see the inhabitants at all. If he put up eventually at any tavern, the place would be gradually filled by droppers-in, who sneaked in to ask such questions as, "Any news from Fredericksburgh?" "Where's Lee's army now?" "Do you think the Yankees will come up the valley again?" &c., all of course "aside," and with a furtive look at some "citizen," who was believed to be a sort of Yankee spy.

It seemed to me, that in spite of all these frontier people had endured, they were even more intensely "secesh" than in the interior of the Confederacy.[4] The constant excitement and terror in which they were kept, with the bugle or drum beating "to arms" every few hours night and day, and scenes of violence passing at their doors continually, seemed only to deepen their loathing for the "Yankee" as they called him. The women of course were, as elsewhere, bitter beyond expression, and Northern Virginia certainly is not subjugated yet. It was impossible not to sympathize deeply with these poor people, and regret extremely to see their lovely country so devastated as it was. There is no doubt that the Valley of Virginia, London County, Page Valley,[5] and, in fact, most of Northern Virginia, is the garden of America—a rich, rolling, well-cultivated country, traversed by noble rivers and hemmed in by chains of mountains, sublime and picturesque in the extreme. I am told that, in the season, over 10,000 acres of red clover can be seen in flower at one time, and all in a patch, on the banks of the Shenandoah River. The people are evidently, or rather were, a well-to-do, intelligent, hardy race of farmers; they will be so again, I trust, before long.

3. On October 21, 1861, at Ball's Bluff near Leesburg, Confederate infantry caught a Union brigade with its back to the Potomac River. The rebels pressed their advantage, and the Federals suffered roughly nine hundred casualties (Faust, ed., *HTIE-CW,* 37).

4. "Secesh" was a label used, often with derogatory tones, for a secessionist (Hendrickson, *Whistlin' Dixie,* 201).

5. Loudoun (London) County is east of the Shenandoah Valley. In 1831, sections of Shenandoah and Rockingham Counties were combined to form Page County (Hagemann, *Heritage of Virginia,* 143, 186).

TWELVE

Impressions of an English Businessman

I t is only right to state, before closing, what the impressions are which these six weeks' residence in the Confederate States have left on my own mind. Reviewing the state of the country, as it bears on the all-important question, as to whether the South can be subjugated, the following important conclusions seem to me to be established beyond a shadow of doubt. First, the South cannot be *starved out*. It is quite true that the Southern people may be said to have *no* luxuries; but of the necessaries of Southern life (such as Indian corn, wheat, pork, beef, sweet potatoes, rice, sugar, molasses, and poultry) they have an enormous superabundance. It was incessantly repeated in my hearing, "If we see no sign of a settlement before March, we shall not sow a single cotton-seed, but devote our land to breadstuffs, vegetables, and such things as we and the army need most." Any notion that the South is now dependent on any outside people for food is a fallacy, and may as well be given up. Secondly, the pressure for clothing, boots, arms, ammunition, &c. in the South, will not cause the rebellion to collapse. Setting aside the enormous quantities of goods which run the blockade, I may say that many large merchants and capitalists assured me that, in another six or twelve months, the Confederate States would be able, not only to feed, but clothe and arm her whole population.[1]

Before leaving Richmond, I saw samples, for instance, of very neatly-

---

1. Lacking experience and the machinery, the South could not totally arm itself in six to twelve months. Almost all Confederate firearms were antebellum vintage, captured, or purchased from Europe. So heavily did the rebels rely on imported weapons that from April 27 to August 3, 1862, runners brought in 48,510 stands of arms. Fortunately, the machinery taken from the Harpers Ferry armory to Richmond could manufacture and repair some rifles (*OR*, Ser. IV, Vol. II, 52; Lee, *General Lee's City*, 158–59).

made shoes—the upper leather tacked to thin wooden soles, the leather so well tanned, and the soles so neatly made, that they looked like a superior leather shoe. The contractor offered to supply very large quantities, and to increase monthly. Of course, machines were used, and negro labour chiefly employed in making them. These shoes, which would outwear at least two pairs of the ugly brown-paper abominations with which New England formerly supplied the South, were offered at about a third the price of the imported shoe, and a large reduction in price promised. There is no doubt that for negroes these shoes will come into extensive future use, and for the troops will be now both cheap and serviceable.

At one time the probable want of shoes promised to be one of the greatest sufferings to be inflicted on the South by non-intercourse with the North and the blockade. In the spring of 1862, I am told, this necessity was at its height. Wherever I went printed cards were even yet nailed on the inside of the bedroom doors at the hotels, on which were some such words as, "If you put your boots outside your door they will be stolen;" showing plainly that necessity had at one time driven the regular guests to strange shifts.

I was also shown a very serviceable hat of Southern manufacture, made of wool and cotton, and at about one-fifth the price of the imported hats and caps. The manufacturer said he could make them either light and porous, or thick and heavy, so as to suit both summer and winter wear. Several mills had also commenced, in North and South Carolina, weaving very neat materials for women's and children's dresses.[2] They also were composed of cotton and wool; the patterns were checks and stripes chiefly, and of course the colours were few and simply arranged. There is no doubt, however, about these cloths coming into extensive use, and gradually bringing the price of clothing within limits again.

---

2. "A review of antebellum textile development in South Carolina indicates three main periods of activity: (1) 1807–14, (2) 1828–38, (3) 1845–50. South Carolina's peak year was 1849. There were twenty-one mills in operation in the state at that time. Thereafter the number was reduced by subsequent business failures. Most other Southern states followed a similar pattern" (Ernest McPherson Lander, Jr., *The Textile Industry in Antebellum South Carolina* [Baton Rouge, 1969], 80). "In absolute terms, by every measure, by 1850 Georgia's antebellum cotton textile industry was the South's largest" (Carole E. Scott, "Why the Cotton Textile Industry Did Not Develop in the South Sooner," *Agricultural History,* LXVIII [Spring, 1994], 119). By the time the southern states left the Union, "they contained 143 cotton goods establishments" (Current, ed., *Encycl. of the Confederacy,* IV, 1588). By 1864, North Carolinians worked forty textile factories, "half as many as the other Confederate states combined" (Bell Irvin Wiley, *The Life of Johnny Reb: The Common Soldier of the Confederacy* [1943; rpr. Baton Rouge, 1978], 113).

As for cotton goods, spinning and weaving mills are spreading very rapidly, especially in South Carolina and Georgia. "Augusta drills," "Graniteville sheetings," and "Atlanta shirtings," are as well known now by purchasers at auction, and command as high a price, as the productions of Lowell or Manchester. I have spoken before of the busy thriving look which Augusta, Graniteville, and other such towns, have assumed since the numerous mills now in full operation have been built. Those persons who only recollect these places as they were ten or fifteen years ago, would scarcely know them if they approached them now by night, and saw the long rows of windows lighted up, tier above tier, as I did in some of them.[3]

The iron works of Virginia and Tennessee are well known already, and their assistance to the Confederacy has been invaluable. Large forgings and castings, for marine, locomotive, and stationary engines, such as Northern manufacturers never believed the South could produce, have been supplied with great rapidity and of excellent quality.[4] The quantity and quality of the cannon manufactured in the Confederacy have amazed both the North and Europe, and have exercised immense influence on

3. Drill is "a coarse twilled linen or cotton fabric used for summer clothing" (*OED*, IV, 1052). Shirting is used for shirts as well as other garments (*ibid.*, XV, 286). In July and September, 1862, commissions priced good quality drills, seven-eighths' yard wide and three yards to a pound, at sixty-five to seventy cents a yard (*OR*, Ser. IV, Vol. II, 652, 836).

Augusta and Richmond Counties in Georgia also had two cotton gins and two mills before the war. It should be remembered that Augusta was twice the size of Atlanta, and Milledgeville was the state capital (*Appleton's, 1857*, 277–79; Dept. of Interior, *Manufactures, 1860*, 67–68). The Graniteville Manufacturing Company by 1849 had 9,245 spindles and was "by far the largest mill in antebellum South Carolina, if not the entire South" (Lander, *Textile Industry*, 59).

4. It is unlikely that Confederate factories ever built any locomotives. See Dew, *Ironmaker to the Confederacy*, 77, 101; Johnston, *Virginia Railroads*, 11–13. In 1860, the capital investment for eighty-one establishments in Virginia, North Carolina, Georgia, Alabama, and Tennessee in bar, sheet, and railroad iron was $1,184,010. This region employed 1,546 workers, who produced 14,072 tons of bar iron and 2,000 tons of railroad iron. In comparison, Pennsylvania alone boasted eighty-seven factories, with an investment of $10,974,013 and 10,177 employees, who forged 112,276 tons of bar iron, 133,577 tons of railroad iron, 13,000 tons of boiler plate, and 7,000 tons of sheet iron, for a total of 266,253 tons (Dew, *Ironmaker to the Confederacy*, 89).

Remember, "the South did take significant strides in the 1850s. The slave states more than quadrupled their railroad mileage, outstripping the northern pace which merely tripled mileage in that section. Capital invested in southern manufacturing rose 77 percent, exceeding the rate of population growth so that the amount invested per capita increased 39 percent. The value of southern-produced textiles increased 44 percent. But like Alice in Wonderland, the faster the South ran, the farther behind it seemed to fall. While the slave state proportion of national railroad mileage increased to 35 percent in 1860, this was less than the 44 percent of 1840" (McPherson, *Battle Cry of Freedom*, 94–95).

the progress of the war. From these sources have been mainly derived the enormous number of cannon which make Drury's Bluff, Port Hudson, Vicksburgh, Savannah, Mobile, Charleston, or indeed any place which the Southerners deem worth keeping, absolutely impregnable; and every day increases the supply.[5]

The quantity of cannon and field-pieces in the Confederacy really is prodigious. Apart from the immense numbers made there, they have taken enormous quantities from the enemy. Nothing has taken the Federal generals more by surprise than the unexpected strength and efficiency of the Confederate artillery; and it is an ominous fact for the Federal cause, that this arm of the Confederate service is being daily strengthened, so as to render it very probable that, before long, it will overmatch that of the Federal army, so unmistakeably, as to make Victory even more averse than she has been thus far to perch on the Federal banners; and that is needless, Heaven knows!

The quality of the Confederate artillery made in the Confederacy seemed very good. I was shown on board the iron-clad ram and battery the *Richmond* (or *New Merrimac,* as some people persist in calling her), at Richmond, four splendid pivot-guns of immense strength and perfect finish.[6] As pieces of workmanship they would have done credit to any

---

5. Actually, the quality of Confederate-made arms was, at times, suspect. In June, 1861, Leeds and Company of New Orleans produced its first heavy cannon. "Unfortunately, the weapon failed to pass even the simplest of tests, both poor iron and defective furnaces taking their toll" (Daniel and Gunter, *Confederate Cannon Foundries,* 35). Two years later, the Columbus Iron Works of Georgia made a gun from the wheel shaft of a river steamer. "The performance of the weapon was said to have been very poor" (*ibid.,* 34). And there were problems on occasion with the guns made at Tredegar (Dew, *Ironmaker to the Confederacy,* 101). The major cannon foundries were located in the Richmond area, New Orleans, Nashville, Memphis, Charleston, Vicksburg, Huntsville and Selma in Alabama, and Rome, Columbus, Macon, Augusta, and Atlanta in Georgia. Neither Savannah nor the fortifications at Port Hudson, Mississippi, and Drewry's Bluff, Virginia, were the site of notable foundries. Daniel and Gunter estimate the production of Confederate foundries of cannon and mortars for the war to be at least 1,361 field pieces and 732 heavy pieces (Daniel and Gunter, *Confederate Cannon Foundries,* 93).

6. Around October 8, 1862, Emmanuel Shaw, formerly a machinist from Baltimore County and a refugee from the Confederate capital, informed U.S. Navy authorities of the status of the CSS *Richmond.* He claimed the ironclad "would be ready in about two weeks, her engines are old and said to be not of much account. They are making a large rifle gun at the Tredegar Works for this vessel; gun about 15 or 16 feet long, caliber 7 7/8 inches; three bands superposed, each 2 inches thick round the reinforce; wrought-iron, steel-pointed shot; end fashioned diamond wise" (*OR, Navies,* V, 117). The *Richmond* (also known as the *Virginia II* and *Young Virginia*) had been towed from Norfolk to be completed at the Rocketts yard. The vessel's armament had four guns and was similar in design to the CSS *Virginia* (*OR, Navies,* Ser. II, Vol. I, 265; Silverstone, *Warships,* 205–206).

shops in England or France. They were all made at the Tredgar Iron Works at Richmond, were seven and a half-inch bore, rifled; one weighed 20,000 lbs. and the others not much less; they had all been tested with unusual severity, and all pronounced perfect. So perfectly were they balanced, that the largest gun could be moved with very little effort.[7]

Lead and the ingredients for making gunpowder were, until lately, very scarce, but the enormous price which these articles commanded gradually stimulated the industry and vigilance of the people, and the result is, that now there are many extensive manufactories of gunpowder and bullets in Virginia, South Carolina, Georgia, &c., and there seems no lack of ammunition for war purposes.[8]

Everybody seemed agreed that the activity, ingenuity, and energy which were now being directed towards developing the resources of the South were of recent growth, and dated their rise from the time when, about the spring of 1862, their last hope of foreign intervention died out, and they realized the fact that they were standing face to face with a gigantic war in which they must either conquer, or, by defeat, be humiliated to an extent which would render life itself intolerable. Then it was that they resolved to see what they could do to help themselves.[9]

---

7. The banded gun was most likely a Brooke rifle. A "Confederate product from start to finish, the Brooke was a source of pride to the South" (Faust, ed., *HTIE-CW*, 81). Tredegar did not make a 7.5 bore piece but did make a 7-inch rifle in the second half of 1862. The largest cannon made in Richmond were Columbiads (Daniel and Gunter, *Confederate Cannon Foundries*, 4, 94–99; Harold L. Peterson, *Notes on Ordnance of the American Civil War, 1861–1865* [Washington, D.C., 1959], 7).

8. The South did make great strides in the manufacturing of ammunitions, under the direction of future general Josiah Gorgas. As chief of the Ordnance Bureau, he "became one of the South's greatest assets during the Civil War. . . . His success was extraordinary. Gorgas displayed sound judgment and organizational genius in selecting his subordinates and managing what became a huge war industry" (Faust, ed., *HTIE-CW*, 316). See also Theodore P. Savas, "The Life Blood of the Confederate War Machine: George Washington Rains and the Augusta Powder Works," *Journal of Confederate History*, V (1990), 87–110. The Confederates scrambled to find the raw materials to make munitions. The antebellum South had only two lead and shot works, in eastern Tennessee and Arkansas. Members of the Niter and Mining Bureau sought out laborers, machinery, and lead deposits; and mines in Virginia, North Carolina, and Tennessee showed potential for meeting the need. In the summer of 1862, however, a yield of "three and four tons per working day" was not enough to meet the army's demand (*OR*, Ser. IV, Vol. IV, 29, 30). As a result, blockade runners brought in tons of lead to meet the demand. See Frank E. Vandiver, ed., *Confederate Blockade Running Through Bermuda* [1947; rpr. New York, 1970], 74–130; Dept. of Interior, *Manufactures, 1860*, 716.

9. For an interesting and at times amusing look at southern ingenuity, see *Confederate Receipt Book: A Compilation of Over One Hundred Receipts, Adapted to the Times* (1863; rpr. Athens, Ga., 1960). In the nineteenth century, the term *receipts* was used for *recipes,* and this pamphlet contains

They found their country rich, beyond their wildest dreams, in every kind of raw material. All they needed was an abundance of skilled labour to render themselves independent of the foreigner or Yankee. Already they had infant manufacturing enterprises which must be fostered and expanded. So long as cotton, wool, hides, bark, coal, iron, and wood could be depended upon, of course the supply of native manufactures could be kept up, supposing sufficient skilled labour could be found to manipulate them. Here, however, I could see the great difficulty had arisen. Until this war has disclosed the facts, even the Southern people themselves have not been aware how completely dependent they had become on the North for every article of manufacture.

It may be safely asserted that before the war the South manufactured almost nothing. The consequence has been, that the male white population has had to learn the arts of war and peace simultaneously, and in the crucible of actuality too. Nothing short of desperate necessity ever could have developed the latent industry, ingenuity, and ability of the Southern people for manufactures and commerce. They have been *compelled* to become shoemakers, tailors, cotton-spinners, mechanists, and so on; and, whether they consider it a compliment or not, it is a fact that there is enough of the Yankee about them to invent and make machines, and look uncommonly sharp after making them pay well too.[10]

----

directions for making soup, candles, beer, tooth powder, rice flour, medicines, and stain removers, as well as on how to preserve meat with little or no salt. A similar work demonstrated the means to make Confederate gray dye, secession bread, and Confederate cake. See Frances M. Burroughs, "The Confederate Receipt Book: A Study of Food Substitution in the American Civil War," *South Carolina Historical Magazine,* XCIII (January, 1992), 31, 47, 49, 50.

10. Certainly, southern nationalists and industrialists encouraged development of manufacturing. At times they were motivated by a kind of regional nationalism to free the primarily agricultural South from dependence on finished goods from the North and Europe; as cotton prices rose in the 1850s, however, investors became "attracted by the prospect of profit and beguiled by the image of plantation life, [and] Southerners turned even more than formerly toward agriculture and rejected further efforts to diversify their economy" (John McCardell, *The Idea of a Southern Nation: Southern Nationalists and Southern Nationalism, 1830–1860* [New York, 1979], 128). Plantation owners also undermined capitalistic expansion. They "had no desire to surrender even a particle of their pre-eminence to industrialists, and they seldom forfeited an opportunity to lionize themselves as the noblest of southerners and their profession as the highest calling known to man. They were obviously nervous about a challenge to their social and political status from members of the industrial or commercial classes" (Wilson and Ferris, eds., *Encycl. of Southern Culture,* 715).

"Slaves provided the backbone of the workforce in the Southern iron industry from its inception in the first decades of the eighteenth century." For example, "on the eve of the Civil War, the Tredegar Iron Works of Richmond, Virginia, the South's leading iron company, employed 900 workers, one-half of whom were slaves." The same was true for the naval stores production (Miller and Smith, *Dictionary of Slavery,* 368, 519–21).

There can be no doubt that among the negroes, male and female, a great deal of available mechanical skill exists; and this is being worked up rapidly. Then, again, Southern women have taken to work. At the dinner-hour many of the streets of Richmond and other cities are thronged with thousands of young women hastening to or from the large clothes, cartridge, or cotton factories.[11] Boys are not allowed to grow up idle either. As soon as ever they are fit to leave school, the universal activity around seems to infect them: they must either go to work or be in the army. The truth is, that the Southern folks have "woke up," as they say, and the old dislike to mechanical employment or labour of any kind among white people is dying away.

This is one of the good results which every well-wisher of the South will hope to see grow out of the sad present; and it may have been worth the price, after all, if a people so noble as they, are purged by their trials of some of the great prejudices which in the past have hindered their happiness and progress. I am anxious not to seem to exaggerate either the energy, industry, or ingenuity, of the Southern people, nor the fruits which they are bearing; but without doing that, it is a great fact, which no traveller in the South can overlook, that she has at last found out that she possesses the raw material and skill necessary to become, to some extent at least, a manufacturing country. Once started, these enterprises must increase; and I am therefore forced to the conviction that the South will never henceforth be compelled to succumb for want of the necessaries of life and war, either in food, clothing, arms, or ammunition. The growth of these manufacturing interests will very likely have an important influence on the future tariff of the Confederacy.

There is no doubt that if peace had come before these interests had been called into existence, a very low rate of duty, at least on European imports, would have been selected; but now immense sums have been, and are being, daily invested in all kinds of mining and manufacturing enterprises, and beyond doubt their projectors will claim protection in their tariff against the Yankee and foreigner. Having come to the help of the Confederacy in her hour of need, they will ask this protection boldly, as a measure of national safety, and with a great deal of justice on their side.

My own conviction is, that they will obtain what they ask; for, in truth,

---

11. White southern women smuggled supplies into the Confederacy, toiled as factory workers, clerks, nurses, spies, and overseers, and volunteered their skills to knit and mend clothing (Wiley, *Confederate Women*, 140–79).

it would be the height of madness for the Confederate States ever to run the risk of having in time of war to go through such an ordeal as they are now passing through, simply because they are dependent on foreigners for manufactures. The population of the South had better pay an extra ten or twenty per cent. for staple goods than be caught again without mills and foundries in active operation, and capable of clothing and arming the people.

The desire to make cheaper to themselves than to their foreign rivals all the staples which their country produces, will doubtless persuade the Confederate Government to impose export duties on cotton and naval stores, and very likely on rice, sugar, and tobacco too.[12] Not only will a large revenue be thus raised, but an advantage will be given to the Southern manufacturer. So that the rate imposed is small, it cannot prevent the consumption by foreign countries, at remunerative prices, of every ounce of these staples the South can raise. Two years of blockade have proved to the world that, without the South, Europe has practically to go almost without cotton and naval stores, and has to pay enormous advances on everything else usually obtained from the South.[13] The Confederate planter and farmer can afford to snap his fingers at anything which "Cotton-growing Associations," &c. can do. He knows that when the ports are opened, and American cotton in the market again, his bales will be sold before any others are looked at, and the bales of mere "waste," from India, &c., over which people are chuckling so much now, will be consigned, as they once were, to the mattrass-maker.[14]

---

12. After much debate, the Confederate Congress adopted a moderate export duty early in its history. The taxed items were naval stores, lumber, syrup, cotton, sugar, and molasses. "Although similar proposals were put before Congress, the Act of February 28, 1861, was the only export duty the Confederacy ever attempted" (Ball, *Financial Failure and Confederate Defeat,* 208).

13. By the end of 1862, cotton surpluses in England were low. Furthermore, obtaining cotton from India was problematic despite British efforts to promote the Asian crop and break the South's hold on the cloth industry. Indian growers would not increase yields to meet demands, Indian cotton strains had shorter fibers that resulted in inferior finished cloth, and the Indian industry was hampered by a poor internal transportation system, wasteful cultivation methods, and troubles with peasant laborers. See Owsley, *King Cotton Diplomacy,* 3–14; E. R. J. Owen, *Cotton and the Egyptian Economy, 1820–1914: A Study in Trade and Development* (Oxford, Eng., 1969), 89–92. Before the Civil War, 80 to 90 percent of the British and Continental supply of cotton came from America. But with American sources almost gone during the hostilities, England looked to the brightest jewel in the British crown, and "when the war ended England was getting 85 percent from India" (Owsley, *King Cotton Diplomacy,* 551, 552).

14. "Chucklers" are members of a low caste in southern Indian society and are tanners or cobblers. Therefore, "chuckling" would be activity related to the output of cottage industries (*OED,*

The next fact which is strongly impressed on my mind is, that there is *absolutely no Union sentiment in the South.* The North and the whole world seem now to have admitted this to be true; and I can safely assert, that I never met with more than three persons (and two of them were ladies) who were hostile to the Southern cause.[15] Beyond any doubt, Secession took the vast mass of the Southern merchants, planters, and population generally, as much by surprise as it did the people of the North.[16] I think there is no doubt that personal dislike, disappointment, dissensions, and ambitions, between the comparatively small section of the Southern people called "politicians," and the similar class in the Northern or Free States, first suggested the idea of Secession. It is equally certain also, I think, that the movers on the side of the South, no more anticipated the bloody and desperate struggle which has followed, than their rivals at the North did. If "Secession" had been as long and as completely nursed as some people pretend, the Southern leaders, who for so many years had the control of the purse, skill, and credit of the United States, were either more scrupulous or less far-seeing than their enemies and friends assert them to be. Otherwise, what were they doing not to have had in commission, commanded by safe men, or building in friendly yards, as powerful a fleet as money and skill could produce? If that had been the case, a blockade would have been impossible; the rivers of Tennessee, Kentucky, and Arkansas could never have been opened, and there is no reason why peace could not have been dictated, before Christmas in 1861, even in Faneuil Hall itself.[17]

III, 195). Corsan did not mention the boom in Egyptian cotton growing. "The cause of this sudden metamorphosis was the American Civil War, which, by depriving the European textile industry of the greater part of the supplies of American cotton on which it was largely dependent, drove up the price of cotton to enormous heights and conferred great prosperity on those countries which, like Egypt, were able to take advantage of the favorable situation" (Owen, *Cotton and the Egyptian Economy,* [89]).

15. Corsan's belief that "there is *absolutely no Union sentiment in the South*" is, of course, incorrect. First, he neglected the view of over three million African Americans. Second, he passed through, for the most part, the Mississippi Delta, Gulf Coast, and mid-Atlantic tidewater regions. An examination of Hilliard's *Southern Agriculture Atlas* shows these areas had a high concentration of slaves. Consequently, the citizens in these sectors supported the Confederate cause. Whites in the Appalachian Mountains owned far fewer slaves and did not universally back the new central government (Hilliard, *Southern Agriculture Atlas,* 34–37).

16. On this point, Corsan is on firmer ground. Very few Americans anticipated a war that would consume over six hundred thousand lives and maim tens of thousands more. Many people assumed that any fighting would quickly result in victory for their side (Jones, *Union in Peril,* 58).

17. Originally built in 1742, Boston's Faneuil Hall was "a meeting hall and marketplace for the general public." It was also renowned as a "gathering place of revolutionaries and abolitionists" (Fred Pelka, "Witness to History," *Americana,* XX [1992], 45).

Be that as it may, however, I am satisfied that the Secession movement came on the Southern people like a thunderclap, whether the politicians knew of it or not. Unfortunately, however, for the peace of the continent, the movement chimed in too well with the smothered hatred of the Southerner towards the "Yankee," as he calls him, and offered too fair a chance to be thrown aside of breaking through the shackles of high tariffs, navigation-laws, and financial dependence, with which the keen, industrious, scheming, ingenious North had, for years, been slowly binding him hand and foot.[18] Nothing but this can account to me for the spontaneous uprising of the South in this matter: the dislike of a lifetime forced them forward.

The merchants in Augusta, Charleston, Richmond, &c.,—who saw their customers year after year compelled, by the operation of tariffs, to go North and buy their goods, instead of purchasing near home, as they once did—saw a chance of making their own cities what the great cities of the North were, if they could only ship their produce direct to Europe and import their goods direct from Europe. Every owner of slaves snatched at the opportunity of cutting off for ever from a set of neighbours who seemed bent on making their property worthless.[19] Free-trade, direct shipments, their ports crowded with the ships of every nation, undisturbed possession of their slaves, and freedom from the "peddling Yankee," as they call their restless compatriots, were among a few of the blessings which successful Secession promised.[20] They complained that, in past times, no distinguished foreigner was ever permitted to come further south than Washington. "The climate was unhealthy," they said he was told; "there are few or no good roads, poor hotels, wretched residences, and nothing to eat worth talking about. Then, the population is brutal, uneducated, and the state of the slaves such as to make a foreigner's heart bleed."[21]

---

18. The American Yankee had a strong sense of independence, was quick to act against oppression, was capitalistic and concerned with material wealth yet philanthropic, and religious. See Richard L. Bushman, *From Puritan to Yankee: Character and the Social Order in Connecticut, 1690–1765* [New York, 1970], 286–87).

19. Southern planters had a tremendous investment in slaves; one estimate places their total value in 1860 at $2.4 billion (Ball, *Financial Failure and Confederate Defeat*, 300).

20. "The West as well as the South were the principal losers from the protection of manufacturing" before the war (C. Knick Harley, "The Antebellum American Tariff: Food Exports and Manufacturing," *Explorations in Economic History,* XXIX [1992], 398); Scott, "Cotton Textile Industry," 109.

21. "The South's defensive-aggressive temper in the 1850s stemmed in part from a sense of

In the good time coming, they expect to have their country specially visited, themselves and their belongings placed fairly before the polite and educated society of Europe, and their just position conceded.

In spite of all this, however, I am quite certain that, so long as the Federal Government adhered to their declared determination of prosecuting the war only for the purpose of restoring the Union *as it was,* there were many people in the South willing to give in, rather than wade through seas of blood, pestilence, and famine to freedom. It was only when the Southern people began to see that the Federal Government had resolved to use *any* means to subdue them, no matter how inhuman or contrary to the Constitution, that they resolved on "liberty or death!"

The attempt to destroy the harbour of Charleston, by sinking a "stone fleet;"[22] the nameless and hideous atrocities of their German mercenaries in Kentucky, Missouri, Tennessee, Northern Alabama, and Northern Virginia;[23] the scheme for cutting off Vicksburgh "for ever" from the

---

economic subordination to the North" (McPherson, *Battle Cry of Freedom,* 91). "The South carried a heavy burden of the infectious and noninfectious diseases common to the North and to Europe, somewhat exacerbated by the region's climate and social conditions" (Ronald L. Numbers and Todd L. Savitt, eds., *Science and Medicine in the Old South* [Baton Rouge, 1989], 152). Most salient were epidemics of yellow fever that hit Memphis, Norfolk, Portsmouth, Savannah, Vicksburg, Mobile, and Natchez. New Orleans, as the "principal port of entry, was considered the yellow fever capital of the South" (Roller and Twyman, eds., *Encycl. of Southern History,* 1367).

Travelers and scholars alike have speculated about the origins of the "shiftless southerner" stereotype. Some of the causes postulated for creating this image are the evils of slavery, poor diet, poverty, agricultural practices, ill health, and poor climate (David Bertelson, *The Lazy South* [New York, 1967], vii).

22. The "stone fleet" consisted of older vessels, many from the New Bedford whaling industry, that the Federals started to sink in Charleston harbor in mid December, 1861, to prevent blockade runners from entering the port. It was known as the stone fleet because about seventy-five hundred tons of rock were used for ballast to keep the ships anchored. The fact that whalers could be sacrificed, and that many of their old captains sailed them to block the Ashley and Cooper Rivers, signaled a decline in this maritime industry in the East. The event inspired Herman Melville to pen "The Stone Fleet: An Old Sailor's Lament." Because of changes in the current and for other reasons, the effort finally was unsuccessful. The last stanza of Melville's poem reads:

> And all for naught the waters pass—
> Currents will have their way;
> Nature is nobody's ally; 'tis well,
> The harbor is bettered—will stay.
> A failure, and complete,
> Was your old Stone Fleet.

[Pardon B. Gifford *et al.*], *Famous Fleets in New Bedford's History: Stories of Wooden Ships and Iron Men* (New Bedford, Mass., 1939), 28.

23. Americans of German ancestry and recent German immigrants who fought as Union soldiers

Mississippi; the declaration by the *Tribune* newspaper (the leading Government party-organ in New York), that Charleston "must be razed to the ground and sown with salt;" the vindictive language of such preachers as Beecher, Cheever, Bellows, &c., and their churches, organs, and imitators;[24] the leaden hand of General Butler in New Orleans; the negro-stealing at Beaufort, Port Royal, Newburn, &c., and the raising of negro troops there and at New Orleans;[25] the purposeless waste, murder, and devastation in Virginia and North Carolina, and specially at Fredericks-burgh; and finally, the declaration of the Emancipation Policy of the Federal Government, which, so far as they could do it, handed over the whole male and female population of the South to lust and murder;—all these, following rapidly on each other, had burned into the minds of the whole Southern people, when I was there, the conviction that they had to do with an enemy bent on their annihilation.[26] Hence they were

---

were not mercenaries. Both sides offered a bounty, and soldiers could be paid to serve as substitutes. Because many Germans came to America for freedom, the feeling that all people should be free was very strong. Southerners also singled out German settlers in Missouri for acts of violence, which impelled the immigrants to support the Union and to join the army by the thousands (Ella Lonn, *Foreigners in the Union Army and Navy* [1951; New York, 1969], 14, 48, 146). Many southerners believed that ethnic German soldiers committed "hideous atrocities." In her diary, for example, Emma Holmes recounts hearing in the summer of 1862 that the guards of "Dutch" (*i.e., Deutsch,* or German) background had brutalized captured southern privateersmen who found their way back to Charleston. These same privateers vowed never to take a "Dutchman prisoner" (Marszalek, ed., *Holmes Diary,* 188, 189).

24. Henry Ward Beecher (1813–1887), born in Litchfield, Connecticut, was a famed clergyman and abolitionist. Family members Thomas Kinnicut Beecher (1824–1900), Harriet Beecher Stowe (1811–1886), and Frederick H. Beecher (1841–1868) also opposed slavery. The first was a chaplain in the 141st New York Infantry; the second wrote the legendary *Uncle Tom's Cabin; or, Life Among the Lowly;* and the third was an officer in the 16th Maine Infantry and was severely wounded at Gettysburg (*Who Was Who in America: Historical Volume,* 49, 77, 511; Sifakis, *Who Was Who in the Union,* 27, 395). Of the same view were George Barrell Cheever (1814–1890) and Henry Whitney Bellows (1814–1882). Cheever was a Congregationalist preacher, an editor, and author of *God Against Slavery.* Bellows was a well-known minister in New York City and cofounder and head of the United States Sanitary Commission, an organization that cared for the health, welfare, and morale of armed servicemen (*Who Was Who in America: Historical Volume,* 51, 103; Sifakis, *Who Was Who in the Union,* 27, 29, 395).

25. On July 11, 1862, the U.S. Congress passed the Second Confiscation Act. It was one of the earliest steps to liberate slaves. "Under the act, Confederates who did not surrender within 60 days of the act's passage were to be punished by having their slaves freed" (Faust, ed., *HTIE-CW,* 157). Furthermore, the legislation liberated bondsmen who fled to advancing Union divisions in the South. This law especially affected the chattels on the coast of the Carolinas where Federals had made some inroads (Rose, *Rehearsal for Reconstruction,* 186, 196).

26. A large number of white southerners believed strongly that the real function of Lincoln's

fighting, not to keep out of the Union, but to prevent their being beaten by an enemy to whom pity, honour, or moderation were unknown; who would destroy their plantations, steal their negroes, make mistresses of their women, and slaves of themselves and their children. Hence the ferocity and utter indifference to life with which they fight. Numbers, loud threats, and imposing equipments have no terrors for them: they fling themselves into the fray with the conviction that their cause is just, and that Heaven fights on their side. Stung by the recollection of what others have suffered, and wound up to the pitch of madness by the thought that, unless they succeed, even their own dear ones at home may have to suffer similar wrongs, they count life as nothing, if its sacrifice can avert dishonour and defeat.

I shall not soon forget the effect produced on the troops and population in Richmond, on the Saturday and Sunday, at the end of November, as train after train arrived from Fredericksburgh, filled with the refugee population of that city, to whom General Burnside had given twenty-four hours to escape before the bombardment commenced. There they were, sick women, little children, delicate ladies, all sorts of scared, weeping, unhappy people, turned out into the streets of a strange place suddenly, some with and some without hastily-collected household valuables or necessities—all homeless, ruined, and dependent on the charity of strangers. On the Sunday, about 3,000 out of the 5,000 total population of Fredericksburgh arrived in Richmond; and Broad Street, where the cars stopped, was such a scene of confused, helpless misery for hours, as would make any one's heart bleed. The churches were thronged with these refugees, sermons pertinent to the occasion were preached, and of course the hatred of the enemy deepened beyond eradication. How is it possible for "Union feeling" to survive such scenes?[27]

Emancipation Proclamation was to create a mass insurrection in the Confederacy by freeing only those slaves not in Union hands. The proclamation went into effect January 1, 1863, but had been announced the previous fall after the battle of Antietam. This well-publicized event generated fear and hatred in the South. Jefferson Davis "condemned it as encouraging slaves to assassinate their masters" (Eaton, *Jefferson Davis,* 144). So great was the apprehension that British warships positioned themselves to give refuge to their countrymen and English consuls in southern ports. See Courtemanche, *No Need of Glory,* 113; Miller and Smith, *Dictionary of Slavery,* 219–20.

27. In 1860, the population of Fredericksburg was 5,023 people; of that number, 3,309 were white, 1,291 were slaves, and 422 were free blacks. The town rested south of the Rappahannock River halfway between Washington, D.C., and Richmond. "In the second winter of the war the largest mass displacement was that of the Fredericksburg citizens, and the appeals for assistance again met with a generous response but less was contributed than the year before" (Mary Elizabeth Massey, *Refugee Life in the Confederacy* [Baton Rouge, 1964], 253); Dept. of Interior, *Population, 1860,* 291.

The last impression produced on my mind which I intend to notice, is this—that all expectation of a rising among the negroes, in consequence of their being declared free, or of any negro regiments being able in any way to even *face* the Confederate troops, must be abandoned as fallacious. How any sane man could ever expect the negro to "rise" I cannot imagine. Isolated on plantations chiefly, in small numbers, remote from each other, mostly unable to read, naturally docile and attached to their homes and masters, more than any other existing race devoid of the power of combination, absolutely without leaders or self-reliance, what could such a people do? Even the city negro, no matter how near white he is, exhibits none of the dissatisfaction with his condition, nor power to draw together and hold faithfully together for a common object, nor courage to look upon himself as equal in a fight to at least two white men, which must precede even a possibility of resistance. At so low a value do the Southerners in the cities rank the chance of servile insurrection, that they never allow the presence of a negro to interfere with anything they are talking about, no matter how nearly it may touch the black man's interest: any negro who can read, or can learn, may read just what and as much as he likes, and no one even thinks of asking, "What does the negro think about this?"

I know many families, for instance, in Richmond, where the newspaper-vendor as regularly delivers the *Despatch* every morning at the kitchen-door, as he does the *Examiner* or *Whig* at the counting-house or front entrance. The significance of this will be appreciated, when it is known that every imaginable question (and slavery among others) is fully and ably discussed in all the papers, and that all President Lincoln's "proclamations," "orders," and "messages," even the grand declaration of freedom itself, on January 1st, 1863, are printed in all the papers *verbatim et literatim!* To put arms in the hands of negroes is a most fatal mistake. No number of coloured men, however well armed, will ever stand against the white soldier. I am convinced that to put negro regiments into battle with the Confederates, is tantamount to murdering them. It is not reasonable to expect them to stand: their antecedents, physical qualities, mental habits, all tell fearfully against their chance of success.

It is only right to say that, with the foregoing strong impression on my mind, I see very little chance for the North in the task she has undertaken. Really, the contest is narrowed down to this point and question—"Which section has the largest number of men capable of bearing arms who will fight and be killed?" Considering that the South is acting on the defensive—never putting ten men where two will do the work; ever on the watch to save her strength—while the North seems to aim at crushing suddenly by numbers and lavish expense, which does not succeed, I am inclined to think that the reserve of power is very near equal.[28] If the North ceases to be unanimous on the War Question, then the balance leans to the South, and the end is near. It is quite true that, if all the points are pricked out on a map where Federal troops are, the Confederacy seems encircled, and even eaten into very seriously, especially in the South-west. But when we know how completely isolated all the Federal outposts would be but for their command of rivers and the sea, and how utterly impossible it has been found to advance inland, this method of estimating the position of the two parties rather tells in favour of the South. If it is a fact that, in spite of the North keeping up a strict blockade and holding all the western rivers, the South, united and resolved, is still able to feed, clothe, and arm herself, can rely on the obedience and aid of the negroes, and is able without exhaustion always to oppose a force at any threatened point sufficient to repel the enemy, it is plain that neither the wealth, population, credit, nor patience of the North will bear the strain, and that the independence of the South must sooner or later be admitted.

In conclusion, I have only to express a hope that the preceding pages, exhibiting, as I have wished them to do, without prejudice, the true state of affairs very recently in the Confederate States, may cause reflecting men to ask themselves, whether it is not time that an attempt so hopeless as that of subjugating the South should be abandoned? No man can blame the Northern Government for *trying* to bring the South back. With the knowledge in their possession early in 1861, and holding the views they did on State Rights, I cannot see how they could escape the terrible necessity of making the attempt to reconstruct the Union.[29] But every

28. The North had three population advantages over the South that, even though they were never fully exploited, still provided a flow of manpower. Unlike those in the South, northern ports still accepted immigrants, some of whom found their way into military service; also, many African Americans willingly joined the fight. By October, 1864, there were more than one hundred thousand black soldiers in 141 regiments and eight heavy artillery batteries. Finally, the Union's base population provided "more than 3.5 times as many white men of military age as the Confederacy" (McPherson, *Battle Cry of Freedom,* 322, 606–608; Cornish, *Sable Arm,* 257).

29. "States' rights constitutionalism holds that in the Federal system the states retain rights and powers that cannot be taken from them." One of these rights was the choice to leave the Union. So it was that white southern citizens and representatives elected to secede from the United States, and that then these states were accepted into the Confederate States of America. Northerners, like Lincoln, opposed the right to leave the Union (Wilson and Ferris, eds., *Encycl. of Southern Culture,* 816).

man who has gained even middle life, has undertaken some things which he *could not* do. So it may and really must be with nations. It is no disgrace to the North that she cannot subdue the South. If she had all Europe with her, they could not accomplish it. Nations, no matter how small and unmeritorious, *cannot* be annihilated. They may be put down and even divided up, and their name erased from the roll of nations; but the generic spark is there, and will flame up to the end of time distinct and inextinguishable! How vain, then, is the task of "crushing out" a "rebellion" in which between twelve and thirteen millions of human beings, two-thirds of them Anglo-Saxons, are implicated![30]

There is no reason in the world why the South and North should not live amicably and prosperously apart; and it will be for their own happiness, as much as for that of other nations, if this desirable consummation should come to pass in 1863 instead of 1873.

---

30. Corsan used *Anglo-Saxons* to refer to all whites, even though the word more properly refers to strictly English peoples of Germanic tribe origin. The South did have white citizens of German, Irish, Scotch-Irish, Scottish, Welsh, French, and Spanish ancestry. In comparison to the North, however, the white population did appear very homogeneous. Finally, southerners and many northerners were convinced the Confederates, especially Virginians, were descended from the noble Norman-Cavalier line, as opposed to the more common Saxons. The false air of nobility did give certain southerners an aura of self-confidence. See Wilson and Ferris, eds., *Encycl. of Southern Culture,* 1283–84, 541–42; McMurry, *Two Great Rebel Armies,* 47–49.

Bibliography

Manuscript Sources

Mariners' Museum, Newport News, Va.
   Marion. Eldredge Collection of Vessel Histories.
National Archives, Washington, D.C.
   Passenger Lists of Vessels Arriving at New Orleans, 1802–1902.
      Roll 259, December 1, 1860–March 31, 1866. Record Group 36,
      Microcopy 237.
   Passenger Lists of Vessels Arriving at New York, 1820–1897.
      Roll 223, September 11–October 16, 1862. Record Group 36,
      Microcopy 237.
Public Record Office, London
   Passport Index and Passport Register for 1862, Kew,
   Richmond, Surrey. Foreign Office Records, 611/11, 610/32.
Sheffield Library, England
   1861 Census, County of York, Borough of Sheffield, Town of Sheffield.

Books

American Numismatic Association. *Selections from the Numismatist*. Racine, Wis., 1960.
Anderson, Patricia J., and Jonathan Rose, eds. *British Literary Publishing Houses, 1820–1880*. Dictionary of Literary Biography Series. 134 vols. Detroit, 1978–93.
Appleton's Illustrated Hand-book of American Travel. New York, 1857.
Bacon, Edward. *Among the Cotton Thieves*. 1867; rpr. Bossier City, La., 1989.
Ball, Douglas B. *Financial Failure and Confederate Defeat*. Urbana, Ill., 1991.
Barrett, John G. *The Civil War in North Carolina*. Chapel Hill, N.C., 1963.
Barton, E. H. *The Cause and Prevention of Yellow Fever at New Orleans and Other Cities in America*. New York, 1857.
Becnel, Thomas A. *The Barrow Family and the Barataria and Lafourche Canal: The Transportation Revolution in Louisiana, 1829–1925*. Baton Rouge, 1989.
Bergeron, Arthur W., Jr. *Confederate Mobile*. Jackson, Miss., 1991.
———. *Guide to Louisiana Confederate Military Units, 1861–1865*. Baton Rouge, 1989.

Bertelson, David. *The Lazy South*. New York, 1967.

Blackie, W. G., ed. *The Imperial Gazetteer: A General Dictionary of Geography, Physical, Political, Statistical, and Descriptic*. 2 vols. London, 1860.

Blosser, Susan Sokol, and Clyde Norman Wilson, Jr. *The Southern Historical Collection: A Guide to Manuscripts*. Chapel Hill, N.C., 1970.

Blunt, Edmund M., and G. W. Blunt. *The American Coast Pilot*. New York, 1857.

Boatner, Mark Mayo, III. *The Civil War Dictionary*. New York, 1987.

Boritt, Gabor S., ed. *Why the Confederacy Lost*. New York, 1992.

Bowman, John S., ed. *The Civil War Almanac*. New York, 1983.

Bradbeer, William West. *Confederate and Southern State Currency*. Mt. Vernon, N.Y., 1915.

Broadfoot, Tom, *et al*. *Civil War Books: A Priced Checklist with Advice*. Wilmington, N.C., 1990.

Bullock and Crenshaw. *Catalogue of Drugs, Pharmaceutical Preparations, Utensils, Apparatus, Surgical Instruments, Anatomical Preparations, Offered to Physicians by Bullock & Crenshaw*. Philadelphia, 1860.

Burns, Zed H. *Confederate Forts*. Natchez, Miss., 1977.

Bushman, Richard L. *From Puritan to Yankee: Character and the Social Order in Connecticut, 1690–1765*. New York, 1970.

Butler, Benjamin F. *Butler's Book: A Review of His Legal, Political, and Military Career*. Boston, 1892.

Capers, Gerald M. *Occupied City: New Orleans Under the Federals, 1862–1865*. Lexington, Ky., 1965.

Carter, Hodding, and Betty Werlein Carter. *So Great a Good: A History of the Episcopal Church in Louisiana and of Christ Church Cathedral, 1805–1955*. Sewanee, Tenn., 1955.

Case, Lynn M., and Warren F. Spencer. *The United States and France: Civil War Diplomacy*. Philadelphia, 1970.

Casey, Powell A. *Encyclopedia of Forts, Posts, Camp Names, and Other Military Installations in Louisiana, 1700–1981*. Baton Rouge, 1983.

Chase, P. H. *Paper Money of the Confederate States of America and Cross Index to Types*. Philadelphia, 1947.

Christovich, Mary Louise, *et al.*, eds. *New Orleans Architecture: The American Sector*. Gretna, La., 1972. Vol. II of Christovich *et al.*, eds., *New Orleans Architecture*. 7 vols.

Cocke, Edward J. *Monumental New Orleans*. New Orleans, 1968.

Commager, Henry Steele, ed. *The Blue and the Gray: The Story of the Civil War as Told by Participants*. 1950; rpr. New York, 1982.

Confederate Receipt Book: A Compilation of Over One Hundred Receipts, Adapted to the Times. 1863; rpr. Athens, Ga., 1960.

Connelly, Thomas L. *The Marble Man: Robert E. Lee and His Image in American Society*. Baton Rouge, 1977.

Conrad, Glenn R., ed. *A Dictionary of Louisiana Biography*. 2 vols. New Orleans, 1988.

Cordasco, Francesco, ed. *Dictionary of American Immigration History*. Metuchen, N.J., 1990.

Cornish, Dudley Taylor. *The Sable Arm: Negro Troops in the Union Army, 1861–1865*. 1956; rpr. New York, 1966.

Coulter, E. Merton. *Travels in the Confederate States: A Bibliography*. Norman, Okla., 1948.

Courtemanche, Regis A. *No Need of Glory: The British Navy in American Waters, 1860–1864*. Annapolis, 1977.

Crute, Joseph H., Jr. *Confederate Staff Officers, 1861–1865*. Powhatan, Va., 1982.

Cullen, Joseph P. *The Peninsula Campaign, 1862: McClellan and Lee Struggle for Richmond*. New York, 1973.

Cunningham, H. H. *Doctors in Gray: The Confederate Medical Service*. 1958; rpr. Gloucester, Mass., 1970.

Current, Richard N., ed. *Encyclopedia of the Confederacy*. 4 vols. New York, 1993.

Cushing, William. *Initials and Pseudonyms: A Dictionary of Literary Disguises*. New York, 1886.

Daniel, Larry J., and Riley W. Gunter. *Confederate Cannon Foundries*. Union City, Tenn., 1977.

De Kerchove, René. *International Maritime Dictionary*. Princeton, N.J., 1961.

Dew, Charles B. *Ironmaker to the Confederacy: Joseph R. Anderson and the Tredegar Iron Works*. New Haven, Conn., 1966.

Dickens, Charles. *American Notes*. 1842; rpr. Gloucester, Mass., 1968.

Dickey, Thomas S., and Peter C. George. *Field Artillery Projectiles of the American Civil War*. Mechanicsville, Va., 1993.

Dillon, William. *Life of John Mitchell [sic]*. 2 vols. London, 1888.

Directory of the City of Charleston to Which Is Added a Business Directory. Charleston, 1860.

Donald, David, ed. *Why the North Won the Civil War*. New York, 1971.

Douglas, Henry Kyd. *I Rode with Stonewall*. Chapel Hill, N.C., 1940.

Dunglison, Robley. *A Dictionary of Medical Science*. Philadelphia, 1855.

Dunn, Richard S. *Sugar and Slaves: The Rise of the Planter Class in the English West Indies, 1624–1713*. New York, 1973.

Eaton, Clement. *Jefferson Davis*. New York, 1977.

Evans, Eli N. *Judah P. Benjamin: The Jewish Confederate*. New York, 1988.

Farrow, Henry, and W. B. Dennett. *Directory for the City of Mobile, 1859*. Mobile, Ala., 1859.

Faust, Patricia L., ed. *Historical Times Illustrated Encyclopedia of the Civil War*. New York, 1986.

Ferslew, W. Eugene, comp. *Second Annual Directory for the City of Richmond to Which Is Added a Business Directory for 1860*. Richmond, *ca.* 1860.

Fraser, Walter J., Jr. *Charleston! Charleston!: The History of a Southern City*. Columbia, S.C., 1989.

Fremantle, Arthur James Lyon. *Three Months in the Southern States: April–June 1863*. 1863; rpr. Westport, Conn., 1970.

Gardner, Charles, comp. *Gardner's New Orleans Directory for the Year 1859*. New Orleans, 1859.

Gaskell, Philip. *A New Introduction to Bibliography*. Oxford, Eng., 1979.

Gifford, Pardon B., *et al. Famous Fleets in New Bedford's History: Stories of Wooden Ships and Iron Men*. New Bedford, Mass., 1939.

Glasgow, Vaughn L. *A Social History of the American Alligator: The Earth Trembles with His Thunder.* New York, 1991.

Goff, Richard D. *Confederate Supply.* Durham, N.C., 1969.

Gooding, James Henry. *On the Altar of Freedom: A Black Soldier's Civil War Letters from the Front.* Edited by Virginia M. Adams. Amherst, Mass., 1991.

Griffith, R. Eglesfeld. *A Universal Formulary: Containing the Methods of Preparing and Administering Officinal and Other Medicines.* Philadelphia, 1850.

Hagemann, James. *The Heritage of Virginia: The Story of Place Names in the Old Dominion.* Norfolk, Va., 1986.

Hall, Edward H. *Appleton's Hand-book of American Travel: The Southern Tour.* New York, 1866.

Hamersly, Thomas H. S., comp. and ed. *Complete Regular Army Register of the United States: For One Hundred Years (1779 to 1879).* Washington, D.C., 1881.

Hamilton, Edith. *Mythology.* Boston, 1942.

Harder, Kelsie B., ed. *Illustrated Dictionary of Place Names: United States and Canada.* 1976; rpr. New York, 1985.

Harwell, Richard. *Confederate Music.* Chapel Hill, N.C., 1950.

Hellier's New Orleans Business Directory for 1860 and '61 with Commercial Register of Business Men of New York City. New York, 1860.

Hendrickson, Robert. *Facts on File Encyclopedia of Word and Phrase Origin.* New York, 1987.

———. *Whistlin' Dixie: A Dictionary of Southern Expressions.* New York, 1993.

Hilliard, Sam Bowers. *Atlas of Antebellum Southern Agriculture.* Baton Rouge, 1984.

———. *Hog Meat and Hoecake: Food Supply in the Old South, 1840–1860.* Carbondale, Ill., 1972.

Homans, J. Smith, and J. Smith Homans, Jr., eds. *A Cyclopedia of Commerce and Commercial Navigation.* New York, 1859.

Huber, Leonard V. *Jackson Square: Through the Years.* New Orleans, 1982.

———. *Landmarks of New Orleans.* New Orleans, 1984.

Huber, Leonard V., and Samuel Wilson, Jr. *The Basilica on Jackson Square: The History of the St. Louis Cathedral and Its Predecessors, 1727–1987.* New Orleans, 1987.

Hunter, Louis C. *Steamboats on the Western Rivers: An Economic and Technological History.* Cambridge, Mass., 1949.

Huston, James L. *The Panic of 1857 and the Coming of the Civil War.* Baton Rouge, 1987.

Jefferson, Thomas. *Notes on the State of Virginia.* Edited by William Peden. 1787; rpr. New York, 1954.

Johnston, Angus James, II. *Virginia Railroads in the Civil War.* Chapel Hill, N.C., 1961.

Jones, Howard. *Union in Peril: The Crisis over British Intervention in the Civil War.* Chapel Hill, N.C., 1992.

Jones, John B. *A Rebel War Clerk's Diary at the Confederate States Capital.* Edited by Howard Swiggett. 2 vols. 1866; rpr. New York, 1935.

Jones, Katharine M. *Ladies of Richmond: Confederate Capital.* Indianapolis, 1962.

Jones, Terry L., ed. *The Civil War Memoirs of Captain William J. Seymour: Reminiscences of a Louisiana Tiger.* Baton Rouge, 1991.

Kemp, Peter, ed. *The Oxford Companion to Ships and the Sea*. London, 1976.

Kennedy, James, *et al*. *Dictionary of Anonymous and Pseudonymous English Literature*. 7 vols. Edinburgh, 1926–34.

Lander, Ernest McPherson, Jr. *The Textile Industry in Antebellum South Carolina*. Baton Rouge, 1969.

Lane, Mills. *Architecture of the Old South: Louisiana*. New York, 1990.

Lee, Richard M. *General Lee's City: An Illustrated Guide to the Historic Sites of Confederate Richmond*. McLean, Va., 1987.

Leeper, Clare d'Artois. *Louisiana Places: A Collection of the Columns from the Baton Rouge "Sunday Advocate," 1960–1974*. Baton Rouge, 1976.

Loehr, Charles T. *Of the Old First Virginia Infantry Regiment, Army of Northern Virginia*. 1884; rpr. Dayton, Ohio, 1978.

Long, E. B., with Barbara Long. *The Civil War Day by Day: An Almanac, 1861–1865*. New York, 1971.

Lonn, Ella. *Foreigners in the Confederacy*. 1940; rpr. Gloucester, Mass., 1965.

———. *Foreigners in the Union Army and Navy*. 1951; rpr. New York, 1969.

———. *Salt as a Factor in the Confederacy*. 1933; rpr. University, Ala., 1965.

Low, Sampson, comp. *The English Catalogue of Books with the Dates of Publication in Addition to the Size, Price, Edition and Publisher's Name*. 4 vols. 1863–91; rpr. New York, 1963.

Lytle, William M., *et al*. *Merchant Steam Vessels of the United States, 1790–1868*. Staten Island, N.Y., 1975.

McCardell, John. *The Idea of a Southern Nation: Southern Nationalists and Southern Nationalism, 1830–1860*. New York, 1979.

McMurry, Richard M. *Two Great Rebel Armies: An Essay in Confederate Military History*. Chapel Hill, N.C., 1989.

McPherson, James M. *Battle Cry of Freedom: The Civil War Era*. New York, 1988.

Marszalek, John F., ed. *The Diary of Miss Emma Holmes, 1861–1866*. Baton Rouge, 1979.

Massey, Mary Elizabeth. *Refugee Life in the Confederacy*. Baton Rouge, 1964.

Matthews, James M., ed. *Meeting Directory of the City of Charleston, to Which Is Added a Business Directory*. Charleston, S.C., 1860.

Miller, Randall M., and John David Smith, eds. *Dictionary of Afro-American Slavery*. New York, 1988.

Morgan, James F. *Graybacks and Gold: Confederate Monetary Policy*. Pensacola, Fla., 1985.

Morris, Richard B. *Encyclopedia of American History: Bicentennial Edition*. New York, 1976.

Morris, William, and Mary Morris. *Morris Dictionary of Word and Phrase Origins*. New York, 1977.

Mulvey, Christopher. *Transatlantic Manners: Social Patterns in Nineteenth-Century Anglo-American Travel Literature*. Cambridge, Eng., 1990.

Nash, Jay Robert. *Encyclopedia of World Crime: Criminal Justice, Criminology, and Law Enforcement*. 6 vols. Wilmette, Ill., 1989–90.

Nevins, Allan, *et al*., eds. *Civil War Books: A Critical Bibliography*. 2 vols. Baton Rouge, 1967, 1969.

Nolan, Dick. *Benjamin Franklin Butler: The Damnedest Yankee.* Novato, Calif., 1991.

Numbers, Ronald L., and Todd L. Savitt, eds. *Science and Medicine in the Old South.* Baton Rouge, 1989.

O'Brien, Robert, ed. *The Encyclopedia of the South.* 1985; rpr. New York, 1992.

Owen, E. R. J. *Cotton and the Egyptian Economy, 1820–1914: A Study in Trade and Development.* Oxford, Eng., 1969.

Owsley, Frank Lawrence. *King Cotton Diplomacy: Foreign Relations of the Confederate States of America.* 1931; rpr. Chicago, 1959.

Parker, Sandra V. *Richmond's Civil War Prisons.* Lynchburg, Va., 1990.

Parrish, T. Michael, and Robert M. Willingham, Jr. *Confederate Imprints: A Bibliography of Southern Publications from Secession to Surrender.* Austin, Tex., 1987.

Pember, Phoebe Yates. *A Southern Woman's Story: Life in Confederate Richmond.* Edited by Bell Irvin Wiley. 1959; rpr. St. Simons Island, Ga., 1980.

Perdue, Charles L., Jr., *et al.,* eds. *Weevils in the Wheat: Interviews with Virginia Ex-Slaves.* Charlottesville, Va., 1992.

Peterson, Harold L. *Notes on Ordnance of the American Civil War, 1861–1865.* Washington, D.C., 1959.

Pretz, Bernhard. *A Dictionary of Military and Technological Abbreviations and Acronyms.* London, 1983.

Rable, George C. *Civil Wars: Women and the Crisis of Southern Nationalism.* Urbana, Ill., 1989.

Ripley, Warren. *Artillery and Ammunition of the Civil War.* New York, 1970.

Robertson, James I., Jr. *Soldiers Blue and Gray.* Columbia, S.C., 1988.

————. *The Stonewall Brigade.* Baton Rouge, 1963.

Robinson, William M., Jr. *Justice in Gray: A History of the Judicial System of the Confederate States of America.* Cambridge, Mass., 1941.

Roller, David C., and Robert W. Twyman, eds. *The Encyclopedia of Southern History.* Baton Rouge, 1979.

Rose, Al. *Storyville, New Orleans: Being an Authentic, Illustrated Account of the Notorious Red-Light District.* 1974; rpr. Tuscaloosa, Ala., 1989.

Rose, Willie Lee. *Rehearsal for Reconstruction: The Port Royal Experiment.* New York, 1964.

Royster, Charles. *The Destructive War: William Tecumseh Sherman, Stonewall Jackson, and the Americans.* New York, 1991.

Rudé, George. *Hanoverian London, 1714–1808.* London, 1971.

Russell, Charles Edward. *From Sandy Hook to 62°: Being Some Account of the Adventures, Exploits, and Services of the Old New York Pilot-Boat.* New York, 1929.

Sacks, Howard L., and Judith Rose Sacks. *Way Up North in Dixie: A Black Family's Claim to the Confederate Anthem.* Washington, D.C., 1993.

Sanger, Donald Bridgman, and Thomas Robson Hay. *James Longstreet.* Baton Rouge, 1952.

Savitt, Todd L. *Medicine and Slavery: The Diseases and Health Care of Blacks in Antebellum Virginia.* Urbana, Ill., 1978.

Sears, Stephen W. *To the Gates of Richmond: The Peninsula Campaign.* New York, 1992.

Sideman, Belle Becker, and Lillian Friedman, eds. *Europe Looks at the Civil War.* New York, 1960.

Sifakis, Stewart. *Who Was Who in the Civil War.* 2 vols. Vol. I, *Who Was Who in the Union;* Vol. II, *Who Was Who in the Confederacy.* Both New York, 1988.

Silverstone, Paul H. *Warships of the Civil War Navies.* Annapolis, 1989.

Smith, Sidney Adair, and C. Carter Smith, Jr., eds. *Mobile, 1861–1865: Notes and a Bibliography.* Chicago, 1964.

Stevens, Henry, Son and Stiles. *Catalogue New Series 101.* Williamsburg, Va., January, 1993.

Stewart, George R. *American Place-Names: A Concise and Selective Dictionary for the Continental United States of America.* New York, 1970.

Stover, John F. *The Railroads of the South, 1865–1900: A Study in Finance and Control.* Chapel Hill, N.C., 1955.

Symonds, Craig L. *Joseph E. Johnston: A Civil War Biography.* New York, 1992.

Thomas, Emory M. *The Confederate State of Richmond: A Biography of the Capital.* Austin, Tex., 1971.

Thomas, G. F., comp. *Appleton's Illustrated Railway and Steam Navigation Guide.* New York, 1859.

Thornbury, Walter. *Old and New London: A Narrative of Its History, Its People, and Its Places.* 6 vols. London, n.d.

Todd, Richard Cecil. *Confederate Finance.* Athens, Ga., 1954.

Todd, William B. *Directory of Printers & Others in Allied Trades, London and Vicinity, 1800–1840.* London, 1972.

Turner, George Edgar. *Victory Rode the Rails: The Strategic Place of the Railroads in the Civil War.* Westport, Conn., 1972.

Turner, Michael L. *Index and Guide to the Lists of the Publications of Richard Bentley & Son, 1829–1898.* Herts, Eng., 1975.

Tweedale, Geoffrey. *Sheffield Steel and America: A Century of Commercial and Technological Interdependence, 1830–1930.* Cambridge, Eng., 1987.

V & C. *The City Intelligencer, or Stranger's Guide.* Richmond, Va., 1862.

Vandiver, Frank E., ed. *Confederate Blockade Running Through Bermuda.* 1947; rpr. New York, 1970.

————. *Mighty Stonewall.* New York, 1967.

Waitt, Robert W., Jr. *Confederate Military Hospitals in Richmond.* 1964; rpr. Richmond, 1979.

Walkley, Christina. *The Ghost in the Looking Glass: The Victorian Seamstress.* London, 1981.

Wallace, Lee A., Jr. *1st Virginia Infantry.* Lynchburg, Va., 1984.

————. *A Guide to Virginia Military Organizations, 1861–1865.* Lynchburg, Va., 1986.

Watson, Alan D. *Wilmington: Port of North Carolina.* Columbia, S.C., 1992.

Who Was Who in America: Historical Volume, 1607–1896. Chicago, 1963.

Wiley, Bell Irvin. *Confederate Women.* Westport, Conn., 1975.

————. *The Life of Johnny Reb: The Common Soldier of the Confederacy.* 1943; rpr. Baton Rouge, 1978.

Wilson, Charles Reagan, and William Ferris, eds. *Encyclopedia of Southern Culture.* Chapel Hill, N.C., 1989.

Wilson, Samuel, Jr. *The Vieux Carre, New Orleans: Its Plan, Its Growth, Its Architecture.* Historic District Demonstration Study, Conducted by the Bureau of Governmental Research. New Orleans, 1968.

Winters, John D. *The Civil War in Louisiana.* Baton Rouge, 1963.

Wise, Stephen R. *Lifeline of the Confederacy: Blockade Running During the Civil War.* Columbia, S.C., 1988.

Woodman, Harold D. *King Cotton and His Retainers: Financing and Marketing the Cotton Crop of the South, 1800–1925.* Lexington, Ky., 1968.

Younger, Edward, ed. *Inside the Confederate Government: The Diary of Robert Garlick Hill Kean.* New York, 1957.

GOVERNMENT PUBLICATIONS

Acts of the General Assembly of the State of Virginia, Passed at Called Session, 1862, in the Eighty-Seventh Year of the Commonwealth. Richmond, 1862.

Federal Archives in Louisiana. *Ship Registers and Enrollments of New Orleans, Louisiana.* 6 vols. Baton Rouge, 1942.

Humphreys, A. A., and H. L. Abbot. *Report upon the Physics and Hydraulics of the Mississippi River . . . Based upon Surveys and Investigations.* Philadelphia, 1861.

Matthews, James M., ed. *The Statutes at Large of the Provisional Government of the Confederate States of America.* Richmond, 1864.

Mayo, John J., ed. *The Mercantile Navy List and Annual Appendage to the Commercial Code of Signals for All Nations.* London, 1863.

Official Records of the Union and Confederate Navies in the War of the Rebellion. 30 vols. Washington, D.C., 1894–1927.

U.S. Department of the Interior. *Agriculture of the United States in 1860: Compiled from the Original Returns of the Eighth Census.* Washington, D.C., 1864.

————. *Manufactures of the United States in 1860: Compiled from the Original Returns of the Eighth Census.* Washington, D.C., 1865.

————. *Population of the United States in 1860: Compiled from the Original Returns of the Eighth Census.* Washington, D.C., 1864.

————. *Statistics of the United States (Including Mortality, Property, & c.,) in 1860: Compiled from the Original Returns, Being the Final Exhibit of the Eighth Census.* Washington, D.C., 1866.

U.S. Department of the Treasury. *Report of the Treasury on the State of the Finances.* Washington, D.C., 1856, 1860–63.

————. *Report of the Secretary of the Treasury Transmitting a Report from the Register of the Treasury of the Commerce and Navigation of the United States for the Year Ending June 30, 1860.* Washington, D.C., 1860.

U.S. Department of War, comp. *The Official Military Atlas of the Civil War.* 1891; rpr. New York, 1978.

The War of the Rebellion: A Compilation of the Official Records of the Union and Confederate Armies. 130 vols. Washington, D.C., 1880–1901.

Dissertations

Redard, Thomas E. "The Port of New Orleans: An Economic History, 1821–1860." 2 vols. Ph.D. dissertation, Louisiana State University, 1985.

Newspapers

Charleston *Daily Courier,* 1862.
Daily Richmond Examiner, 1862.
Mobile *Register and Advance,* 1862.
New Orleans *Bee,* 1862.
New Orleans *Daily Delta,* 1862.
New Orleans *Daily Picayune,* 1862.
New Orleans *Daily True Delta,* 1862.
New York *Herald,* 1862.
Richmond *Enquirer,* 1862.
Richmond *Examiner,* 1862.
Sheffield (Eng.) *Independent,* 1876.
Wilmington (N.C.) *Daily Journal,* 1862.

Journal Articles

Burroughs, Frances M. "The Confederate Receipt Book: A Study of Food Substitution in the American Civil War." *South Carolina Historical Magazine,* XCIII (January, 1992), 31–50.

Crowther, Edward R. "Holy Honor: Sacred and Secular in the Old South." *Journal of Southern History,* LVIII (November, 1992), 619–36.

Ekelund, Robert B., Jr., and Mark Thornton. "The Union Blockade and Demoralization of the South: Relative Prices in the Confederacy." *Social Science Quarterly,* LXXIII (December, 1992), 890–902.

Everett, Morris. "Confederate 'Rag Tags.' " *Confederate Philatelist,* XXXVI (January–February, 1991), 27–30.

Hallock, Judith Lee. " 'Lethal and Debilitating': The Southern Disease Environment as a Factor in Confederate Defeat." *Journal of Confederate History,* VII (1991), 51–61.

Harley, C. Knick. "The Antebellum American Tariff: Food Exports and Manufacturing." *Explorations in Economic History,* XXIX (1992), 375–400.

————. "International Competitiveness of the Antebellum Cotton Textile Industry." *Journal of Economic History,* LII (September, 1992), 559–84.

Higginbotham, R. Don. "The Martial Spirit in the Antebellum South: Some Further Speculation in a National Context." *Journal of Southern History,* LVIII (February, 1992), 3–26.

Johnson, Ludwell H., III. "Trading with the Enemy: Some New Lincoln Documents." *Manuscripts,* XXXIX (Winter, 1987), 29–39.

Jones, Allen W., ed. "A Georgia Confederate Soldier Visits Montgomery, Alabama, 1862–1863." *Alabama Historical Quarterly,* XXV (Spring/Summer, 1963), 99–113.

Lash, Jeffrey N. "A Yankee in Gray: Danville Leadbetter and the Defense of Mobile Bay, 1861–1863." *Civil War History,* XXXVII (September, 1991), 197–218.

Olliff, Martin T. "Life and Work in a Progressive Cotton Community: Prattville, Alabama, 1846–1860." *Agricultural History,* LXVIII (Spring, 1994), 151–61.

Pelka, Fred. "Witness to History." *Americana,* XX (1992), 44–48.

Pittman, Walter E., Jr., "Trading with the Devil: The Cotton Trade in Civil War Mississippi." *Journal of Confederate History,* II (1989), 132–42.

Rhett, Claudine. "Sketch of John C. Mitchel of Ireland, Killed Whilst in Command of Fort Sumter." *Southern Historical Society Papers,* X (1882), 268–72.

Rogers, William Warren. " 'In Defense of Our Sacred Cause': Rabbi James K. Gutheim in Confederate Montgomery." *Journal of Confederate History,* VII (1991), 112–22.

Scott, Carole E. "Why the Cotton Textile Industry Did Not Develop in the South Sooner." *Agricultural History,* LXVIII (Spring, 1994), 105–21.

Soltow, James H. "Cotton as Religion, Politics, Law, Economics, and Art." *Agricultural History,* LXVIII (Spring, 1994), 6–19.

Surdam, David G. "Cotton's Potential as an Economic Weapon: The Antebellum and Wartime Market for Cotton Textiles." *Agricultural History,* LXVIII (Spring, 1994), 122–45.

Wyche, Billy H. "The Union Defends the Confederacy: The Fighting Printers of New Orleans." *Louisiana History,* XXXV (Summer, 1994), 271–84.

CORRESPONDENCE

Michael A. Ermilio to Benjamin H. Trask, February 24, 26, 1993.

George Griffenhagen to Benjamin H. Trask, October 14, 1992.

D. Hindmarch to B. H. Trask, September 17, 1993.

William E. Lind to Benjamin H. Trask, March 11, 1993.

New York Public Library to Benjamin H. Trask, September 29, 1993.

E. F. Thomson to B. H. Trask, September 29, 1993.

G. Ridgley to Patrick Flood, September 3, 1992.

(All letters are part of the editor's files in Williamsburg, Va.)

Index